Praise for *Judging Iran*

"Judge Brower's *Judging Iran* delivers on its stated purpose: it tells a gripping story about the career of a highly esteemed international lawyer, and in the process lays out and defends, with sophistication, our contemporary system of international dispute settlement."

—Sean D. Murphy, Manatt/Ahn Professor of International Law, George Washington University; Member, U.N. International Law Commission

"This remarkable personal story of one of the greatest international law practitioners of our time presents international law in action. Charles Brower, leadership patron of the American Society of International Law, sat in at least 133 international cases as arbitrator or judge, including in three cases as judge *ad hoc* at the International Court of Justice. In addition, he acted in a number of cases as lead counsel, for both investors and governments. Having advised the State Department (including as its acting legal adviser for an extended period) and President Reagan at a critical moment of his presidency in early 1987, Brower's book offers unique insights.

I recommend this memoir, elegantly written and highly readable, to all interested in better understanding the challenges besetting the settlement of international disputes, in particular to young lawyers aspiring to pursue a career in international litigation."

—Peter Tomka, Judge and former President of the International Court of Justice

"Charles Brower's memoir vividly portrays the power of international justice and the inestimable value of an orderly dispute resolution system for international peace and security.

It narrates, in lucid and colorful language, how peaceful litigation, arbitration, and the judicial settlement of disputes have gradually triumphed, during the lifetime of the author, over gunboat diplomacy and the force of arms in relations between states."

—Abdulqawi Yusuf, Judge and former President of the International Court of Justice

JUDGING IRAN

JUDGING IRAN

A MEMOIR OF THE HAGUE, THE WHITE HOUSE, AND LIFE ON THE FRONT LINE OF INTERNATIONAL JUSTICE

HON. CHARLES N. BROWER

Judge of the Iran–United States Claims Tribunal

Judge ad hoc of the International Court of Justice (ret.)

Judge ad hoc of the Inter-American Court of Human Rights (ret.)

DISRUPTION
BOOKS

New York   Austin

Published by Disruption Books
New York, New York
www.disruptionbooks.com
Copyright ©2023 by Charles N. Brower

Distributed by Disruption Books

For information about special discounts for bulk purchases, please contact Disruption Books at info@disruptionbooks.com.

Photo of Nixon and Brezhnev, June 19, 1973, reprinted courtesy of *The New York Times*
Cover images courtesy of the author and © Shutterstock / Kiev.Victor
Cover and book design by Sheila Parr

Library of Congress Cataloging-in-Publication Data available

Printed in the United States of America.

Print ISBN: 978-1-63331-070-4
eBook ISBN: 978-1-63331-055-1

First Edition

Dedicated to my father, Charles Hendrickson Brower,
my earliest and longest mentor, who always had
the right answer and believed in me

George W. Jaeger, my academic tutor, who
counseled me the rest of his life

Lawrence ("Larry") B. Morris, because he cared

John ("Jack") R. Stevenson, who as
The Legal Adviser launched my career

and David M. Abshire, who took me with him
everywhere, ultimately to the White House.

*"And what does the Lord require of you but to do justice,
and to love mercy, and walk humbly with your God?"*
—Micah 6:8

"Still bearing fruit in old age; still remaining fresh and green."
—Psalm 92:14

Contents

ACKNOWLEDGMENTS xiii

FOREWORD xvii

INTRODUCTION: The World That Sues Together Hews Together 1

CHAPTER ONE: Street-Fighting Man. 11

CHAPTER TWO: Might Makes Right. 27

CHAPTER THREE: Rug Pulls, Investments, and Shakedowns 49

CHAPTER FOUR: How to Sue a State 73

CHAPTER FIVE: The Iran Connection 81

CHAPTER SIX: Judging Iran, Part I 109

CHAPTER SEVEN: Judging Iran, Part II 121

CHAPTER EIGHT: Iran-Contra: What Reagan Knew 135

CHAPTER NINE: Of Parasites and Lousy Loans 149

CHAPTER TEN: Suing Saddam. 171

CHAPTER ELEVEN: Judging Iran, Part III 183

CHAPTER TWELVE: International Arbitrator, Part I 205

CHAPTER THIRTEEN: International Arbitrator, Part II 225

CHAPTER FOURTEEN: Human Rights. 233

CHAPTER FIFTEEN: The Future. 245

NOTES 255

INDEX 277

ABOUT THE AUTHOR .293

Acknowledgments

I began this book by contacting the legendary "go-to" lawyer for global leaders and celebrities seeking to publish books, Robert "Bob" Barnett of Williams & Connolly LLP in Washington, DC, who as a favor to a mutual friend took me under his wing. As I started this adventure I was already eighty-five years of age and so extremely busy still in winding down my arbitration practice and public duties that I literally had not the time to write the book all by myself and needed a "collaborator." Through Bob I acquired a sensational one, A.J. Wilson.

Of A.J.'s incredibly productive as well as wholly enjoyable collaboration with me I cannot say it better than did the *New York Times* best-selling author of *Anatomy of Terror: From the Death of Bin Laden to the Rise of the Islamic State* Ali Soufan: "First and foremost, I must thank my collaborator throughout this project, A.J. Wilson, without whose intellect, persistence, and way with words this book would simply never have seen the light of day. His wife, Rachel Madan, deserves special mention for her forbearance for the long hours A.J. spent helping me make this book the best it could be."

I also am immensely indebted to Hugh Verrier, the longtime chair of White & Case LLP, the law firm with which I practiced for decades, for his generously volunteering to arrange, without cost to me, for me to be interviewed for some days at length by a professional writer, with everything videotaped and the entire interview transcribed, all of which material afforded A.J. a head start on our collaboration.

I owe A.J. double credit for having introduced me to the publisher of this volume, Disruption Books, led by a troika of skilled, strong, solid, and spectacularly professional women with each of whom it was a joy to work: Kris Pauls, the publisher, who at our first meeting spent as much time gracefully convincing me to publish with Disruption Books as I devoted to selling her on these memoirs, from which our contract quickly emerged; Alli Shapiro, the editorial and production director, and thereby my most frequent, and always welcome, interlocutor; and Janet Potter, the all-important marketing director. I could not possibly have had a better team to perfect and market this book. Those three, of course, were supported by a considerable supporting cast, in particular Sheila Parr, the book's designer, who perforce spent the most time on this book of her cohort. To all of them I am eternally grateful.

It is traditional, also just and well deserved, to cite the importance of the support one has enjoyed from one's family, in my case through-out my life and career. My mother, who at age seventeen held two women's records in track, then graduated from college Phi Beta Kappa, was thoroughly dutiful in caring for her children when sick, helping us with our schoolwork as needed, and doing everything within her considerable power to inspire ambition in us and to prepare us in every way for life.

Since my two children's mid- and later teenage years they have seen much less of me, and I of them, than would be regarded as normal. In law practice many years I was traveling abroad due to my international arbitration work not less than 25 percent of the time and up to 45 per-cent of the year. Then there were the twenty-one-and-a-half years I was resident in The Hague as an international judge and therewith a Member of the Diplomatic Corps. My daughter, Frederica "Rica" Amity, PhD, has lived way out in the western states of our country since she was just turning nineteen, and is currently in Yakima, Washington, on the faculty of a medical school. My son, Charles "Chip" H. Brower, II, spent three years in Moscow after graduating *summa cum laude* from college, then obtained his JD (plus being on the Law Review). For the next three years he was in Minneapolis, first clerking for a judge and then practicing with a law firm. Then he became a professor of international law, first at the University of Mississippi, and for some years now at Wayne State University in Michigan. I find it very gratifying that despite all of my absences from their lives and the geographical distances separating us, they have managed their lives so successfully and that it seems our love for each other has endured and, in my old age, even grown. They always have been, and continue to be, a constant source of pride and also inner strength for me.

Finally, I am enormously grateful to my by now innumerable law clerks, student interns, and assistants in my public positions, as well as those associates and partners with whom I enjoyed practicing at White & Case LLP, in addition to my colleagues in Twenty Essex Chambers, and the many wonderful arbitrators with whom I have sat, all of whom have contributed to my learning as well as to my social pleasure over many years. You all know who you are, and I could not have arrived where I am without each and every one of you.

My only regret about these memoirs is that some lovely, some quite rare, and certain surprising events incidentally punctuated my life, but played no role in my professional career. Therefore I thought to list them here as irrelevant but fascinating footnotes. (1) I slept once in Einstein's bed in his Princeton, New Jersey, home, alone (he had passed away, but the house remained in the family). (2) In the summer of 1956, just turned twenty-one, I worked in the Senate office of Senator Clifford P. Case of my home state of New Jersey, and thus had a pass for the Senate floor, where I observed close up future Presidents JFK and LBJ. (3) In the summer of 1984 I attended one of the Garden Parties traditionally held by Queen Elizabeth II on the grounds of Buckingham Palace. (4) I spent a long day in DC in a room of the Mayflower Hotel with Billy Carter, President Carter's somewhat embarrassing brother, accompanied by my then–law partner, Paul Friedman, who later became a U.S. district judge for the District of Columbia, discussing the possibility of us representing Billy, as the family peanut warehouse was being investigated by an independent counsel. (We weren't hired!) (5) I spent my sixtieth birthday witnessing within the forecourt of Buckingham Palace the changing of the guard, followed by a birthday luncheon in the Queen's Guard Officer Mess surrounded by friends from various stages of my life. (6) Liz Cheney, star of the U.S. House Select Committee to Investigate the January 6th Attack on the United States Capitol, worked for me in the 1990s at White & Case LLP. (7) In 1990 I sat in the Royal box at Wimbledon, watching Stefan Edberg beat Boris Becker in the men's singles finals. (8) In London one memorable summer I was invited into the box of the Marylebone Cricket Club, the most important institution in the cricket world, at Lord's Cricket Ground to observe a test match, a singular treat for a past president and wicketkeeper of the Harvard Cricket Club (me). (9) I shook hands and chatted with Princess Anne of Edinburgh, The Princess Royal, when the 800th anniversary of the sealing of the Magna Carta was celebrated on the field at Runnymede in 2015. (10) I dined with Lord (Thomas) Bingham of Cornhill, the only judge invited by the late Queen Elizabeth II into the Most Noble Order of the Garter (limited to twenty-four persons), and Lady (Elizabeth) Bingham at their home in London as their only guest, an extraordinarily memorable evening.

Foreword

In sharing the story of his career spanning more than sixty years, Judge Charles Brower has traced the course of international dispute settlement over the same period. His individual experiences give the reader insights into past developments and offer food for thought about the future.

Judge Brower reveals in his memoir that, as a student at Harvard Law School, he enrolled in only one course in international law. He explains that he had hoped to find a position as an attorney at a Wall Street law firm upon graduation in 1961 and thought that a transcript filled with international law electives might diminish his prospects for such an opportunity.

This logic was surely correct in 1961. In that year, the International Court of Justice (ICJ) delivered one judgment; its entire output, including procedural orders, consumed a mere sixty-five pages. The Convention on the Settlement of Investment Disputes Between States and Nationals of Other States (ICSID Convention), which would eventually establish a mechanism for the settlement of disputes between a state and a foreign investor, did not open for signature until 1965. Law firms considering applications from members of the class of 1961 would not have seen much value in a student's expertise in international law or the settlement of international disputes.

Twenty years later, when I graduated from law school in 1981, the situation was not very different. In that year, only fifty-three pages were needed to capture a year's work by the ICJ. The ICSID Convention had been in force for fifteen years, but only three awards had been issued by ICSID tribunals. Unlike Judge Brower, however, I was naïve about the prospects for employment in public international law and enrolled in every relevant class that was offered by my law school. I was disappointed when I came to realize that work that law firms described as "international" was largely related to transnational commercial transactions. Outside of academia, the few positions in public international law were almost exclusively found in foreign ministries and international organizations.

In January of 1981, my law school classmates and I crowded around a small television in the cafeteria of Boalt Hall (University of California, Berkeley) to watch the United States hostages being freed after 444 days of captivity in Iran, a result of the Algiers Accords. We paid far less attention to the fact that the Algiers Accords also established a tribunal that would settle certain disputes between Iran and the United States, as well as claims by the nationals of one of these states against the other.

Within a few years, however, it became clear that the Iran–United States Claims Tribunal (IUSCT) would be emerging as a forum that was important not only for the two states and their nationals, but also for the development of international law and dispute settlement. The tribunal's output has been impressive in volume and in scope. For example, as Judge Brower observed when he delivered a course at The Hague Academy on International Law in 1990, the tribunal has addressed important questions of public international law, such as the expulsion of aliens and the expropriation of property.

Because the tribunal's rules of procedure are based on the widely used arbitration rules of the United Nations Commission on International Trade Law and because its awards are publicly available, the tribunal's approaches to procedural matters are widely cited as illustrations of the way that arbitration rules operate in practice. Over his long career, Judge Brower himself has become a repository of expertise on arbitral procedures and on substantive law, having served as arbitrator in numerous proceedings governed by the UNCITRAL rules and other rules of arbitration both in commercial arbitration and in investor-state cases.

Judge Brower became a member of the IUSCT in 1984, having previously served as a substitute member of the tribunal. Elsewhere in The Hague, there was a notable development in international dispute settlement in that same year. Nicaragua filed a case against the United States in the International Court of Justice (ICJ), leading to a judgment on the merits in 1986 in which the court upheld most of Nicaragua's claims. While some commentators may exaggerate the impact of this one case on the subsequent growth in the court's docket, Nicaragua's success undoubtedly served as a reminder to many states of the potential for settling disputes in the ICJ.

Judge Brower's presence in The Hague in 1984 meant that he was able attend the oral proceedings in *Nicaragua v. United States* in that year. His involvement with the ICJ eventually went far beyond that of an informed observer. As his memoir describes, during the most recent decade, he was appointed as a judge *ad hoc* in three ICJ cases, participating on equal footing with the elected members of the court until he decided, as of his eighty-seventh birthday, that it was the right time for him to step down from that role.

Judge's Brower's career path demonstrates that the field of international dispute settlement is increasingly rich and dynamic. With this dynamism comes uncertainty about the future. In relation to investor-state dispute settlement, reference is sometimes made to "backsliding,"i.e., doubts about this form of dispute settlement that have been expressed in various contexts. Changes and potential improvements in investor-state dispute settlement are being actively debated, and we can expect some evolution in this mechanism.

One can also identify clouds over state-to-state dispute settlement, illustrated by events such as the ongoing difficulties confronting the Appellate Body of the World Trade Organization. There have also been occasional refusals by respondents to participate in proceedings before international courts and tribunals, including the ICJ. Because the ICJ is the principal judicial organ of the United Nations, the broader challenges faced by that organization also have the potential to weaken the role of the court.

What conclusions should today's law students draw from the present state of international dispute settlement? A student might ask, "What if states lose faith in international adjudication and arbitration, leading the field to contract just as I begin my career?" I am confident that Judge Brower, known as an enthusiastic mentor of younger colleagues, would tell students not to shy away from international law courses, as young Charlie Brower did, but instead to seek out electives in international law and arbitral procedure. Through active and sustained involvement in the field, today's young lawyers will be equipped to shape the future of international dispute settlement. Judge Brower's memoir of his own career should inspire them to do exactly that.

Joan Donoghue
President, International Court of Justice
The Hague
October 15, 2022

The World That Sues Together Hews Together

In my library, amid the books, papers, and memorabilia of five decades in international law, I keep a handsome scale model of a ship, the CSS *Alabama*. My son, a professor of international law at Wayne State University, gave me the model as a present for my eightieth birthday. It was a singularly appropriate gift from one international lawyer to another.

As her prefix indicates, the CSS *Alabama*—a copper-bottomed sloop-of-war from the overlap between the twilight of sail and the dawn of steam—saw service on behalf of the short-lived Confederate States of America. But she was not built in any Southern shipyard. The Union's naval blockade—part of Gen. Winfield Scott's "Anaconda Plan"—was too threatening for that. Instead, the *Alabama* was constructed in England, at Birkenhead on the Mersey.

Great Britain's role in the Civil War was a fraught one. One month to the day after the fall of Fort Sumter (April 12–13, 1861), Prime Minister Lord Palmerston's Liberal government had declared itself neutral in the conflict and recognized the Confederacy as a legitimate belligerent—but, crucially, *not* an independent state. The textile industry, accustomed to receiving shipments of cheap cotton from the South, pressed for pro-Confederate intervention. Although the Palmerston administration flirted with the idea more than once, it ultimately held to its policy of neutrality and nonrecognition.

Nevertheless, a few British shipyards knowingly undertook to build vessels for the Confederacy. This they did more or less openly, with barely a fig leaf of plausible deniability in the form of dubious middle-men and false papers. One offending yard was that of John Laird, Sons & Company, which constructed the *Alabama* in 1861. Thomas Dudley, the U.S. consul in Liverpool, furnished Britain's Foreign Office with ample evidence that the Laird hulls were meant for the Southern war effort. Yet the government made only token efforts to stop their construction.

On her maiden voyage, the *Alabama* was sailed out to the Azores, where she was armed with eight cannon and manned by a gray-coated Confederate crew captained by one Raphael Semmes, formerly a com-mander in the United States Navy. From there, she went on the rampage. Her modus operandi matched that of her sisters: Fly a false British flag. Get close to U.S. merchant ships. Seize them, take their crews prisoner, and burn the ship and its cargo. During a two-year reign of terror, the *Alabama* pursued this policy from Newfoundland to French Indochina, stopping along the way at Cape Town and Singapore—both British colonies. Meanwhile, sister Confederate ships found refuge at the Baha-mas and Melbourne, also under British rule. The raiders had by then destroyed dozens of Union vessels, and the founder of the Laird yard, then a Conservative member of Parliament, declared in the House of Commons that he "would rather be handed down to posterity as the builder of a dozen *Alabama*s than as the man who applies himself delib-erately to . . . cry up the institutions of another country."[1]

Finally, when two more keels were laid at the Laird yard—this time for ironclads equipped with battering rams—the U.S. ambassador in London told the British foreign secretary, "It would be superfluous in me to point out to your Lordship that this is war."[2]

Britain impounded the vessels.

The *Alabama* patrolled the seas for another nine months before she was at last cornered by the Union sloop-of-war *Kearsarge* near Cherbourg on June 19, 1864. There she lies to this day, thirty-three fathoms deep in the English Channel. Having survived the battle, her captain went on to practice law, further blurring the already tenuous boundary between lawyer and pirate. The *Alabama* alone had destroyed in total some sixty-four Union ships, leading naval historian William Dudley to observe that she and her British-built sisters had "virtually swept the Union merchant fleet from the seas."[3]

After Lee's surrender at Appomattox in April 1865, anti-British sentiment ran high in the North. Top of the list of grievances were the depredations of the *Alabama* and her British-built sister ships. Clearly, the United States would require some form of compensation for what had become known as "the *Alabama* claims."

The Johnson-Clarendon Treaty, negotiated in the fall of 1868, would have settled the matter, but the Senate rejected it by 44–1 after Sen. Charles Sumner of Massachusetts, whose near-fatal 1856 beating on the Senate floor had been a harbinger of the Civil War, made a lengthy, fiery speech denouncing the treaty. He demanded restitution not only for direct losses but for the entire cost of carrying on the war for the two additional years by which he claimed the *Alabama* and her sisters had prolonged it. He put the total at more than $2 billion, an astronomical sum amounting to more than twice the size of the entire world economy at the time.[4] Nobody expected the United Kingdom to bankrupt itself, so in lieu of payment Sumner demanded that Britain cede Canada to the United States. This was an equally ludicrous proposition, but the Senate, and a good portion of the American people, seemed ready to accept nothing less.

The United States thus reached an impasse in its relations with the world's then-dominant power.

What do two states do when they cannot settle their differences by treaty? For almost all of human history, the alternative to negotiation has been war—the "continuation of politics by other means," as military theorist Carl von Clausewitz wrote a generation before Gettysburg. In the late 1860s, armed conflict between Britain and America was not as unlikely a prospect as it seems today. After all, the two countries had been at war before, and within living memory at that: Reverdy Johnson, the U.S. ambassador who negotiated the treaty, had been an eighteen-year-old law student when the redcoats burned the White House (or Presidential Mansion as it was then called) in 1814. Now, a reopening of hostilities seemed shockingly possible—this time, perhaps, on the industrial scale first glimpsed in the Civil War.

At just the right moment, however, President Ulysses S. Grant fell out with his former ally Sumner over a different matter. The breach between the two men suddenly defrosted the *Alabama* issue, freeing the two sides to try a different tack. British and American commissioners were appointed to negotiate a more durable settlement, and the Treaty of Washington was signed on May 5, 1871. To ensure Senate ratification, Grant engineered Sumner's removal as chair of the Senate Foreign Relations Committee.

Here, at last, we see the importance of the CSS *Alabama* to an international lawyer, for the centerpiece of the détente was an international arbitration. Article 1 of the Treaty of Washington referred the *Alabama* claims to a specially convened arbitral tribunal of five members. The United States and Great Britain would each appoint one, while the remaining three would be selected by neutral third powers. Article 2 named Geneva as the venue, and article 6 gave the governing law— essentially, the principles of international law, subject to three overriding rules on the obligations of neutrals. Article 11 stated that the result of the arbitration was to constitute "a full, perfect, and final settlement of all the claims hereinbefore referred to."

The United States pressed claims in relation to the activities of some thirteen ships, including the *Alabama*. Befitting stereotypes about the two countries' legal professions, the American written case was, in the words of Lord Bingham, "hard-hitting [and] adversarial," while the British reply was "dignified and professional."[5] The tribunal duly met and held its substantive hearings at the city hall of Geneva in July 1872. With remarkable alacrity for an arbitral body, it issued its award a mere two months later.

On the claims related to the CSS *Alabama* herself, the tribunal decided unanimously in favor of the United States. In relation to the depredations of other vessels, the votes varied, and a handful of claims were unanimously rejected. Ultimately, the panel awarded the United States $15.5 million, including interest. This was a far cry from the $2 billion Sumner had demanded, but the amount was still fully 5 percent of the British government's annual budget.[6] On this basis, the equivalent sum for the United States today would be considerably more than $200 billion.[7]

But the Crown paid, on time and in full, and a new era of transatlantic cooperation dawned. The British politician and biographer Roy Jenkins summed up the event's importance for world history:

> [T]he settlement not only was the greatest nineteenth-century triumph of rational internationalism over short-sighted jingoism, but also marked the breakpoint between the previous hundred years of Anglo-American strain and the subsequent century and more of two world wars fought in alliance, a Cold War conducted by the American-led but partly British-created NATO, and several decades in which at least some people in both Washington and London believed strongly in a special relationship between the two countries.[8]

In the case of the *Alabama* claims, then, international arbitration constituted one of the most successful peacemaking efforts in history. It would not be the last time.

Let us say that you are out walking one day, and, out of the blue, you are hit by a FedEx truck. From such an incident, you can expect there to flow certain consequences. The driver might be charged with a crime. You (or your insurance company) might sue FedEx for damages. We are none of us above the law; that is the social contract into which we are born. To be sure, a handful of powerful individuals and corporations might be able to get away with certain misdeeds; but these cases stand out precisely because they are the exception, not the rule. For most people and most businesses most of the time, the authority of the state keeps us in line.

What if the offending party is itself a state? Domestically, its own laws apply. At least in developed countries, the state can generally be sued in its own courts; thus, if the offending FedEx truck were instead a vehicle belonging to the U.S. Postal Service, you would likely not be at a material disadvantage. But on an international scale, all states are equally sovereign. There is no ultimate authority; no "sheriff" to hold everyone to the same code. In the absence of Leviathan, the default state of being is *bellum omnium contra omnes*—"the war of all against all," as the philosopher Thomas Hobbes put it.[9] Exceptions like the *Alabama* arbitration notwithstanding, historically there has been but one guiding principle of international relations: Might Makes Right.

In such a world, the most precarious position was that of the stranger in a strange land. Governments would routinely confiscate the assets of foreigners, change the law to disadvantage them, impose dubious additional "taxes" on them, and commit a hundred other slights. Strangers who complained might be thrown in jail. In my legal practice, I have seen all of these things and more, as this book will show.

Those wronged by a foreign government had but two options: to throw themselves on the tender mercies of their hosts or to persuade their own government to intervene on their behalf. Neither was likely to work; and the latter, if successful, came freighted with the risk of sparking a confrontation between two states or else an ugly bout of gunboat diplomacy—the "empire trap" described by economic historian Noel Maurer in his book of that name.[10]

For the most part, then, wronged foreigners abroad were left in effectively the same position as the master of the *Brilliant*, an American merchant vessel that had the misfortune to encounter the CSS *Alabama* in the North Atlantic. Cmdr. Raphael Semmes, the captain of the *Alabama*, wrote in his memoir that he sympathized with the master's plight:

He was a hard-working seaman, who owned a one-third interest in her. He had built her, and was attached to her, and she represented all his worldly goods. But I was forced again to steel my heart. He was, like the other masters who had remonstrated with me, in the same boat with the political rascals who had egged on the war; and I told him he must look to those rascals for redress.[11]

The *Brilliant* burned upon the waters, "lighting up the Gulf Stream for many miles around." There was little the master, or any of her other part owners, could do about it.

Today, however, we find no shortage of international courts and tribunals that routinely hand down judgments and awards against sovereign states. These, like the *Alabama* award, are usually paid. For example, the International Court of Justice—the lineal descendant of the *Alabama* tribunal, as the late Lord Bingham has pointed out[12]—has awakened from decades of somnolescence to a boom in state-to-state claims. Disputes over maritime boundaries, a bugbear of international relations since time immemorial, are now often settled by a combination of arbitration and the International Tribunal on the Law of the Sea. The International Criminal Court, together with the special tribunals for Rwanda, the former Yugoslavia, and other conflict-affected regions, pursues war criminals and genocidaires. The United Nations Compensation Commission has processed millions of claims arising from Saddam Hussein's unlawful occupation of Kuwait. Arbitral tribunals, constituted under the rules of bodies such as the International Centre for the Settlement of Investment Disputes, adjudicate claims involving sovereigns on a routine basis.

Perhaps the poster child for this new culture of state accountability is the international tribunal on which I have served since 1983: the Iran–United States Claims Tribunal. For the whole history of the tribunal, the two parties have enjoyed no diplomatic relations; indeed, the severing of such ties by President Jimmy Carter in 1980 was a precipitating factor in its creation. Throughout the intervening decades, Iran and the United States have frequently been at loggerheads. More than once, they have drawn sabers on each other. In practical terms, there would have been little to stop either party walking away from the tribunal. Yet they have not done so. Instead, the tribunal has done its work. American, Iranian, and third-country judges have processed hundreds of claims—in the process awarding more than $2 billion to American parties against Iran, and around half as much in the other direction.[13]

When I began my legal career in the 1960s, almost none of the abovementioned institutions existed. The International Court of Justice was considered moribund, and, with the occasional much-ballyhooed exception, there was no international arbitration to speak of. I have therefore witnessed, and in many cases participated in, the rise of this new system of peaceful dispute resolution, first as a State Department official, next as an international lawyer in private practice, and finally as a judge and arbitrator. In addition to my service on the Iran–United States Claims Tribunal, I have sat on the International Court of Justice, the Inter-American Court of Human Rights, and dozens of international arbitrations. Just a generation earlier, this career trajectory would have been next to impossible.

It is far from a coincidence that the same period, from the 1960s to the present, has witnessed an unprecedented boom in cross-border investment flows. Political risks (discrimination, expropriation, conflict, and so forth) increase the price of investment; indeed, for the poorest countries, these factors may make it prohibitively expensive. The development of rules of the road by which states must play, and of mechanisms to enforce those rules, has helped mitigate these risks and build a stable foundation for international investment on a scale that has transformed economies and lifted millions from poverty.

Unfortunately, this system of peaceful dispute resolution is now under threat. In recent years, opinion has turned against international tribunals. The left sees them as biased in favor of large corporations and against developing countries. The right dislikes the idea of nationals being subject to "foreign" jurisdiction and wants to keep investment money at home. States themselves—at all income levels, from the European Union through middle-income countries like India to the poorest nations—have tried to rewind the clock on international arbitration, in order to claw back some of the power they perceive themselves as having lost. Without vigilance, we might sleepwalk back to the bad old days, when might made right, there was little recourse against states, and the developing world was a place where responsible investors feared to tread.

In this book, therefore, I want to do three things. First, tell a compelling story that will be of interest to aspiring lawyers, judges, diplomats, and foreign-policy wonks of all stripes. Second, trace the development of the system just described. And third, offer a full-throated defense of that system. For international dispute resolution, whatever flaws it may possess, whatever setbacks it may from time to time inflict upon this or that party, ultimately remains just what it was when Grant was president: a form of peacemaking.

CHAPTER ONE

Street-Fighting Man

THE INADVERTENT LAWYER

I never intended to be a lawyer—at least not for long. My true calling, I felt, was diplomacy. In high school, I took German and became so good at it that, when our teacher left unexpectedly, I was essentially appointed the substitute at the age of seventeen. By the time I finished college, I spoke the language fluently, as well as decent French and some Russian. I had lived overseas for extended periods. I had experience in government to boot, having spent the summer after my junior year working for Sen. Clifford P. Case of my native New Jersey. As part of this work, I had held a pass to visit the Senate floor and had stood within feet of towering figures like the future presidents John F. Kennedy and Lyndon B. Johnson. By the time of my graduation, I had passed all the exams for the U.S. Foreign Service and my appointment was held open for me as I spent a year as a Fulbright Scholar in West Germany.

It was my Harvard tutor George Jaeger who first talked me into going to law school. Born in Austria with Jewish lineage, George had been forced to flee the Nazis at thirteen, so he knew how unpredictable life could be. In Sen. Joseph McCarthy's anti-communist witch hunts—a dark episode that had only ended with McCarthy's censure halfway through my sophomore year—George saw disturbing parallels with Hitler's early purges. McCarthyism showed that government service, particularly at the State Department, was no longer the stable career option it had once been. George therefore advised me to create a fall-back position. To this end, he said I should acquire either a PhD or a law degree. A life of academic poverty did not tempt me; maybe there was something to the law school idea.

My father, who went from being a poor boy to chairman and CEO of one of the topmost advertising agencies on his way to the cover of *Time* magazine, reached the same conclusion by a different path.

"All the CEOs of my clients are lawyers," he told me. "So whatever you want to do—foreign service, politics, business, whatever—getting a law degree is the thing to do." I followed the advice of my mentors and plumped for Harvard Law School to follow that year in Germany.

If my fallback were to be the law, I wanted to set it up properly by obtaining a summer job with the best firm I could. Unfortunately for this plan, my first year at law school was an academic disaster. For the first time in my life, I was sitting on a C-plus average. "Harvard Law" on my CV was enough to secure interviews with most of the big New York firms, but I could tell that the interviewers were on autopilot. They read my grades and their interest in me evaporated.

The sole exception was Larry Morris, a corporate partner with White & Case, a firm whose roots went back to 1901. He alone looked at the totality of my résumé and encouraged me. He said, "You graduated *cum laude* from Harvard College. You were a Fulbright Scholar. You can do better than this."

"I know I can," I said. "I intend to."

Morris sighed. "Look, we can't hire you for the summer between your second and third year. Your grades are just not good enough. But if you pull them up in your second year, I want you to give me a call."

This, it turned out, was just the carrot I needed to complement the stick of those terrible grades. As soon as my second-year results came in,

I called Morris. It was too late for a summer associateship at White & Case, but the improvement was enough to land me lunch with various partners in order to argue my case for a full-time job upon graduation. Just over a year later, on September 18, 1961, I began my career with White & Case at the princely salary of $7,200.

I had not given up my goal of joining the foreign service. To the contrary, I felt that by spending a couple of years with one of the topmost firms in the country, I would have punched a ticket that would stand me in good stead for the rest of my career.

From my beginning at the firm, however, I was captured by the law forever. My longing for the foreign service soon disappeared—though not my thirst for the international life, as will be seen. I preferred litigation over Larry Morris's domain of corporate deal-making. The main reason for this was my impatience. In corporate work, at least with the megadeals on which White & Case advised, it would be a long time before you would be trusted with conducting the negotiations. With litigation, on the other hand, you could pick up smaller cases and be in court arguing right away.

The litigation bug bit me hard. I took on all kinds: criminal trials, personal injury, divorce proceedings, you name it. I defended the publisher McGraw-Hill and the credit-reporting agency Dun & Bradstreet against accusations of libel. At one point, I helped prevent Howard Hughes from taking over ABC, and we debated whether it was Hughes himself or one of his famous body doubles who showed up in the courtroom.

Amid this jack-of-all-trades practice, I somehow became the go-to lawyer for defending claims that involved exploding beer bottles. One of the most memorable was *Simon Savoie v. Anheuser Busch*. Savoie was a French Canadian working as a bartender at a hotel on Madison Avenue. One day, he was tending bar when a bottle of Budweiser exploded in his hand. He said the injury thus suffered was bad enough to put him out of bartending work permanently. He sued Anheuser Busch for $100,000— more than $800,000 in today's money.

Savoie brought suit in a thoroughly blue-collar part of Queens County. We knew the jury would instinctively be on the side of the working man allegedly wronged by a big, faceless corporation. But there was something fishy about Savoie's claim. We hired a private investigator to tail him using a van equipped with a hidden movie camera pointed through a hole drilled in the side (state-of-the-art spy gear in the 1960s). The PI filmed Simon Savoie, among other things, picking up his dry cleaning on wire coat hangers and moving furniture, including picking up a folding metal card table—all with his "injured" hand.

Savoie had said he could no longer pursue his profession; but when we tried to schedule a medical examination of his injuries, his lawyer stupidly let slip that his client had a job as a bartender at the F&M Schaefer Brewing Company pavilion at the 1964–65 New York World's Fair in Queens. As luck would have it, the Shaefer company also was a client of White & Case! I went to interview the head bartender at the pavilion and told him that Savoie claimed he could not do things with his injured hand.

The head bartender laughed. "I saw no evidence of that," he said. "You know, if anything, he was a little too quick with his hand." I asked him what he meant, and he explained that Savoie had been caught pilfering tips meant for the common pot and been fired for it.

Needless to say, this was all interesting when it came time to try the case. Savoie was under no obligation to testify; but he did, suggesting that his lawyer (who was working on contingency and so incentivized to push the damages as high as possible) thought the case would be a slam dunk before a sympathetic working-class jury.

I cross-examined Savoie about his claim that he could not work, and he stuck to his guns. I asked him if he would be able to move furniture with that injured hand.

"No."

"What about a little card table? Could you even pick one of those up?"

"No, I couldn't do that."

"Could you carry clothes home from the dry cleaner on those wire hangers they use?"

"Oh no, I couldn't possibly do that!"

By my count, that made at least four lies he had told on the stand. We introduced testimony from the head bartender at Schaefer. We played the detective's film. We also introduced his pre-"injury" tax returns, which showed tip income so absurdly minimal that a working-class jury would know it to be falsely reported. The jury found against Savoie. After it was all over, one of the jurors approached me outside the courtroom.

"Mr. Brower," he said, "I want you to know that I am a working man. I have always been for the working man. But that son-of-a-bitch Savoie was *lying*!"

SPIES AND SWINDLERS

Every so often, the partners at White & Case would receive calls from judges in the criminal courts who would say that defendant so-and-so needed counsel and could not afford to pay. They would ask the firm to send over a capable young associate to defend the impecunious accused. Litigation partners dared not say no to judges before whom they often had to appear; and besides, it was a good deal for the associates, who would receive valuable courtroom experience. Eager for as much exposure as I could get, I made clear early on that I wanted to be considered for such assignments.

At first, the clients I acquired this way were run-of-the mill offenders: purse snatchers, drug addicts, street brawlers, pimps, and so forth. For a nice small-town kid like me, it was an eye-opening experience. My third year as an associate saw the publication of Claude Brown's *Manchild in the Promised Land*, a semiautobiographical novel dealing with the author's childhood in the slums of Harlem, over the course of which he starts his career in robbery at age five, is shot when he's thirteen, and escapes drug addiction only because he cannot stomach narcotics. I read the book when it came out and instantly recognized the world most of my indigent clients came from.

To interview my clients, I was taken to what were known as "the cages"—huge jail cells crammed with those who had been arrested on drug charges and were in various stages of withdrawal. Between the sight of prisoners writhing in agony on the concrete floor, the sounds of their groans, and the foul smells, the cages were as close to a Dantean vision of hell as I have seen with my own eyes.

In the New York criminal courts, I learned all the tricks of a brass-knuckle trial attorney. Which assistant district attorneys could be trusted and which were inveterate liars. How to sway a courtroom by producing priests and schoolteachers to say nice things about the defendant as character witnesses. How, on appeal, to pick apart a judge's instructions to the jury.

Soon, I was working on bigger criminal cases in federal courts. Two stand out in particular. In 1964 and 1965, I represented Yeoman First Class Nelson Cornelious Drummond, a seventeen-year veteran of the United States Navy. Drummond had been charged with espionage, and they had him dead to rights. In the first criminal case to rely on videotape evidence, Drummond had been recorded entering the secure files area at Naval Station Newport in Rhode Island, extracting a stack of highly classified documents on anti-submarine warfare, and driving with them to a diner in the New York suburbs. Waiting for him there were two officials from the Soviet mission to the United Nations. Also waiting, less conspicuously, was a group of FBI agents. At his trial (in which, I hasten to add, White & Case was not involved), Drummond put forward the slightly desperate defense that he was using the documents only as bait to lure the Soviet agents to his car so he could assassinate them in a show of patriotism. It did not wash: he was sentenced to life imprisonment.[1]

White & Case came in at the appeal phase. At this time, the landmark case *Miranda v. Arizona* was on its way to the Supreme Court. This was the case that established the requirement for the famous warning everyone knows from watching cop shows: "You have the right to remain silent . . ." Drummond had not received the warning, and we argued to the United States Court of Appeals for the Second Circuit, before the usual panel of three judges, that he should have. In light of other ongoing *Miranda* litigation before other three-judge panels of the

Second Circuit, the chief judge decided to submit the case to the court *en banc*—meaning that the final decision would be that of all eight judges of the Court of Appeals, not just the three who had heard it. We lost by a majority, but there was one point of pride for the White & Case team: the three judges who dissented were the same three before whom we had appeared and argued!

This did not help Drummond, of course; nor did the Supreme Court's later *Miranda* decision itself, because it was held not to apply retroactively. So we could not spare Drummond prison; but we did manage to get his sentence reduced. At Lewisburg Penitentiary in Pennsylvania (home, at various times, to such luminaries as James "Whitey" Bulger, John Gotti, and Alger Hiss), Drummond turned out to be a model prisoner. I went before the trial judge, District Judge Thomas Murphy, and told him of Drummond's good deeds: among other things, he had become personal secretary to the warden and organized his fellow inmates to help arrange adoptions for Korean orphans on behalf of Catholic charities (the Catholic part was, I thought, likely to appeal to an Irish American judge). Plus, I argued, espionage is the one crime where there is no chance of recidivism: once your cover is blown, your spying career is over. Judge Murphy agreed to give the parole board discretion to bring Drummond's parole date forward. As a result, Drummond was paroled after just seven years of a life sentence—and went straight into a job as a Pennsylvania probation officer.

The second standout case was different but no less colorful. Lowell McAfee Birrell was a big-time stock trader in the 1940s and 1950s, when he had been known for a time as "the Wizard of Wall Street." The son of an itinerant Presbyterian minister in the Midwest, Birrell hauled himself out of poverty to graduate from Syracuse University at the age of eighteen and the University of Michigan Law School at twenty-one, securing a position at the venerable firm of Cadwalader, Wickersham & Taft. From there, he started a career in business, gained control of dozens of companies, and became a millionaire many times over.[2]

To call Birrell a bon vivant would be an understatement. In Manhattan, he ran his operation out of a suite in the Park Lane Hotel. He became famous around town for schmoozing with starlets and sports stars, drinking with them all night at the then-famous Stork Club on Fifty-Eighth Street. He was such a regular at the club that the staff would on occasion let him sleep there. His 1,200-acre farm in Bucks County, Pennsylvania, was supposedly equipped with an artificial lake for sailing his yacht[3] and "a row of slot machines that were said to have paid off about as often as watered stock."[4] One Christmas, his wife gave him a fire truck; another Christmas, an elephant.[5]

But behind the jovial façade and Horatio Alger backstory, Birrell was a crook. He once told an investor he ran into at a restaurant, "You put money into one of my companies? That was a mistake, sir. Nobody makes any money in my companies except me."[6] Birrell watered stocks, issuing millions of unregistered shares to himself and selling them at grossly inflated prices. He secretly stripped companies of their valuable assets, talked up the stock, and sold out before they collapsed. He laundered transactions through Swiss bank accounts and middlemen in Cuba. The Securities and Exchange Commission (SEC) called him "the most brilliant manipulator of corporations in modern times."[7]

In 1957, the SEC finally caught up with him and issued a subpoena. Birrell fled to Cuba and again to Brazil when Castro came to power in 1959. After a military coup five years later, the junta in Brazil ratified an extradition treaty with the United States. Tired of fleeing, Birrell returned to face the music.[8] He had been charged with conspiring to rig the stock of American Leduc Petroleum and selling three-and-a-half million unregistered shares in the company.

Birrell was now penniless, or at least said that he was. Around my thirty-second birthday, I was assigned to defend him. This was in June 1967, and the trial was to take place that December, meaning I had five months to get to grips with the affairs of a man who had purposefully made them as difficult to understand as possible. Worse, the case was assigned to Judge William Herlands of the Southern District of New York. Herlands had been a district attorney in the 1930s, padlocking New York speakeasies by the dozen. Following his elevation to the bench, he had developed a reputation as a hanging judge, unfavorably disposed toward defendants in general. He was unlikely to look kindly upon my client, a notorious drinker who had been on the lam for years. I told the firm I could do it, but I would need to dedicate myself completely to the case for the next six months.

I soon found a gap in the government's armor. The prosecution had gotten hold of about forty file cabinets of documents from the farm of one of Birrell's Bucks County cronies. Before I entered the case, a previous judge had ruled that the search warrant that had produced the trove of documents was defective, meaning that everything in those file cabinets was inadmissible in court. (The judge had admitted Birrell to $15,000 bail, which someone posted on his behalf.)

This gave rise to the complicated question of whether the prosecution could prove its case without relying on those tainted documents. If we saved those issues until after the trial and Birrell were convicted, he might have to languish in jail while we unraveled the admissibility question, only to find he should not have been convicted in the first place because the evidence was tainted. From what I had heard about Judge Herlands, it seemed he would be only too happy to lock Birrell up while the court took its time deciding the issue.

I therefore wanted the prosecution to show in advance that they could try a clean case. Twenty years later, this would be done before the trial of the Iran-Contra conspirator Lt. Col. Oliver North, to ensure that the prosecution case did not rely on immunized testimony from congressional hearings. But in Birrell's case, predictably enough, Judge Herlands would have none of it, and the Supreme Court denied my petition to reverse his decision. The trial would go ahead as planned.

The original indictment had been drawn up by an ace prosecutor, Arthur Liman. Liman had left the U.S. Attorney's office while Birrell was in Brazil, but now returned from private practice to argue the case before a jury. (Liman's path and mine would cross again when he went on to counsel the Senate committee investigating Iran-Contra in 1987.)

Birrell's trial lasted almost the whole month of December 1967. It was a ferocious flu season in New York City. So many jurors got sick that we used up our supply of alternates. If one more juror had dropped, we would have had a mistrial. Even Liman was hospitalized briefly during the trial, having taken too many aspirin for what he described as "a persistent cold."[9] (Against doctor's orders, Liman returned to deliver the closing speech to the jury.) For my part, I just prayed I could get through the trial in one piece.

I did my darndest for Birrell, as I would for any client. I cross-examined a handwriting expert, forcing him to admit that matching handwriting based on just eight letters in a signature was a tenuous proposition. My vigorous cross-examination of Birrell's co-conspirator, who had turned state's evidence, was a classic of the genre, in which I forced him to admit that his eventual sentence might depend upon how "helpful" to the prosecution's case he proved. It made the front page of the *Wall Street Journal*. When Liman in his closing speech introduced the well-known aphorism about one rotten apple spoiling an entire barrel, I turned it around on him, telling the jury: "The only rotten apples here are in the prosecution's barrel."

The jury convicted Birrell on all counts related to selling unregistered stock. That was inevitable because the evidence was all there in black and white in the company's books. But the jury could not reach a verdict on any of the counts of stock rigging, resulting in a mistrial on those counts.[10] Arthur Liman approached me after it was over and expressed his astonishment at my having hung a jury in such a case. "I just hope that the partners at White & Case appreciate what you've achieved here," he said. "And by the way, the 'rotten apples' thing was very good."

In the immediate term, this success did not help Birrell, who was ordered locked up pending a determination of whether the prosecution's case had been clean of the mass of unlawfully seized documents. After the foreman read the verdict, Birrell leaned over to me and whispered, "Ask the judge for marshal's tickets." I had no idea what a marshal's ticket was, but I did as I was told, and Judge Herlands granted his mysterious request. I found out later that marshal's tickets allowed the federal marshals to take a prisoner out for dinner before delivering him into custody. In Birrell's case, they apparently did this in the style to which the defendant had become accustomed, for the marshals finally deposited him at the West Street Jail at five in the morning, just the way he liked to be at that hour—drunk as a skunk.

I felt that I had already spent enough time on this case, and I was not eager to pore over the contents of forty-plus filing cabinets, so I asked Judge Herlands to release me from my court-appointed assignment. He agreed, thank God. But two months after the end of the trial, the senior partner who had handled my assignment called me into his office. "I've just had a call from the chief judge of the Second Circuit," he said. "He tells me that Lowell Birrell has been before the court this morning representing himself appealing Judge Herlands's denial of bail. Birrell specifically asked that 'your young man Brower' be appointed as his counsel."

My heart sank. Hadn't I had enough? Nevertheless, rising yet again to a challenge, I said I would do it, assuming the firm agreed.

Herlands had denied bail on the basis that Birrell was a flight risk. The judge had a point: Birrell's flight to Copacabana Beach via Batista's Cuba had been reported in all the newspapers, and there wasn't a snowflake's chance in hell of my convincing anyone, let alone a Second Circuit judge, otherwise. So I tried a different tack. I researched what sentences over the years had been handed out in the Southern District of New York to those convicted specifically of selling unregistered stock—the only crime of which Birrell had been convicted, thanks to the hung jury.

The answer turned out to be, on average, exactly two months longer than Birrell already had spent in the pokey, pre- and post-trial. So my argument was simply, "Why would a man of sixty-plus years flee the country to avoid just two more months of incarceration?"

Before I could open my mouth, however, the chief judge asked, "Mr. Brower, how much bail can your client make?" I recited that I was court-assigned under the Criminal Justice Act on the basis of the appellant's affidavit of poverty. I had no more information than that. The argument proceeded but was brief.

The next morning the clerk of court phoned me. "Mr. Brower, you have an order. Your client is admitted to $30,000 bail." When I asked where he was being held, the clerk told me, "He's already out. Some guy in dirty boots and workmen's clothes came and bailed him out." Evidently, Birrell still enjoyed certain connections.

Not long after that, Judge Herlands died in the middle of the evidentiary trial, and the prosecution, facing the prospect of running the entire case again, formally abandoned the indictment on which I defended Birrell. From what I read, he had some more criminal legal problems before he died years later; but I remain proud of what I achieved on his behalf.

THE SHAPE OF THINGS TO COME

New York City is a tough place to be a litigator; in fact, it is a tough place to be just about anything. But, to paraphrase Frank Sinatra, if you can make it there, you can make it anywhere. For those with the stomach for a fight, a career as a street-fighting Big Apple trial attorney can be tremendous fun, as it certainly was for me. But there was an element missing: my eight years of practice never took me north of Schenectady, west of Philadelphia, or south of Washington. My international itch, in other words, remained unscratched.

There was one case that suggested the shape of things to come, and it was—of all things—a personal injury matter. Chemical Bank, a venerable Wall Street institution dating back to 1824, was a client of White & Case. One day, the company's vice chair, Hulbert Aldrich, was in a cab coming down Park Avenue, turning left to head for JFK, when a limousine coming up Park Avenue slammed into the side of the taxi and injured him. This limo turned out to be the official car of the Hungarian Permanent Representative to the United Nations. Aldrich engaged us to sue.

My exposure to international law in school had been slight; in fact, I had taken only one course in the subject. I wanted to build the foundation of my fallback career with a big Wall Street firm, and I thought that if such firms looked at my curriculum vitae and saw a roster of electives in international law they might think me some kind of weirdo. So I didn't know much, but I did know that foreign ambassadors enjoyed more or less blanket immunity from lawsuits.

In the splendidly named British sovereign immunity case *Rahimtoola v. The Nizam of Hyderabad*, Lord Denning had said (very much *obiter dictum*, as was his wont):

> *It is more in keeping with the dignity of a foreign sovereign to submit himself to the rule of law than to claim to be above it, and his independence is better ensured by accepting the decisions of courts of acknowledged impartiality than by arbitrarily rejecting their jurisdiction.*[11]

It almost goes without saying that most sovereigns, most of the time, have not been this high-minded. On the contrary, they guard their immunities with the watchfulness of a mother hen. If you wanted to sue a foreign government in the United States in the 1960s, either the defendants would have to waive their immunity, or the State Department would need to say that an exception applied, in which case the courts would generally follow that determination. Neither possibility was particularly likely.

There are sound reasons for a general policy of immunity before foreign courts. One would not want states blackmailing each other by victimizing diplomats. But this was a personal injury matter in which the only victim was my client, a private citizen. Looking more deeply at the case, I discovered that the Hungarians had purchased liability insurance on the car. If they thought they needed liability insurance, I reasoned, they must have contemplated the possibility of liability in the local courts. I therefore argued that by securing the insurance, the Hungarian mission had impliedly waived their immunity. This brought the Hungarians to the table, and we settled the case favorably for my client.

I do not think, however, that they settled because of the brilliance of my argument, which frankly was a little far-fetched. They settled because they did not want bad publicity. Diplomats, especially in New

York City, were (and still are) notorious scofflaws, routinely parking illegally, racking up parking tickets, and using immunity to avoid paying. The Hungarians settled the case because they did not want the distraction of opening up this can of worms in the press. This, therefore, was a valuable early lesson in the degree to which outside considerations affect litigation against states. I may not have realized at the time but, as far as my career was concerned, suing states (and defending them) would define the shape of things to come.

While I forged ahead at White & Case, across the river in my home state of New Jersey I also was pursuing another early love, politics. As a high schooler, I had been selected to attend a summer camp called Boys State, where we spent a week on the Rutgers campus, practicing our civic political system in a mock election by running for state office, campaigning, and voting. I ran for state senator from my assigned county under the slogan "Put Brower in Power, the Man of the Hour!" I lost.

As an adult, however, I enjoyed a bit more success. A lifelong northeastern "liberal Republican"—a philosophy now considered tantamount to a contradiction in terms but in those days a political category being championed by such heavyweights as Rockefeller and Javits—I got myself elected to the Somerset County Republican Committee, then also to the Township Committee, the five-member governing body where I lived, and I harbored ambitions of rising in the political world. My inspiration was Senator Case, for whom I had worked the summer before my college graduation. Case himself had been a partner in Simpson, Thacher & Bartlett in New York City, as well as a municipal councilman and a state assemblyman, before going to Congress. I myself began seriously to contemplate a career in elected office.

In November 1968, near the beginning of my eighth year as an associate at White & Case, Richard Nixon was elected president. This was exciting to me, given my growing interest in a political career, and all the more so because Nixon entered office explicitly as a foreign policy president. To shape his foreign policy, he brought in as national security adviser a brilliant Harvard professor, Henry Kissinger, then a relatively young forty-five years of age. While at law school, I had taken Kissinger's defense policy seminar, which was more or less what the Germans would call a *raupensammlung* (literally a "caterpillar collection," but used jokingly to refer to any display of assorted items). Each week, we were treated to a fresh grandee from Kissinger's already formidable Rolodex: the former head of the Office of Management and Budget, the former prime minister of France, and on and on. I wrote my thesis off the back of that seminar, titling it, rather grandly, "The Dialectics of National Purpose." Kissinger read it, and his teaching assistant gave it an A.

After Nixon's election, I told my mentors in the firm that if there were a job for me in the administration, I would take it. In retrospect this may not have been such a smart move; but it did not seem to hurt me because, to my delight, the firm nevertheless made me a partner on July 1, 1969.

I thought that a post in the State Department would appeal most to me, so I set out on the hunt for a position there. The first administration job for which I interviewed was that of special assistant to Elliot Richardson, then undersecretary of state. I lost out to a fellow lawyer, Bert Rein, later the cofounder of the powerful Washington firm Wiley Rein and to this day a good friend. Bert had clerked at the Supreme Court, as had Richardson, and it will always be hard to trump that kind of pedigree. But soon enough, another role came up: assistant legal adviser for European affairs, reporting to State Department Legal Adviser Jack Stevenson, a partner of the Wall Street firm Sullivan & Cromwell.

"I don't know," I told my State Department contacts. "I've been beating my brains out in the law for eight years. I want to do important things. Policy-related things."

"You don't understand the job," they said. "It's maybe 20 or 25 percent law. The rest is policy. You would be working on international negotiations. Career foreign service people will come to you for advice because they know you are smart and separate from their hierarchy."

I agreed to speak to Jack Stevenson about the role. We hit it off immediately. Stevenson was about thirteen years older than I, and I admired his career path. In addition to his law degree, Jack held a doctorate in law—something that was almost unheard of at the time, even among professors, and showed his genuine fascination with the law. We shared each other's liberal Republican politics.

For his part, Jack seemed to think it impressive that a brand-new partner at another Wall Street law firm would choose to quit four months later to join him as assistant legal adviser. I had excellent credentials for working in European relations, where Germany was the most critical country, alongside the Soviet Union. We clicked right away. I was sold on the job, and it seemed he was sold on seeing me in it. As will be seen later, he promoted me steadily and became one of the two greatest mentors in my professional life until he passed away in 1997.

When I left White & Case, just four months after being made partner, some of my colleagues could not understand it. The sentiment was along the lines of, "Well, I could understand if they wanted him for secretary of state. But assistant legal adviser for European affairs? What is that?" But following that meeting with Jack Stevenson, there was no doubt in my mind that this would be a good move. It would turn out to be the beginning of the rest of my life. I asked Jack what I should do to prepare. He told me to read the entire *American Law Institute Restatement of the Foreign Relations Law of the United States*, a dry tome of some six hundred pages. It was good advice, for I still knew too little about international law. That reading assignment was my crash course in a subject that was to consume much of the rest of my career.

CHAPTER TWO

Might Makes Right

THE BERLIN CONNECTION

Shortly before I joined the State Department in November 1969, Willy Brandt was sworn in as chancellor of West Germany. Right away, Brandt set to work implementing his promised *Neue Ostpolitik* (new eastern policy)—beginning with the easing of relations between West and East Germany. It was an exciting time to be the newly minted assistant legal adviser for European affairs. The Nixon administration had already begun pursuing its own policy of détente with the Soviet Union, and the legal and political status of a divided Berlin was to prove a key component of that policy. Clearly, the city would loom large in my portfolio.

On a personal level, moreover, I had long enjoyed a connection with Berlin. At my public high school in Westfield, New Jersey, students could study three modern languages: French, Spanish, and German. The French teacher was considered a little odd; he had been gassed in World War I and was rumored to have a metal plate in his skull. The Spanish teacher spoke the language well, but with a grating American accent. The German teacher spoke with an impeccable accent (she was American, but one of her parents was German) and during World War II had been a sergeant in the U.S. Women's Army Corps. She was by far the most rigorous of the three. I took her class and excelled.

During my senior year (1952–53), an organization called The Experiment in International Living visited my high school and delivered a presentation about their program of homestays abroad, including placements in West Germany. I decided on the spot that I had to go. Having persuaded my parents it was a good idea, I found myself spending the summer with a doctor's family in the charming medieval town of Soest in Westphalia.

Soest was a peaceful town, far from any industrial area; but even here, eight years after the war had ended, there remained evidence of the intense Allied bombardment. The Möhne Dam near the town had been breached by the famous Dambusters Squadron of the British Royal Air Force, and it still bore surface scars. A boy around my age from one of the host families had on display in his room part of a bomb casing that he had retrieved from the street after a raid when he was no older than ten.

We did go on trips outside Soest—to Bavaria, Austria, and Switzerland. But there was no talk of visiting Berlin, perhaps because it was not considered safe. On June 17, 1953, shortly before my arrival in Germany, workers had risen against the Communist puppet government in East Berlin and hundreds of other towns in East Germany; the uprising had been ended by Soviet tanks, with dozens of deaths. Eight years before the Berlin Wall went up, Churchill's "Iron Curtain" was already making its presence felt.

That September, I started my undergraduate studies at Harvard. I originally majored in German, but I switched to government because, while I have always been an admirer of German culture and language, the thought of spending months on end ploughing through Goethe or Schiller was just too much (I would no doubt have felt the same about Whitman or Baudelaire). But I would not stay away from Germany, returning to the country on a Fulbright scholarship in 1957. I started out studying in Bonn but later transferred to West Berlin, partly to attend

the Hochschule für Politik, the country's premier political science institution, and partly to spend more time with my girlfriend, Oda, a fellow
Fulbright scholar I had met on the ten-day ocean voyage from New York
to Bremerhaven as she was returning home to Germany from her year at
Lawrence College in Wisconsin.

Together we would go to East Berlin to visit her relatives, take in
excellent operas and concerts, or attend the theater, where Bertolt Brecht's
widow, Helene Weigel, still performed in his plays (the East German cen-
sors seemed unaware that Brecht's critique of nationalist authoritarianism
might apply equally to them). The severe Soviet architecture of East Berlin's
main boulevard, the aptly renamed "Stalinallee" (now Karl-Marx-Allee)
seemed purpose-built to leech the joy out of life. The Berlin Wall was still
four years away, but your nose always told you which side of the divide
you were on, courtesy of the pungent exhaust from East Germany's low-
grade diesel fuel.

On one occasion, a professor at East Berlin's Humboldt University
arranged for me to attend the lectures on Marxist-Leninist dogma that
the Communist government had made mandatory for every student. It
felt unreal to know, sitting there, that shortly I could go to my home
in West Berlin and continue relegating Karl Marx to historical study,
while those around me were trapped in his world. Such a far cry from
Harvard—or even from the Hochschule für Politik just a few miles away.

The summer after my first year of law school, Oda and I were married at the seven-hundred-year-old St.-Annen-Kirche, a village church
in the Dahlem-Dorf area of West Berlin. Two years later, in 1961, we
returned to the city for six weeks before I was due to start my legal
career at White & Case in New York City. On August 13, however, over
breakfast on a beautifully sunny day, we heard on the radio that the
East German regime was closing the border between the two halves of
the city. For many weeks, East Germany had been bleeding thousands
upon thousands of refugees into West Berlin; apparently the authorities had had enough. We went down to the dividing line and saw East
German *Volkspolizei* (people's police) and teenage factory militias string-
ing barbed wire down the dividing streets. West Berliners stood around,

jeering and blowing raspberries at the Communists. This new barrier was the first iteration of the Berlin Wall.

The United States' reaction was swift. An armored infantry brigade thundered up the autobahn from West Germany to reinforce the Berlin Brigade. We saw their arrival, which the locals greeted with cheering and flowers. The White House dispatched Vice President Lyndon B. Johnson to reassure the city, together with Gen. Lucius Clay, the hero of the 1948–49 Berlin Airlift, after whom a major street in West Berlin had been renamed. Oda and I saw Johnson's speech at the Rathaus Schöneberg, where two years later Kennedy would intone, "*Ich bin ein Berliner.*" From the steps of the building, LBJ delivered a message to the people of East Berlin: "Do not lose courage, for while tyranny may seem for the moment to prevail, its days are numbered."

Unfortunately, the number of its days would prove many, and their toll steep. Less than a week after Johnson's speech, on August 24, a tailor named Günter Litfin became the first person shot dead attempting to escape East Berlin.[1] He would be far from the last. Within a few years, the East German authorities would build not one but two permanent barriers, clearing buildings between them to create a "death strip," where snipers could pick off any would-be escapees. Between 1961 and 1989, more than one hundred and forty people died during their attempts to cross the wall and reach the West.

The wall upended lives in other ways, too. The elder of my two brothers-in-law, Dr. Ulf Rohde-Liebenau, was in 1961 engaged to a woman who lived on the other side of the wall and could not leave. We seriously considered lending her my wife's West Berlin ID card. Oda and my prospective sister-in-law looked somewhat alike, and there was a ten-day grace period allowing West Berliners to enter and leave East Berlin; in the end she wisely decided it was too risky. If the border guards had smelled a rat, she would have been arrested on the spot, and we would never have heard from her again. Eventually she got out—presumably for an exorbitant fee—through one of the secret tunnels that were later dug between East and West.

I WAS A THIRTY-FOUR-YEAR-OLD BRIGADIER GENERAL

Talks on the status of Berlin were already in the works when I arrived in Washington in late 1969.[2] Within a month, I was briefing Secretary of State Bill Rogers face-to-face on the United States' legal position regarding Berlin. Rogers was an accomplished lawyer who had served as Eisenhower's attorney general; but the scuttlebutt around town was that Nixon had appointed him precisely because he saw Rogers as a neophyte in international affairs. The president wanted to control U.S. foreign policy directly from the White House through Henry Kissinger. As I knew him, however, Rogers was an agreeable straight shooter with a lot of sense and much to offer. He was an alumnus of Thomas E. Dewey's 1930s racket-busting team in Manhattan's district attorney's office before Dewey became governor and a presidential candidate. He then went on to work as a Hill staffer with Rep. Richard M. Nixon on the Alger Hiss case. When Nixon, running in 1952 as Dwight D. Eisenhower's vice presidential candidate, came under attack—to the extent that Eisenhower had considered dropping him from the ticket—it was Rogers who advised him to give what became known as the "Checkers speech," the defense that rescued Nixon. Eventually Rogers served as Eisenhower's attorney general, and I have always thought that if Nixon as president had consulted Rogers in 1972, as he had in 1952, he might well have avoided the Watergate scandal.

Legally speaking, while West Germany was now a state in its own right with the city of Bonn as its capital, Berlin remained occupied territory, as it had been since the end of World War II, when it was subdivided into British, French, American, and Soviet sectors of occupation. West Berlin consisted of the first three sectors, but it did enjoy a degree of self-government, with its own legislature and mayor, an office in which Chancellor Willy Brandt had been serving in 1961 when the first barbed-wire wall went up.

The position of East Berlin was murkier, however. According to the United States and its allies, its status was the same as that of the other three sectors—occupied territory. According to the Soviet Bloc countries, however, East Berlin was properly the capital of East Germany, and the Western occupation of the rest of Berlin merely a temporary inconvenience.

For propaganda reasons, East German maps sometimes represented West Berlin as a gaping blank space, evoking the *hic sunt dracones* ("here be dragons") scrawled along the edges of medieval navigation charts.[3] An enclave of freedom some one hundred miles inside Communist territory, West Berlin was in constant danger of being cut off from the outside world. In 1948, the USSR had blockaded West Berlin for almost a year; the city was sustained only by aerial shipments of supplies, known to history as the Berlin Airlift, the success of which ultimately convinced the Soviets to lift the siege. Thereafter it was possible to travel by road or rail across East German territory between West Germany and West Berlin. But the Soviets periodically threatened renewed blockades, so keeping the borders open required constant vigilance. Reinforcing that right of access, and shoring up West Berlin's position more generally, was to be a major preoccupation of my first two years at State.

Berlin was, not surprisingly, the major destination for my first official trip. When I arrived, my U.S. military escorts seemed not to know quite how to treat me. "What is your equivalent military rank?" they asked. I hadn't a clue, so we looked it up. At thirty-four years old, serving in an office just two steps below assistant secretary of state, it turned out that I was the equivalent of a brigadier general! Needless to say, the phantom stars on my shoulders garnered me a certain amount of respect—and nice quarters at the Harnack-Haus, the U.S. Army's "hotel" for visiting dignitaries, to boot.

As part of my trip, I rode along with one of the daily Army intelligence helicopter tours of the entire ninety-six-mile border between the Democratic and Communist halves of the city. From the air, the differences between East and West were even more apparent. East Berlin had a great deal more devastation still left over from the war, and infill buildings stood out as dark, heavy boxes. The border bisected the city like a scar: two parallel barriers separated by the death strip.

Toward the southwest apex of our flight, closer to Potsdam than to Berlin proper, we flew out a little way over East German soil and touched down in the hamlet of Steinstücken, a thirty-one-acre shard of West Berlin surrounded by the East. There existed a dozen such enclaves, created by various accidents of history. Most consisted of farms or allotments; only Steinstücken was permanently inhabited.

Steinstücken had fewer than two hundred residents, and I was surprised that even that many had stayed. Watchtowers loomed over the enclave, which was hedged with barbed-wire fences. The death strip beyond was patrolled by East German guards who handily outnumbered the residents, even without counting their ever-present sniffer dogs. At night, the inhabitants' sleep would be disturbed by floodlights and sporadic gunfire. In 1972, a corridor to "mainland" West Berlin would be ceded and a proper road built; but for now the residents' only access to jobs and schools in the city was to drive or walk two-thirds of a mile through a wooded stretch of Communist territory, passing through not one but two death strips each way.

From time to time, crises would erupt over Steinstücken, including one in 1956 when border guards refused to allow a repair man access to fix the lone refrigerator in the enclave's only grocery store.[4] Regular U.S. helicopter visits had begun in 1961 when Gen. Lucius D. Clay insisted on visiting in person and stationed a small detachment of U.S. military police. At first, East German authorities threatened to shoot down the helicopters as a violation of their airspace (which, by clear provision of the governing agreements, it categorically was not); but by the time of my visit in 1970, the flights had become routine.[5]

Until the situation of Germany as a whole normalized, Steinstückeners were completely dependent on U.S. support for their security and freedom. Still, it was not all bad; as one elderly resident told a reporter from the *New York Times* the year after my visit, the neighborhood's isolation also kept out tax collectors.[6]

SPANDAU

Colleagues at the State Department urged me to add another item to my itinerary: an inspection of Spandau Allied Military Prison, a rare relic of the 1945–48 four-power rule of Berlin as a whole. Spandau had been built to hold hundreds of inmates, but by 1970 just one remained: the former deputy führer of the Third Reich, Rudolf Hess, sentenced to life imprisonment in 1946 at the Nuremberg Trials. The prison was physically located in the British sector, but as the internment site of convicted Nazi war criminals it was guarded by British, French, American, and Soviet military contingents in monthly rotations.

I happened to visit on a day when control was passing to the Soviet contingent. The Soviets were always pleased to be at Spandau because it gave them a chance to show their presence inside West Berlin, where their only other foothold was a tiny ceremonial guard at the Soviet War Memorial in the Tiergarten. When their turn came (three times each year), the officers and their wives would celebrate by holding a multi-course luncheon with all the trimmings. On this occasion, they invited me, and I sat swapping jokes with high-ranking KGB officials, conducting my own version of détente in miniature.

Hess's cell was a large, sparse room with bars across the windows. The deputy führer complained a great deal about his predicament, and I got little sense that he felt any remorse for the suffering and death he had caused. In fact, he felt hard done by. On May 10, 1941, shortly before Hitler's planned invasion of the Soviet Union, he had flown himself to Scotland and bailed out in a harebrained attempt to make peace with the Western Allies. This hardly excused his crimes, however; besides, as the Nuremburg tribunal noted in its judgment, Hess's quixotic peace overture was most likely in reality a cynical attempt to secure Germany's western flank and pave the way for the imminent Nazi incursion into Russia.[7]

The deputy führer had claimed insanity at Nuremberg and, while this was not sufficient to postpone his trial, a panel of physicians did find him "unstable" and paranoiac.[8] Was Hess crazy? After so long in captivity, perhaps a little. But looking into the senior Nazi's eyes, I could see the gears still turning. I concluded he was rather, as the expression goes, crazy like a fox. He knew the evil he had done.

No human punishment could match the severity of the crimes that Nazis like Hess had committed. Some had eventually faced justice—but only after Germany lost a war that lasted nearly six years and cost millions of lives. The Soviet Union, too, visited evil on the world for nearly forty-five years following the defeat of Germany. But for its victims, whether in Berlin or anywhere else, there was no justice. The USSR, a nuclear-armed empire, was too big and too powerful to hold to account. As so often happened in international relations, might made right.

BINDUNG, VERBINDUNG: TOMAYTO, TOMAHTO

As my tenure at the State Department went on, the importance of Berlin only grew. Nixon was seeking to hold talks in Moscow with the Soviet premier, Leonid Brezhnev, as the centerpiece of his strategy of détente. Over the course of 1970 and 1971, an agreement easing the situation of West Berlin came to be seen as a necessary preliminary to these talks.

Negotiations began serenely enough, but their intensity ramped up as Kissinger took increasing notice and began to link the agreement on Berlin to the other aspects of détente.[9] As assistant legal adviser for European affairs, I advised the American delegation and periodically traveled to Bonn for high-level meetings of the three Western delegations with our West German ally. The Soviets deployed their usual dirty tricks. In their Russian "translation" of the final text, they reinserted terms that had been rejected. When they were called out, they protested, "But *we* are the masters of the Russian language!"

This led to the absurdity of two separate German-language texts—one from the East, translated from Russian, the other from the West, translated from English. The differences between them were far from trivial. One text would describe the ties between West Germany and

West Berlin as a *bindung*—a "relationship"—while the other would say *verbindung*—a "link"—words that implied different levels of closeness. No sooner had the parties agreed on one term than the other would surface in the East German text. Finally, an accompanying side letter from the Soviet Union was agreed upon, stipulating that the Russian, English, and French versions all had the same meaning—and *neither* German version was official.

The Quadripartite Agreement on Berlin, as it came to be known, recognized the existing relationship between West Berlin and West Germany, provided for unfettered civilian traffic between the two, and ensured West Berliners' right to visit East Berlin and East Germany. (The Soviets would never allow East Berliners the same rights in reverse—that would have led to a mass exodus.)

The agreement was brought into effect by a final protocol signed on June 3, 1972, at the Berlin Kammergericht, the court building in the American sector that had served as the headquarters of the long-moribund Four-Power Allied Control Council. I had the honor of presiding over the signing ceremony with the four foreign ministers: Bill Rogers of the United States, Andrei Gromyko of the United Socialist Soviet Republic, Sir Alec Douglas-Home of the United Kingdom, and Maurice Schumann of France. Despite the national egos involved, it was an impressively civilized affair, with no jostling for the limelight. After the ceremony, we immediately exercised our newly reconfirmed right of access: I hopped in a motorcade with Secretary Rogers, and we drove through East Berlin with the Stars and Stripes flying from the hood of the car.

The agreement was important to West Berliners, at least psychologically, for it lessened their feeling of isolation. Its wider significance, however, was that it punched Nixon's ticket to the May 1972 Moscow summit, at which the United States and the Soviet Union reached historic agreements on weapons control, making a nuclear exchange between the superpowers much less likely.

As far as Germany was concerned, the Quadripartite Agreement paved the way for further détente between East and West. Personally,

I was not pleased with all of those steps, especially when the Soviet Union was permitted to establish a consulate in the American sector of West Berlin. I felt it was inconsistent with the legal status of Berlin as occupied territory, and I tried to persuade Kissinger's office to drop its support for the provision, ultimately to no avail. To make matters worse, the site the East chose for its consulate wound up being a few blocks from the house where Oda's parents lived. My in-laws were indeed displeased. "What on earth, Charlie?" they said. "You couldn't even keep them out of our *neighborhood?*"

TALKING TO THE SOVIETS

As time went on, my relationship with Jack Stevenson deepened. I became his confidant and sounding board. Sometimes we would chat in his office; but when he had something really important to discuss, he would say, "Let's go have lunch at the Metropolitan Club!" just a couple of blocks from the White House.

In the spring of 1971, about a year and a half into my tenure, Jack made this relationship official by promoting me to deputy legal adviser the first time such a slot opened. When he left the department in early 1973, I took over as acting legal adviser on Jack's recommendation. I was only ever "acting" in that role, for two reasons. First, some of the higher-ups thought me, at age thirty-seven, too young for the job (my efforts to look older by dressing in three-piece suits with a pocket-watch on a gold chain notwithstanding). Second, by that point Secretary Rogers felt so stymied by the White House's "Prussians" (John Ehrlichman and Bob Haldeman) rejecting his picks for presidential appointments that he had stopped bothering to send them for approval. Consequently, at least half of those at assistant secretary level were "actings," anticipating by more than four decades similar dysfunction during the Trump administration. Nevertheless, I was allowed to move into Jack's office—a nice perk that came with its own bathroom and two secretaries—but only because there seemed to be a chance that President Nixon would nominate me to be the legal adviser. On the one hand, I was sorry to see Jack, who had been such a close friend and supporter, leave. On the other hand, I indeed was very pleased that he, ever my "angel," had as his last act convinced Secretary Rogers to install me, the most junior of four deputy legal advisers, in an office traditionally reserved for the most senior deputy legal adviser.

International negotiations were always a major part of my portfolio. Indeed, my first assignment as assistant legal adviser for European affairs had been to advise the chief American negotiator with Spain, Undersecretary of State for Political Affairs U. Alexis Johnson, in negotiations to extend U.S. operating and basing rights there. The bases were crucial because they served our nuclear deterrent in the shape of B-52 bombers and Polaris submarines, allowing them to stay in the air or under the sea for longer stretches of time. Nevertheless, the negotiations had to be handled with care. A powerful faction on the Senate Foreign Relations Committee, led by Democratic Sen. J. William Fulbright of Arkansas, would balk at any suggestion of the United States cozying up to a country that was still ruled by the fascist Generalísimo Francisco Franco, then seventy-seven years old.

My 1970 visit to Berlin had included a brief stop in Madrid, with trips out to two of the American bases. I was flown by military transport from Morón Air Base outside Madrid by the son of Gen. Jimmy Doolittle—famed for the daring 1942 bombing raid on Tokyo—to the critical Atlantic Polaris submarine base at Rota, across the bay from Cadíz. There I boarded a Polaris submarine and marveled at the claustrophobia of its quarters and the fortitude of its crew, who had to remain submerged for months on end carrying out missions critical to the defense of the United States.

By coincidence, I was the senior U.S. official in Spain that day: Ambassador Hill was elsewhere and the senior military officer, Air Force Gen. David Burchinal, was in Germany. So Uncle Sam was left with me. Thus I found myself the guest of honor at a long luncheon table otherwise occupied by Marine Corps officers responsible for the security of the base. They were respectful, the meal delicious, the conversation fascinating; but in retrospect, those senior Marines must have been wondering why they were having lunch with some thirty-four-year-old political twerp. I nevertheless attracted good reviews for my work on the Spain negotiations, including from Undersecretary Johnson, who described me in his memoirs as "a lawyer who could always find ways of doing what was needed instead of pleading it was impossible."[10] High praise indeed!

The following year, in the fall of 1971, I headed the American delegation to the conference that produced the Montreal Sabotage Convention. We addressed attacks on civilian aircraft—a response to events such as the 1970 bombing of Swissair flight SR-330, in which forty-seven people had died. The convention required states either to prosecute or extradite perpetrators of such atrocities. Years later, as we will see, it would come into play in the aftermath of the bombing of PanAm flight 103 over Lockerbie, Scotland, and I would find myself addressing the International Court of Justice about the proper interpretation of the convention.

The most delicate talks, however, were invariably the ones with the Soviet Union. A good portion of my work at the State Department involved assisting Americans—and in some cases, aspirant Americans— in trouble overseas. Often these were people who had gotten themselves arrested, sometimes by misadventure, other times through no fault of their own. We would press their captors to grant them access to U.S. officials, which they were obliged to do. Unsurprisingly, the worst offenders were usually the Soviets. I worked for a while on the case of Alexander Dolgun, an American who had been held in the gulag on false charges of espionage. After Stalin's death in 1953, Dolgun was released from the labor camps but not allowed to leave Russia until we finally negotiated his exit in 1971.

One day in November 1970, one of the desk officers for Soviet affairs, Edward Killham, appeared in my office. He explained that the previous day a seaman from Lithuania—then part of the vast Soviet empire—had leapt from his ship onto the deck of the U.S. Coast Guard cutter *Vigilant* during talks over fishing rights off the coast of Massachusetts. The sailor, Simas Kudirka, had claimed political asylum in the United States.

"Is there some kind of rule in international law that says we have to return him to the Soviets?" Killham asked me.

I was taken aback. "Not only is there *not* a rule to that effect," I told him, "but under the Refugee Protocol, we absolutely must not turn him back. That's the principle of non-refoulement."

Killham turned white at this. The Coast Guard had already allowed Soviet officers to board the *Vigilant*, beat Kudirka into submission, tie him up, and take him back to the Soviet vessel. Kudirka would eventually be convicted of treason and sent to a prison in Siberia.

I served as one of the State Department representatives at the Coast Guard board of inquiry, which revealed the shocking details—including the fact that a Coast Guard admiral, William B. Ellis, had ordered Kudirka's return on the basis that he was a deserter. The incident drew condemnation from every quarter, including President Nixon himself, and Ellis was forced into retirement. Less fairly, perhaps, the commander of the *Vigilant* was stripped of his command. To this day, the U.S. Coast Guard calls this incident its "Day of Shame."

It had a happy ending, however. From reading media reports, someone figured out that Kudirka's mother had been born in New York City, which meant he was entitled to U.S. citizenship. The State Department pressed his case—as we would for any American detained overseas—and secured his release in 1974.

"RECIPROCAL! RECIPROCAL!"

In 1972, I was seconded to Secretary of Commerce Peter G. Peterson, to advise the delegation he was leading to negotiate a trade deal with the Soviets, as Nixon and Brezhnev had agreed at their first Moscow summit in May of that year. We traveled to Moscow for the negotiations in July, staying in the Gastiniza Rossiya, a surprisingly modern hotel with three thousand rooms, only a few yards from Red Square. A quarter of the restaurant on the top floor was roped off for the American delegation, open 24/7 for its free use and stocked with Russian offerings including endless caviar and vodka. Each floor had its own *dezhurnaya*—an older woman whose job it was to monitor our movements and report them to the KGB. At night one would get honey-trap phone calls in one's room: "Hello, this is Svetlana calling. Would you like me to come up and visit you?" But we knew all the tricks, and we were not fooled.

The big substantive legal issues in the negotiations for which I was especially responsible were highly technical: copyrights, double taxation, and arbitration. I had to get smart on each of these topics in a hurry. To get to grips with the first two, I consulted with expert delegation members from the Treasury Department and the U.S. Copyright Office. I naturally felt that the third issue, arbitration, was more in my wheelhouse as a litigator, and it particularly caught my eye.

The U.S.-Soviet negotiations illustrate some of the challenges that made international arbitration increasingly necessary. In the Soviet Union, as in all countries that followed the Marxist-Leninist precept of "state ownership of the means of production," most commerce was carried out by state-owned enterprises. If you were an American doing business in the USSR and you had a claim against your Soviet counterparty, Soviet law said you had to arbitrate that claim in Moscow before the Foreign Trade Arbitration Commission—which, of course, also consisted of government employees. Private American companies could scarcely be expected to rely upon such a body to dispense impartial justice. The result was that Americans could not do business behind the Iron Curtain with any level of confidence. If left unaddressed, this problem would defeat the purpose of any trade agreement we might sign.

The solution was to allow such disputes to be arbitrated before a neutral tribunal. In contrast to many other areas of law, weighed down by centuries of precedent, international arbitration was something fresh and vibrant, a new dispute-resolution mechanism spurred by the postwar boom in global commerce. The involvement of states as parties added another layer of fascination, in that they respond to a range of motivating factors far beyond strictly commercial concerns, to include domestic politics, national security, and their relations with other states. For me, international arbitration combined my passion for litigation with my interest in foreign affairs.

In the early 1970s, however, the field was in its infancy. The New York Convention, the cornerstone treaty that today makes it possible to enforce an arbitral award in almost any country, had been in force for barely a decade. Even wholly private arbitrations were relatively rare; those involving states were few and far between. I knew when I joined White & Case that the firm had recently wrapped up an arbitration against Saudi Arabia. But that case was done and dusted, and it seemed implausible that another one like it would soon come along. Times do change, however.

For the U.S.-Soviet agreement, we considered establishing a dedicated dispute-resolution mechanism, but decided it would take too long. Instead, we used the 1966 arbitration rules of the UN Economic Commission for Europe, a body specifically established to promote East-West trade; both the United States and the Soviet Union were charter members. The rules provided for dispute resolution by a three-arbitrator panel. Each party would name an arbitrator, and the chair would be appointed by the other two or, if they could not agree, by an independent appointing authority, usually a chamber of commerce in a neutral third country. The arbitration itself would take place neither in the United States nor in the USSR; eventually, Stockholm, Sweden, was to become the go-to venue for claims under the trade agreement.

Article 7 of the agreement did not require such arbitration, but only "encouraged" it. The actual selection of a dispute-resolution mechanism would be left to individual contracts. But we thought the endorsement of neutral arbitration by the Soviet foreign trade ministry would give American companies sufficient basis to refuse contract provisions calling for hometown justice in Moscow.

Throughout the negotiations, the Russians would always demand that the parties' benefits be kept equal. "Reciprocal! Reciprocal!" they would cry, in English. "Reciprocal!" became their number-one buzzword. (Of course, this was their way of endeavoring to achieve a position better than could be achieved on the basis of their actual bargaining strength.)

As part of the festivities around the final negotiations and signing ceremony in Washington in October 1972, the Motion Picture Association of America, naturally interested in selling American movies to the Soviet Union, laid on a buffet and film screening for the two delegations. In its infinite wisdom, the MPAA selected *The Russians Are Coming, The Russians Are Coming*, a screwball comedy starring Alan Arkin and Carl Reiner in which a Soviet submarine runs aground off New England.

When the lights came up at the end, I asked the Soviet deputy foreign trade minister, Manzhulo, what he thought.

"Very good!" he boomed. "Americans are looking just as stupid as Russians! Absolutely reciprocal!"

In the end, technically, the agreement never entered into force, since due to the Jackson-Vanik Amendment to the Trade Act of 1974, Congress failed to approve "most favored nation" treatment, a central provision of the agreement under which Soviet goods would have enjoyed the lowest applicable tariffs. The rest of the agreement, however, did not require congressional approval and, as a practical matter, became effective. The Soviet Union did become a party to the Universal Copyright Convention. When Brezhnev came to Washington, DC, the following year for his second summit with President Nixon, the U.S.–USSR Double Taxation Convention was signed. And the arbitration provisions, being baked into the text, required no further action to take effect.

Trade between the United States and the Soviet Union rose twenty-two-fold, from $200 million per year in 1971 to a peak of $4.4 billion by the end of the decade. Granted, these were not stellar amounts, even by 1970s standards; but the more important consequence was better relations between the two parties. For as commercial ties grow, it becomes harder and harder to fight.

The same applies to other types of peaceful relations. By the time that Brezhnev arrived in Washington, DC, for that second summit in 1973, we had already negotiated the U.S.–Soviet Accords on Exchanges in Technical and Cultural Matters, which provided for cooperation in transportation, agriculture, oceanography, education, media, and the performing arts. By then acting legal adviser, I presided over a signing ceremony in the Benjamin Franklin State Dining Room at the State Department, and another in the East Room of the White House, both in the presence of President Nixon and Chairman Brezhnev. As will be seen, that would not be my last time in the White House.

THE PENTAGON PAPERS AND CAMBODIA

One day in June 1971, Jack Stevenson called me into a meeting in his office with two other Nixon administration lawyers, one destined for Watergate infamy, the other soon to be known for attempting to shield the president from Watergate blame. They were, respectively, Assistant Attorney General Robert Mardian and General Counsel of the Department of Defense J. Fred Buzhardt. Both were experienced veterans of the Republican right—Mardian had successfully managed Barry Goldwater's 1964 presidential bid in several states, while Buzhardt had worked for Strom Thurmond, South Carolina's segregationist senator. This provenance hardly endeared either of them to me, or for that matter to Jack.

That weekend, the *New York Times* had blindsided the administration by publishing excerpts from a classified study on the Vietnam War, which the newspaper called "the Pentagon Papers."

"Who leaked it? Was it him?" Buzhardt said, passing a note to Mardian with the initials "D.E." written on it. Mardian nodded.

"D.E." meant Daniel Ellsberg, the defense analyst who had indeed leaked the study. I didn't know Ellsberg, but I had dated his now-wife, the toy-company heiress Patsy Marx, while I was at Harvard and she was at Radcliffe. It hadn't worked out between us—though not because I suspected her of being any kind of screaming radical leftist.

Mardian explained that the Department of Justice intended to block further publication and they wanted a senior diplomat to testify that publication would harm national security. It was a stupid argument. The Pentagon Papers were of historical interest only; their analysis stopped in 1968. Nobody at the State Department could truthfully testify that such a document would harm national security. But with the White House behind them, Mardian and Buzhardt could be fiercely insistent. Jack and I decided to make it our business to "cooperate" with the two men, while shielding senior diplomats from any pressure to make fools of themselves. At one point, Mardian fixated on Philip Habib, a hugely respected foreign service officer then serving as U.S. ambassador to South Korea. We told them Habib had a heart condition, which was true enough but probably would not have barred him from testifying.

"If he's got a heart condition," Mardian retorted with cold menace, "maybe he shouldn't be on the front line so close to the Demilitarized Zone!"

In the end, we succeeded in shielding Habib and other nonpolitical personnel from the attention of Mardian and his cronies. Nixon lost the Pentagon Papers case, thank God; but he and some of those around him were evidently becoming addicted to abuses of power. Four years later, Mardian was convicted of conspiring to obstruct justice in the Watergate investigation by ordering the release of the burglars, though his conviction was eventually overturned on appeal, and he was not retried.[11] Buzhardt became special White House counsel for Watergate and a fierce defender of the president, though it was not enough to exonerate Nixon.[12]

FIRST, MAKE NO NEWS

Keeping the president's enforcers at bay was one thing, wrangling Congress quite another. Jack Stevenson assigned me to work with the assistant secretary of state for congressional relations, a smooth-spoken Tennessean named David M. Abshire who, as it turned out, was to play a pivotal role throughout my career. Nine years my senior, and a West Point graduate who had seen combat in Korea and been decorated for valor before earning a PhD in history, Abshire went on to cofound the Center for Strategic and International Studies (CSIS) with former

Chief of Naval Operations Adm. Arleigh Burke. Abshire was an old-fashioned Southern gentleman who treated everyone with kindness, from the grandest senator to the most junior clerk. Later, as U.S. ambassador to NATO when I was in The Hague, he would invite enlisted Marine guards to Thanksgiving Day dinner at his official residence right alongside the bigwigs of Brussels, visiting relatives from Tennessee, and me. Unfailingly courteous, Abshire never to my knowledge lost his temper, even in the most trying circumstances. Needless to say, these qualities are not common at the highest levels of government.

Abshire was a consummate negotiator, but he was not a lawyer, and that was where I came in. In his work with both the House and the Senate, he was having to deal more and more with a range of legal issues, constitutional and international. He had asked Jack to second to him "one of your best lawyers." Thus we became a double act on Capitol Hill as well as at regular White House meetings of the Legislative Inter-Agency Group chaired by the president's chief of staff. On the Senate side, our main antagonist was the usual suspect: Sen. William J. Fulbright, Rhodes Scholar, Justice Department attorney, and law professor (whom I, of course, privately worshipped as the progenitor of the Fulbright Scholarship that had taken me to Germany years earlier and greatly influenced my future career).

Fulbright would raise all kinds of issues, from bills he didn't like to the administration's alleged overuse of the courtesy title "ambassador," but our most memorable battle was over war-powers legislation. The Constitution gives Congress the power to declare war, but the president is commander in chief of the armed forces. In the age of pitched battles and long sea voyages, this inherent conflict did not matter so much; states would declare war on one another formally, and the actual fighting might not take place until months afterward. But supersonic jets and cruise missiles have compressed this timetable to the point where the president often needs to respond to hostilities without time to seek Congressional approval first. The issue was (and still is): how far do the president's war powers go?

On Capitol Hill, there was a move to limit the president's ability to intervene overseas, which its proponents presented as a means of preventing a second Vietnam. We in the administration saw this as misguided, unconstitutional, and potentially dangerous, insofar as it might limit the country's ability to respond swiftly to emergencies.

In the midst of this debate, a crisis blew up over the administration's continued bombing of Vietcong forces on their way through Cambodia to attack the Americans, which had been held secret for some years. This brought the issue of war powers to the front pages. On what authority did the president order the bombing? Frankly, we didn't have a politically acceptable answer to that question, which meant that dodging it became de facto administration policy.

One day in April 1973, Secretary Rogers called me up to his office. "Look, I promised Jake Javits that I would come up and testify on Cambodia, but I've decided not to."

I'll bet you have, I thought. *This is a political minefield.* I braced myself for the kicker.

"So I will tell the senator I'm sending you instead." The secretary did not add, *And if any of this embarrasses me or the administration in the papers, you are toast.* He didn't have to.

I'd be damned before I would be a sacrificial lamb, so I resolved to hew religiously to the party line, not get upset, and make my reasoning as impenetrably legal as possible. My testimony on April 12, 1973, was an exercise in polite deflection. Secretary of Defense Elliot Richardson had made a noncommittal statement on the president's authority, to which I referred the senators, saying that Richardson and Rogers had "illuminated the issue."

"I don't think they have illuminated it at all," Senator Fulbright retorted. But I stuck to the line.

Senator Javits himself challenged me to name the laws on which my argument relied. "All laws passed by Congress with respect to Cambodia," I told him, shining about as much light on the matter as the two secretaries had done. The next day, the *Washington Post* reported that the Senate Foreign Relations Committee had tried "to obtain from the Nixon administration a more precise accounting for its authority to continue

American bombing in Cambodia," but had been "unsuccessful."[13] On the popular news show *Face the Nation*, Fulbright complained that Rogers and Richardson had dodged his committee, instead sending "Mister—his name slips my mind—he's from the State Department." CBS reporter Marvin Kalb had to supply my name for the senator.[14]

Well, my mission had been to make no impact in the media. So I suppose: mission accomplished.

Nixon vetoed the restrictive War Powers Act, but in the wake of the notorious "Saturday Night Massacre" in which Attorney General Elliot Richardson and his deputy both resigned rather than carry out President Nixon's order to fire Independent Counsel Archibald Cox, a cataclysmic event in the Watergate saga, Congress overrode the veto by a handful of votes. Decades of wrangling over war powers ensued. I have always believed that, absent Watergate and the Saturday Night Massacre in particular, the War Powers Act would not have become law at that time. But the concerns that gave rise to it continue even today, with questions over the scope of the authorization to use military force granted after 9/11. The issue, in short, is not going away.

CHAPTER THREE

Rug Pulls, Investments, and Shakedowns

GAMEKEEPER TURNS POACHER

Under other circumstances, I might have stayed at the State Department; but by the middle of 1973 the writing was on the wall, and it had nothing to do with Watergate. Rogers had finally decided I was too young for the post of legal adviser. He wanted to nominate an older fellow named Stuart Scott, a partner at Dewey Ballantine, who had worked with Rockefeller interests. Indeed, Scott Beach at the former RockResorts Caneel Bay Resort on St. John's in the U.S. Virgin Islands (now sadly destroyed by a hurricane) was named after him.

By this time, the feud between Kissinger and Secretary Rogers had become open political warfare, and Kissinger was winning. It had become painfully clear that Nixon intended to fire Rogers and replace him with Kissinger, guaranteeing Kissinger's supremacy in matters of foreign policy. I don't think Kissinger had any personal animus against me—he probably wouldn't know me from a hole in the wall, despite having once been my professor at Harvard—but he had built a team around him that he would transplant into the State Department, and that team included Carlyle E. Maw, his personal lawyer and a partner in the firm of Cravath, Swaine & Moore, whom Kissinger intended to appoint as legal adviser.

Stuart Scott never got his turn as legal adviser. Having relocated to Washington on the strength of Rogers's promise, he received instead the consolation prize of becoming ambassador to Portugal. I resigned from State effective September 1, 1973, two days before Rogers's own resignation took effect.

What to do next? In the past, I had thought about running for Congress. It seemed that soon enough a seat might open. I was on good terms with Peter Frelinghuysen, the moderate Republican congressman from my home district in New Jersey, who after twenty years' service was finding it necessary to rebuff rumors of retirement.[1] As the saying goes, "Never believe anything until it has been officially denied"—Peter stepped down at the next election. In a telephone conversation with Peter after he announced his retirement, he exclaimed, "I thought you would be running for my seat!"

"So did I," I said. "But I'm not."

Having seen the reality of Capitol Hill during my work there with David Abshire, the prospect seemed less appealing. Even back then, representatives did too much fundraising and too little legislating. The Democrats had controlled the House for decades and showed no signs of budging. Besides, while I continue to believe that politics in a democracy should be the noblest profession, I nevertheless concluded that I thrived on purely intellectual combat—the kind that went on in a negotiation or a courtroom. So perhaps a return to White & Case lay in my future?

Or perhaps not. While I was still acting legal adviser at State, the head of the firm called to ask me whether I would come back to New York City to take charge of the multidistrict litigation against the accounting firm Arthur Young & Company (now Ernst & Young). Later a more enticing prospect was put before me: a supporting role in a significant commercial arbitration at the Stockholm Chamber of Commerce.

In both cases, I respectfully declined, saying I was not ready to leave the State Department, which at the time was true. But on a more mundane level, I'd had my fill of living in New Jersey and commuting forty miles every day into Manhattan. More strategically, international arbitration (the kind that involved states as parties) had captured my attention ever since the landmark trade negotiations with the Soviets. That was where I saw my career going.

As a result, when I left the State Department in September 1973, I entered a state of bohemian unemployment—for two weeks. Then White & Case decided to open an office in Washington, DC, and I was invited to rejoin as a partner and be on the front line of setting it up. Also worthy of mention: I was invited to take a position in the American Bar Association's section of international law, which I accepted. Eventually, I would wind up chairing the section; serving on the ABA's governing body, the Board of Governors; and sitting in its House of Delegates for fifteen years. I became active in the American Society of International Law—and was president from 1996 to 1998—and the Center for American and International Law's Institute for Transnational Arbitration—whose advisory board I would chair from 1994 to 2000.

These activities might lack the swashbuckling élan of a New York courtroom or the intrigue of a position at the State Department; but they are no less vital to the legal profession. I built my career in part on the knowledge I gained—and the connections I made—through these organizations. Later, when I served these groups in more senior roles, I was able to "give back" by using my own roster of contacts to convene some of the best minds in the world to educate members about international arbitration.

Every profession is a community, and a community needs to be nurtured; that is why I have been willing to give so much of my time to extracurriculars over the years. Anyhow, on with the story!

DUST-UP IN BOURBON COUNTRY

The main point of having an office in Washington, DC, of course, is to sue the federal government. A partner in the firm, Roger M. Blough, quipped that he had realized the federal government might occasionally need reining in when he was serving as CEO and board chairman of U.S. Steel. In 1962 he had met in the Oval Office with President John F. Kennedy to announce, to the latter's immense displeasure, that contrary to Kennedy's publicly known wishes, steel prices would indeed be raised, as the industry felt higher prices were necessary to modernize and compete with foreign plants. The president's reaction was so strong that soon Blough was awakened at his home in the middle of the night by FBI agents sent by Attorney General Robert Kennedy to interrogate him on the subject.

Suing the government lacked the courtroom cut and thrust of my earlier litigation work; cases tended instead to be decided "on the papers"—that is, on motions for summary judgment or to dismiss for failure to state a claim, without witness-stand drama or climactic speeches to the jury. But it was not without its satisfactions. To the contrary, I have always said that when you sue the government for doing something stupid, you are doing a public service. Thus I continued in public service, and gratefully with a vastly improved income.

A prime example from my post–State Department stint at White & Case is *Brown-Forman Distillers v. Matthews*. At the heart of the matter lay an interagency turf war for which Washington was notorious. If you are a drinking person, you might be familiar with the warning labels on liquor bottles—the ones that contain the "Surgeon General's Warning" alongside other information about the libation within. Just about everyone agrees that some such labeling is necessary to protect drinkers from deception or harm. For decades, the task of regulating them fell to the Bureau of Alcohol, Tobacco, Firearms and Explosives (ATF) and its predecessors.

In 1974 and 1975, the ATF considered introducing new regulations requiring alcohol producers to list ingredients on their labels. It issued proposed regulations, held six days of public hearings, and collected more than a thousand written comments. Ultimately, the ATF decided not to regulate, citing five reasons, including the excessive cost of labeling and the fact that only "a small segment of the public" actually wanted it.[2]

Distillers and winemakers breathed a sigh of relief; but the respite was short-lived. Out of the blue, the Food and Drug Administration (FDA) announced it would introduce its own regulations requiring ingredient labeling of alcohol. This ran contrary to the FDA's explicit policy of thirty-five years, under which alcohol labeling was the sole province of the ATF. To the producers, who had just spent two years arguing successfully (or so they believed) against exactly this kind of labeling, this felt like a rug pull of epic proportions. A group of them, representing 95 percent of distillers and 80 percent of winemakers by volume,[3] engaged me to sue the FDA.

Naturally, we wanted to get the case filed in Kentucky, the center of the U.S. whiskey business. I consulted with a legend among Louisville lawyers, John Tarrant of Wyatt, Tarrant & Combs.

"Listen, Charlie," he told me. "The man you want is Jim Gordon. He's a federal judge in the Western District. He lives in his hometown, which is Madisonville. You won't see this written down anywhere, but he has an arrangement where any case filed in Madisonville goes to him. He's the only federal judge in town. You'll like him!"

Madisonville, it turned out, was smack dab in the middle of whiskey country—both Kentucky and Tennessee whiskey. In other words, perfect for our needs! File in Madisonville we did, and just as John Tarrant had promised, the case went to Judge Gordon, who soon called the two sides down for a conference in his chambers. On the desk, he had a model of a yellow school bus, a souvenir from the fight to integrate the schools in Louisville, when he ordered the busing of more than twenty thousand students and sent armed guards to protect the buses.[4]

Judge Gordon smoked a cigarette as he listened to our arguments. When we were done, he turned to counsel for the FDA, a pencil-necked bureaucrat straight out of central casting, and said, "Well, Mr. So-and-So, I got to tell you. Us folks down here are kind of getting tired of you all from Washington coming down and telling us what we ought to do and ought not to do. First you tell us we shouldn't be smoking." He took a long drag and tipped the ash into an ashtray. "Then you tell us we shouldn't be mining our coal. Now today here you are telling us we shouldn't be drinking our whiskey." He smiled. "And we're not happy about that."

I turned to my associate and whispered, "I think he gets it. Let's ask him to decide it on the papers." The FDA agreed.

In his judgment, Judge Gordon dug into the legislative history and concluded, sensibly, that "it was Congress's intention to place exclusive jurisdiction to regulate the labeling of alcoholic beverages in [the ATF]. To accept the [FDA's] argument we would have to believe that Congress intended to *inflict* upon the alcoholic beverage industry conflicting labeling requirements. We refuse to make such an assumption."[5]

The decision was met with scorn in certain quarters; one law professor called it "bad law" resting on "a pillar of tapioca."[6] But the government (under two successive administrations, Ford and Carter) elected not to appeal.[7] Instead, the Carter White House directed the ATF and FDA to work together on a compromise.

Federal agencies cooperating with one another? Imagine that! The head of the Distilled Spirits Council, one of my clients in the case, called the outcome "one small but significant victory in the endless struggle to make government make sense."[8] That was certainly something I could get behind.

SHAKEDOWN IN LAGOS

Making the federal government behave itself was always satisfying. But my experience at the State Department had whetted my appetite for international dispute resolution. And in this regard, the 1970s represented an exciting time of transition. As the economic historian Noel Maurer wrote in his landmark study *The Empire Trap*:

> *Before 1945, the only substantive recourse available to an American company caught in an investment dispute with a foreign*

government was to call on the coercive power of the U.S. exec-
utive branch. By the 1990s, American investors had access to
an array of mechanisms to protect their property rights that did
not depend on executive discretion. Private investors could now
take foreign governments to arbitration without the intervention
of their home government.[9]

During my second stint at White & Case, I was living through that transition. "Gunboat diplomacy" was a thing of the past; but the old-school coercive system died hard.

In a series of moves over the course of 1976 and 1977, Nigeria's military government of Gen. Olusegun Obasanjo announced it was "Nigerianizing" (read: stealing) a controlling interest in the Nigerian subsidiary of American International Group.[10] David Abshire (who, no surprise, knew AIG's pugnacious chairman, Maurice "Hank" Greenberg, professionally) recommended that I be hired to advise on a response.

Under international law, states are allowed to take property from private parties for a public purpose on a nondiscriminatory basis; but when they do, they must pay "prompt, adequate, and effective compensation." The principle had been established by the Permanent Court of International Justice as early as the 1920s in a famous case involving the expropriation of a German-owned factory in Poland, known as the *Chorzów Factory* case.

Lately, however, a group of developing states had been attempting to water down that standard of compensation. Notably, in 1974 they had caused the UN General Assembly to adopt a resolution embodying a charter of economic rights and duties of states, which asserted the weaker standard of "appropriate compensation . . . taking into account [the expropriating state's] relevant laws and regulations and all circumstances that the state considers pertinent."[11]

Given the dismal history of colonial exploitation, it was easy to see why a developing state might seek to protect its economic interests. But to my mind, this was the wrong way to go about it. One of the charter's stated goals was: "The attainment of wider prosperity among all countries."[12] That could come only through a combination of international aid and private investment. But what investor in its right mind would invest in a state where it could be expropriated at will, with the compensation (or lack thereof) entirely the gift of the host state? Moreover, it was simply wrong to invite a foreign investor to come in and spend time and money building a business in your country, only to turn around and steal that business when it started doing well.

I drafted a brief reflecting the state of the law as I understood it: notwithstanding the General Assembly resolution (which was not binding), Nigeria had to offer, according to the *Chorzów Factory* standard, "prompt, adequate, and effective compensation." That was what AIG now demanded. In response to the company's entreaties, however, the Nigerian government offered AIG only the par value of its shares, which amounted to less than 7 percent of their real value—hardly adequate or effective.[13] Legally speaking, AIG had a strong case. But in a military dictatorship like 1970s Nigeria, the courts would never in a million years take the side of a foreign investor against the government. Nor, at the time, was there any mechanism for resolving the dispute via international arbitration.

This left only one option: political pressure. So we began lobbying the State Department to pressure Nigeria for a fairer deal. I prepared a long and detailed legal brief and handed it to the U.S. ambassador to Nigeria, Donald Easum, in Washington in October 1977.[14] The embassy tried to put pressure on the Nigerian government but found itself spurned at every turn.

Then, on March 21, 1978, Nigeria retaliated for AIG's recalcitrance by sending armed men to arrest and jail the managing director of AIG's Lagos office, Louis LeFevre, on charges of mortgage fraud—vague, trumped-up charges clearly meant to intimidate.[15] Over the weeks that followed, LeFevre was subjected to an ordeal worthy of Kafka, all for the sake of pressuring his employer to accept a bum deal.

The day after his arrest, LeFevre was arraigned together with his lawyer, Fred Egbe, who had been detained on a similarly hazy pretext. The magistrate offered them bail, but the prosecution made a great show of claiming that bail would only give LeFevre and Egbe an opportunity to "cover their guilt" by destroying evidence. With tremendous courage, they defied the prosecution by refusing bail and were thrown in Ikoyi Prison pending a hearing.

An AIG executive from headquarters, Ron Shelp, called me and asked me to fly to Lagos as a matter of urgency. To say I was reluctant to travel to Nigeria in 1978 would be an understatement. Lagos was notorious for rampant crime and the country was unstable: General Obasanjo had come to power just two years before, when assassination had ended the reign of his predecessor, who himself had seized power in a coup only the year before.

"Well, Charlie," Shelp said on the phone with an edge of annoyance to his voice, "I'm sure there are plenty of lawyers in Washington who would love to go out there and do this."

He had a point. This was an opportunity to impress AIG, a vast company with impeccable bipartisan political ties. Moreover, of course, it was a great challenge. I swallowed my fears. On March 30, nine days after LeFevre's arrest, I flew into Lagos with George Abouzaid, a high-level AIG executive dispatched by Hank Greenberg.[16] The plane was a real rust bucket, and it made several stops in other West African cities before landing in Lagos. By the time I arrived I was a little fuzzy in the head—a problem not helped by the cocktail of vaccinations I had gotten all at once before leaving Washington.

From the airport I went straight to the magistrate's court, where LeFevre was due for a bail hearing. There I met his replacement Nigerian lawyer, the 350-pound Chief Rotimi Williams QC, aka "Timi the Law," a larger-than-life figure in every sense. Among other claims to fame, Williams had the distinction of being the first African appointed Queen's Counsel, a British title reserved for the most accomplished senior litigation attorneys.[17]

After a brief hearing, Williams succeeded in getting LeFevre out on $7,500 bail, which this time he accepted. I accompanied LeFevre back to his home and we spoke at length. I found him an impressive person. Around six feet tall and still physically fit in his late forties or early fifties, he had agreed to be posted anywhere in the world on one condition: it must have a polo club. As to his predicament, he did not seem unnerved. This kind of steadiness, I have found, is not uncommon among professional expatriates; after all, it takes a certain cast of mind to be willing to spend years at a time living far from home in less predictable parts of the world.

At breakfast the next day, the police arrived at LeFevre's home and arrested him once again.[18] This time, no charges were filed; the regime claimed the arrest was made under a military decree that supposedly permitted indefinite detention without the possibility of bail.[19] To make matters worse, the Nigerians now incarcerated LeFevre in Kirikiri, known to be one of the world's most squalid and violent prisons. (My family had the unsettling experience of reading in the newspaper that LeFevre had been arrested again "together with his lawyer," but I was able to send a message reassuring them that it was Egbe, not myself, who had been rearrested.)

Evidently, the courts alone were not going to cut it. But we had an ace up our sleeves; within hours of LeFevre's second arrest, Nigeria was to receive President Jimmy Carter. It was the first state visit of a U.S. president to sub-Saharan Africa. (Why the regime picked this moment to harass AIG I may never understand.) Carter was only there for a long weekend, however, and was due to leave on April 3. The clock was ticking.

I worked the presidential visit for all it was worth. Hank Greenberg enjoyed good relations with Carter's secretary of state, Cyrus Vance, and this helped me to secure a meeting with Vance at the Lagos Holiday Inn, which the delegation had transformed into the "Lagos White House," with coordination courtesy of the U.S. Army Signal Corps.

"Look," I told Vance, "the president of the United States cannot go wheels up on Monday and leave behind an American citizen in custody. You have to get him out." Vance agreed, and his people got to work on it.

At the same time, I had discovered that LeFevre's wife, Carole, was temporarily working for Robert Pierpoint, the CBS News White House correspondent who had arrived in Lagos to cover the state visit. Always on the lookout for a good story, Bob offered to interview Carole on camera. Once the distressed wife and mother appeared nationwide on the *CBS Evening News,* the White House could not possibly have Carter leave Lagos without an agreement for LeFevre's release.

I thought this was a terrific idea, particularly as Mrs. LeFevre was every bit as steady, emotionally and psychologically, as her husband. She knew her role and played it perfectly, as did Bob—the two of them delivering a heartrending interview. Suddenly LeFevre's release from jail became a political priority, and that lit a fire under the Carter administration. On April 3, the day of Carter's departure, LeFevre was again a free man. Pierpoint later gave me a copy of his memoirs, inscribed, "To Charlie Brower, with whom I shared one of the more rewarding experiences of my career as a White House correspondent—and . . . . Only you know the full story!"

The tale still had at least one more chapter, however. Louis LeFevre still faced two sets of false charges and was not allowed to leave Nigeria. I felt that AIG owed it to LeFevre to get him out of the country and back to the United States, allowing him, doubtless in consultation with his employer, to freely choose whether or not to return to Lagos. We were speaking one day when he told me his mother, who was living in Williamsburg, Virginia, had recently suffered a stroke and was not in good shape.

"Aha!" I said. "Time for the old sick-mother routine!" I explained we would ask the court for permission for LeFevre to leave the country for just ten days to visit his deeply suffering mother, perhaps for the last time.

Rotimi Williams said he had never heard of such an application. "I can't imagine why the court would grant it."

I thought for a minute. "Back up a bit," I said. "What if the director of public prosecutions does not oppose it?"

Pausing to think deeply on it, Rotimi Williams put two and two together, and concluded, "Well, if the DPP does not oppose it, I suppose the court would have no option other than to grant it."

"All right. You draw up the papers," I said to Rotimi. "I'll get an affidavit from the doctor for the elder Mrs. LeFevre in America, and I'll work on the DPP."

I didn't go directly to the chief prosecutor, but instead first approached the U.S. Ambassador, Donald Easum. Lagos was not the kind of post bestowed on political donors as a prize; it went to accomplished career foreign service officers. And for a specialist in the region, West Africa's most populous nation was a big-deal posting.

Sure enough, Easum was no slouch. He had already served as assistant secretary of state for African affairs and ambassador to Burkina Faso, and my intuition told me he was not immune to further ambitions in the foreign service. The unique state visit of President Carter to "his" country thrust Easum further into the spotlight; and the fact that he had invited me to a breakfast meeting with his entire senior staff told me that he wanted to do his best for LeFevre.

"Now is the time," I told Easum, "to prove your worth as ambassador." I urged him to speak candidly to the DPP. He could strengthen our project, I told him, by submitting a personal statement to the court that he knew LeFevre (which he did) and was confident that, if allowed the ten days to visit his mother, LeFevre would in fact return (which, as we will see, LeFevre did). Easum, the consummate diplomat, persuaded the DPP and provided the personal statement. In exchange for a financial security posted by AIG, LeFevre's request was granted. We left Lagos together.

Back in the United States, I commissioned research on extradition from the United States to Nigeria. I already knew what we would find: the United States would not have made an extensive extradition agreement with Nigeria under military rule; but it would have done so with the British in colonial times and never denounced the treaty. So it proved. We could have argued that LeFevre wasn't extraditable, but it would have been far from a sure thing. This was all academic, as it turned out, for to my surprise and admiration, LeFevre was determined to go back.

"Number one," he said, "I didn't do anything wrong. Number two, if I don't go back, they'll just put my successor in jail in my place." (Even before his initial arrest, LeFevre had been slated to leave Lagos for a new posting, and his replacement had already arrived from a previous job in Vietnam.)

LeFevre did go back, and I went with him. When the case was about to come up in court, the prosecutor approached me and Rotimi Williams and said, "I've studied the file of this case, and I'm not sure that it should go forward. Will you agree to an adjournment?" The adjournment he proposed was a long one—until November—and I suspected that they just wanted the case to go away. I clarified with the prosecutor that, during the adjournment, LeFevre be allowed to leave the country on condition that he return if summoned.

Rotimi Williams and I argued over how to proceed. Williams wanted to put the government to the test: either pursue this case or withdraw it formally. I thought that was crazy. I issued the lawyerly equivalent of the old bird-in-the-hand adage: "Never force someone who has power over you to make a decision now which that person does not wish to make now." LeFevre looked at me, noted that AIG had provided me to be his lawyer, and sided with me. We agreed to the long adjournment, and off we both went back home. A while later, we got word that the case had indeed been quietly withdrawn.

LeFevre's ordeal was over; but Nigeria's attempted shakedown of AIG continued with a vengeance. The military regime refused to budge; for my part, I kept up the pressure on the State Department. The impasse dragged on, pulling in officials on both sides and creating long-term tension between the United States and an important regional power.

If only there had been a system for deciding these matters once and for all, without dragging the U.S. government into it! That system, of course, was international arbitration, and its hour was almost at hand.

SOVEREIGN IMMUNITY GOES NUCLEAR

We may have freed Louis LeFevre by invoking the power of the White House and State Department; but in other areas it might have been better for all concerned if the executive branch had stayed out of things. One of these areas was sovereign immunity, where State was still, despite my best efforts, obliged to act in a quasijudicial capacity.

For two days in 1972, President Nixon held an economic summit with Prime Minister Tanaka of Japan in Hawaii. One agenda item was the enormous trade deficit the United States had run up—the result of Japan's burgeoning manufacturing sector and America's becalmed economy. In order to "reduce the imbalance to a more manageable size," Japan agreed to buy more than $1 billion worth of U,S. goods and services. The shopping list included, among other items, $320 million of "uranium enrichment services" to fuel Japan's growing nuclear power industry.[20] The uranium would not actually be needed until the end of the decade; but Japan agreed to buy it in advance as a favor to the United States. Accordingly, ten Japanese utility companies purchased enriched uranium from the Atomic Energy Commission, to be stored until needed at the AEC's facility at Oak Ridge, Tennessee.

Down in Oak Ridge, they know nuclear; even the municipal seal features a diagram of an atom. The Appalachian town was established in 1942 by the military as the key plutonium manufacturing site for the Manhattan Project. Known as Secret City, Oak Ridge was indeed kept under wraps until after the war—an impressive feat given the tens of thousands who worked there.[21]

After V-J Day, Oak Ridge was handed over to the Atomic Energy Commission. Being the company town of a government agency came with blessings and curses. On the one hand, Oak Ridge residents enjoy unusual job security, for a nuclear processing facility cannot exactly fold overnight. On the other, the city's opportunities for business taxation are limited at best, since almost all potentially taxable property belongs to the federal government and is therefore immune. The municipality, therefore, is always on the lookout for a revenue boost.

One day toward the end of 1974, someone working at the secure facility in Oak Ridge spotted a clutch of uranium canisters that, instead of the ubiquitous logo of the Atomic Energy Commission, bore the stencils of ten Japanese utility companies. Oak Ridge rejoiced: at last, taxable commercial material! The city and Roane County slapped the Japanese companies with bills for back taxation totaling some $15.4 million and began thinking about how they might choose to spend this windfall.[22]

Taken aback, the Japanese government protested. These advance purchases, they said, had been made only as a favor to the United States; were it not for the Nixon-Tanaka summit, the uranium would never have been stored at Oak Ridge. On that basis, they claimed sovereign immunity.

This was where I came in. The attorney for Oak Ridge and Roane County called up the State Department to ask who decided these things and was put through to a former colleague of mine in the office of the legal adviser. He was told, correctly, that at that time it was the State Department's legal adviser who decided on claims of sovereign immunity.

Straight away the attorney asked, "Do you know any recent legal advisers who are back in private practice?"

"Well, Charlie Brower just left here not so long ago," answered my former colleague, "and you can find him here in Washington at White & Case." Thus I was hired as counsel to the city and the county. Japan engaged the services of the late A. Linwood Holton, the former governor of Virginia and, later, a successor of David Abshire as assistant secretary of state for legislative affairs.[23] And the fight was on!

Under the traditional broad theory of foreign sovereign immunity, practically nothing a state did could be the subject of a claim. The problem with this was the same as the one I had encountered when negotiating arbitration provisions with the Soviet Union: namely that communist countries conducted most of their commerce through state-owned enterprises. Granting practically all business dealings from these countries legal immunity would be absurd and lead to all kinds of injustice. Clearly, the legal theory had to change.

By 1974, this process was well underway. Twenty-one years previously, the State Department had issued the Tate Letter, named after a long-ago predecessor of mine as acting legal adviser, Jack Tate. The Tate Letter recognized a more restrictive view of sovereign immunity—one which did not apply to commercial dealings. I had already encountered it in my legal practice, when I represented Hulbert Aldrich of Chemical Bank in his personal injury suit against the Hungarian ambassador (see chapter 1). The Tate Letter represented a step in the right direction, to be sure; but there were several problems with this system.

First, it left interpretation of the Tate Letter in the hands of the State Department—by no means a politics-free zone. Foreign countries tended, understandably, to see unfavorable applications of the Tate Letter not as by-the-book determinations but as slights against them by the administration of the day.

Second, the executive branch, as any reasonably attentive middle school civics student knows, normally cannot bind the judiciary, separation of powers being fundamental to the Constitution. So as far as the courts were concerned, the State Department could only make suggestions. Usually, the courts followed the department's guidance in such matters—except, of course, when they didn't. This had the potential to create colossal confusion.

Third, with the march of global commerce and state-owned enterprises, the State Department was being called upon to make such "suggestions" more and more frequently. By the time I became acting legal adviser, at least one attorney in my office was dedicated to these matters full time. The office was overworked and under-resourced enough; from our point of view, shedding responsibility for sovereign immunity decisions was an administrative no-brainer.

The final problem was more procedural in nature, but no less absurd. For technical reasons, plaintiffs had to establish jurisdiction in the United States by serving a writ not on a human being but on a piece of property owned by the foreign state. But the gaps in the system were such that, once they obtained a judgment, it was usually impossible to enforce against that same piece of property.

This state of affairs satisfied nobody, with the possible exception of litigation attorneys who billed untold hours untangling the mess. Thus, with the collaboration of the Justice Department, we prepared draft legislation and had it introduced in Congress at the end of January 1973. The text, as amended, would eventually become the Foreign Sovereign Immunities Act, known as FSIA—but not for another nearly four years. By the time I testified before Rep. Peter Rodino's House Judiciary Committee in support of that legislation, revelations about Watergate wrongdoing in the White House were coming out on a daily basis, virtually monopolizing newspaper headlines. The first iteration of FSIA was left to die in committee.

In the Oak Ridge case, therefore, the Tate Letter still held sway. Holton, representing Japan, asked the State Department legal adviser to "suggest" immunity on the basis that the utilities were acting as agents for the government of Japan. In my written response, I argued that this was a commercial transaction; the fact that it was being done as a favor to Richard Nixon was neither here nor there. As the Tate Letter itself said, only the character of the transaction matters; its underlying purpose is irrelevant.

Meanwhile, the case progressed to a hearing before the Tennessee State Board of Taxation in Nashville. Suspecting that state courts might not want to tangle with the niceties of public international law, I presented the case as a simple matter of waiver, with which they would be infinitely more familiar. The U.S.–Japanese Friendship Treaty signed at the end of the U.S. occupation in 1953 provided that sovereign immunity would not apply to "privately owned and controlled enterprises." The utilities were such enterprises; any immunity had been waived—case closed.

Or, as the Oak Ridge city attorney told the *Washington Post*, "Just because it's radioactive doesn't mean it can't be taxed."[24]

For technical reasons, the FSIA would likely not have applied in the Oak Ridge case, even if it had been in force. Nevertheless, the case of the Japanese uranium illustrates some of the problems with the Tate Letter system. Japan was, and is, a key U.S. ally and trading partner in a crucial region of the world; in the mid-1970s, it was pursuing its own détente with China, an initiative the U.S. government regarded as strategically significant. Was it really worth introducing potential irritation into such an important relationship for something as trifling as a local tax dispute? Was it a sensible use of State Department resources? What if, at the end of the day, the State Department and the local courts reached different conclusions?

We never got to test the last question. Just ninety minutes before we were due to present our case to the State Department, and with a decision from the Tennessee Tax Board still pending, word came through that the parties had settled the dispute for $4.5 million. Cue audible sighs of relief from Washington, Nashville, and Tokyo. With its share of the proceeds, the City of Oak Ridge proposed to build a high school and solicited naming proposals. Some local wag floated "Enola Gay High," after the B-29 bomber that dropped the atomic bomb on Hiroshima, a suggestion that, while it might have raised a chuckle at the time, was thankfully not implemented, allowing the U.S.-Japan alliance to survive unscathed.

SAVING THE INDONESIAN ECONOMY

The Tate Letter was not the only route by which politics found their way into disputes between Americans and foreign governments. In 1962, Congress passed the Hickenlooper Amendment to the Foreign Aid Act, named after its main proponent, Sen. Bourke Hickenlooper, Republican of Iowa. Passed in the wake of Brazil's expropriation of U.S. telecoms assets, the amendment forced the U.S. government to withhold bilateral aid from (and vote down multilateral aid to) countries that took American property without "adequate compensation."

The Kennedy administration opposed the measure on the same grounds on which the Nixon administration opposed the War Powers Act: it unduly tied the hands of the executive in foreign affairs. Hickenlooper ridiculed the argument, and his amendment passed the full Senate by acclamation.[25] Kennedy could not veto it without also vetoing the rest of the Foreign Aid Act, so the Hickenlooper Amendment became the law of the land.

The very next year, 1963, Indonesia's increasingly unhinged dictator, Sukarno, began an orgy of expropriation across industries from rubber plantations to the movie business. Anti-Sukarno rhetoric ran high on Capitol Hill, with one senator even accusing the Indonesian president of having asked the Detroit Police Department to act as his pimp during a visit to the Motor City.[26] Lyndon Johnson, like all presidents, wanted to avoid any invocation of the Hickenlooper Amendment, lest it limit his executive power; ironically, though, the only way to do so was by cutting aid himself before Congress could force him to. This only pushed Sukarno further into the Communists' column, as the State Department had warned President Johnson it would; but the drift toward Beijing and Moscow ended in 1965 with Sukarno's removal from power.[27]

One by one, Indonesia settled most of the expropriation claims; but there remained one notable holdout, a New York corporation called Sea Oil & General whose plantations had been taken. On the advice of its attorney, Gen. Donald Dawson, who had been a close Truman aide in the White House, Sea Oil rebuffed Indonesia's offers of compensation. Why? Because Sea Oil, courtesy of General Dawson, believed it possessed the political equivalent of the atomic bomb, in the shape of enough well-disposed senators and members of Congress to force application of the Hickenlooper Amendment and choke off nearly all aid to Indonesia.

Shortly after the election of Jimmy Carter in November 1976, I had traveled to Jakarta with representatives from the "troika" of Indonesia's financial advisers—Lehman Brothers, S. G. Warburg, and Lazard Frères—to confer with the leadership of the country's central bank, known as Bank Indonesia. The proximate cause of my visit was a typical shakedown by the notoriously rapacious Israeli banker Bruce Rappaport. Rappaport specialized in locating the most bribable officials in any country and using them for gain. In this case, he had bribed a corrupt Indonesian general to issue overpriced contracts for the transport of oil by sea. Bank Indonesia had gotten wind of this, and the contracts were canceled, sparking worldwide lawsuits from Rappaport, including in New York, in which altogether he claimed over $1 billion.[28]

Indonesia was in the throes of a delicate recovery from the depredations of the Sukarno years; but the recovery was under threat from a deep financial crisis, exacerbated by Rappaport's depredations. While office towers were just beginning to spring up along Jakarta's skyline, at ground level the streets were choked with traffic—much of it consisting of *becaks*, motorized rickshaws—and frequently flooded. When our drivers from Bank Indonesia got becalmed in the murky water, usually because street boys had stopped the exhaust pipes with the soles of their sandals, killing the motors, we sought quick release by pushing banknotes out the open windows to the same offending boys, who would then push the cars out of the deep waters.

The Bank Indonesia governor, Rachmat Saleh, invited me to lunch with his board. I asked Saleh what he thought of Carter's election. "It is good," he said, "because it means that Robert McNamara will remain as president of the World Bank." This response, swift and clear-cut, showed what mattered most to Saleh and to Indonesia at that time: a stable, reliable flow of multilateral aid. Indonesia was on the verge of an economic transformation; but without international support, the country's economy would stall. Its government might fall apart; and the last time that happened, tens to hundreds of thousands had perished in the carnage.[29]

The campaign General Dawson was waging on Capitol Hill on behalf of Sea Oil was thus little short of politically sponsored blackmail of a struggling foreign nation. But I saw something General Dawson had not. There was an exception in the Hickenlooper Amendment for—what else?—arbitration. Conflicts referred to this form of dispute resolution would not trigger the amendment's ban on aid. There was no treaty or contract in place that *required* arbitration, but we could always offer it.

The law did not specify what *kind* of arbitration, however, so I set out to design a tribunal that would be politically bulletproof. We offered arbitration under the rules of the International Chamber of Commerce (at that time the world's most widely used international arbitration rules) before a sole arbitrator (less expensive than a panel) who would be either the Whewell Professor of International Law at Cambridge or the Chichele Professor of Public International Law at Oxford (arguably the two most respected international lawyers in the world).

In parallel, I called upon the then–State Department legal adviser, Davis Robinson, asking that he issue his written official opinion, for use with Dawson, the Senate, and anyone else, confirming that the offer of arbitration I had designed conformed to the Hickenlooper Amendment. How could he possibly refuse? He couldn't and didn't; the opinion was issued; and Sea Oil went eerily quiet.

In due course, we discovered why. Our client spent a million dollars on private investigators to look into the ownership of the company. After a considerable amount of digging, they located Sea Oil's true owner: a man by the name of Diamantidi, a Greek centenarian living in Vevey, Switzerland. Hickenlooper applied only to American-owned firms, so that was the end of that; the State Department agreed that the Hickenlooper Amendment did not apply at all to this case. Whether General Dawson knew the true owner or not, I cannot say; but in any event, all he had done was waste his client's time.

NINO SCALIA AND THE "WORST JUDGE IN THE WEST"

Sea Oil was not, however, the end of my work for Indonesia. In fact, it was just the beginning. In January 1977, a little more than two months after my first trip to Jakarta, I was watching Carter's inaugural festivities when I was handed a telex from Governor Saleh, asking me whether White & Case would agree to serve as outside general counsel to Indonesia in all of its international dealings, financial and otherwise. Of course, we accepted this choice representation, which has continued ever since.

For seven years, from that first trip until I left for The Hague at the end of 1983, I traveled to Jakarta four times a year for a week to ten days at a time, and witnessed a steady rise in Indonesia's fortunes as aid and investment flowed in.

One of my most significant cases for Indonesia, however, was one in which I did not officially appear. In late 1978, the country found itself sued in Los Angeles—along with the other member states of the Organization of Petroleum Exporting Countries (and by OPEC itself) for fixing the price of oil in alleged violation of U.S. antitrust laws. "Do not touch this with a barge pole" was my advice to the Indonesians. Its best defenses would be sovereign immunity or, failing that, a doctrine known as "act of state," under which U.S. courts lack jurisdiction to opine on political matters internal to foreign states. There would be no sense in appearing before a court that you say has no jurisdiction. As a practical political matter, therefore, OPEC and its member states needed to give the Los Angeles court a wide berth.

This gave rise to a problem, however: if neither OPEC nor any of its member states would appear in court, how could their case be put across? There was more than one way to skin a cat, I told my client. Viz., if nonparties have a stake in the outcome, they are sometimes allowed to submit briefs, and even argue in favor of one side or the other. When this happens, this third participant is referred to as an *amicus curiae*—a "friend of the court." The result of consultations within OPEC was that Indonesia volunteered to take on responsibility for producing an amicus, in this case the Indonesia–United States Business Committee of the Indonesian Chamber of Commerce and Industry. In keeping with my advice to Indonesia, I steered clear of any on-the-record involvement in the litigation. I found a Los Angeles firm to represent the amicus. But from behind the scenes, I ran the show. By night, I huddled with this legal team for the amicus, plotting strategy. By day, while the team was in court, I sat around the outdoor pool of my LA hotel reading the previous day's transcripts.

The case had been assigned to District Judge A. Andrew Hauk, who shortly before had been dubbed the "worst judge in the West" in a centerfold spread in the *Legal Times* for the frequent disparaging comments he dispensed from the bench.[30] In the transcripts, Judge Hauk referred to the case—properly *International Association of Machinists & Aerospace Workers (IAM) v. Organization of Petroleum Exporting Countries (OPEC)*—as "the I-AM-ers versus the OPEC-ers." I noticed, too, that at the start of each session Hauk would greet somebody called "General Hershey Bar." The general, I found out, was a courthouse character who would turn up to random trials dressed up as a banana republic dictator in a white uniform festooned with gold. But for all his bombast, Hauk rendered a thoughtful judgment. OPEC, Indonesia, and the other defendants won the case on precisely the grounds we had forecast: sovereign immunity and act of state.

Ultimately, I was not happy with the performance of the Los Angeles firm—I forget why. But when it came time for the appeal to the Ninth Circuit, I knew just the right lawyer to represent our amicus: the attorney who, as assistant attorney general, had argued before the Supreme Court and was the leading authority on the "act of state" doctrine. But my prospect, a hotshot University of Chicago Law School professor, was, as luck would have it, doing a visiting year at Stanford Law School. This was Antonin "Nino" Scalia, whom I had met when I was in the State Department and he was working at the Nixon White House.

Later, of course, Nino would be elevated, first to the U.S. Court of Appeals for the District of Columbia Circuit and then to the Supreme Court. I disagreed with many of his more controversial opinions, but he was formidable as an advocate and charming and extremely funny as a person. So much so, in fact, that he and his wife, Maureen, were among the guests at a very small farewell dinner friends arranged for me on the eve of my second departure for The Hague at the end of 2000. Besides, it impressed my Indonesian client to no end when they heard, not long after the OPEC case was done, that the lawyer I recommended had just been nominated to the prestigious DC Circuit!

It was upheld on appeal, which Scalia argued alone for the chosen amicus.

My work for Indonesia continued; and the next big case for that client would show just how far the burgeoning field of international arbitration had come in just a short time.

CHAPTER FOUR

How to Sue a State

INDONESIA GOES TO ICSID

Just as I had planned, I began to make my way into the new field of international arbitration. My first big arbitration was a contractual dispute between the U.S. aerospace company Lockheed Martin and the Swedish construction firm Skanska. Saudi Arabia had hired Lockheed to modernize its air traffic control system, both civilian and military, and Lockheed had subcontracted to Skanska for all of the building work. Lockheed was withholding payment from all of its subcontractors, allegedly because nobody in Saudi Arabia could agree how much of a kickback was owed to Adnan Khashoggi, the notorious Saudi fixer who had put the deal together.

Lockheed also enjoyed a perverse incentive to hang on to the money because—this being the relentlessly inflationary 1970s—they were making 15 percent interest on it, compared to the 6 percent they would have to pay to Skanska under New York's rules, yielding a net profit of 9 percent for *failing* to pay their subcontractors!

So we went to arbitration and soon sought a preliminary ruling on the applicable rate of interest. The arbitral panel, sitting under ICC rules, held that the New York 6 percent rule applied only to court cases, not arbitrations, and ruled that a commercially "realistic rate" of interest was applicable to Skanska's claim.[1] Lockheed promptly settled, as we assumed they would.

Lockheed v. Skanska was a big deal; but it wasn't the same as suing a foreign state.

A brief detour into terminology may be in order. Lawyers often categorize arbitrations as either "investor/state" or "commercial," according to whether the language requiring the parties to go to arbitration was contained in a treaty between two states ("investor/state") or in a contract between a state and a foreign investor ("commercial"). This distinction may be of academic interest; but to my mind, the real difference is between purely private arbitrations, like *Lockheed v. Skanska*, and those in which a state is itself a party. When I delivered the Chartered Institute of Arbitrators' annual flagship Alexander Lecture in 2013, I coined a portmanteau, "investomercial," to obviate the traditional distinction and highlight the more pertinent one.[2]

This begs the question: Why does the presence of a state as a party make such a big difference? Because states behave in ways that are fundamentally different from the ways individuals and corporations act. First, they are more used to making laws than obeying them. As sovereign entities, with all the rights that status implies, states too often do not deal on equal terms with private parties. They can at any point change domestic law in a way that hurts foreign investors, for example by imposing sudden, excessive "taxes" or by nationalizing whole industries overnight. They are entitled to take private property away for reasons of public policy that could not be invoked by a company or a citizen.

From time to time, it is true, a state may go broke. But the state will not cease to exist as a result, and international mechanisms, like the World Bank and International Monetary Fund, exist to prop up impecunious states for the sake of global stability as well as humanitarian concerns. *Governments*, on the other hand, may face overthrow, whether by ballots or bullets. Much more than commercial imperatives, therefore, states respond to the dictates of politics—principally domestic, but also international. Their motivations, in short, can be extremely complex. It is all part of the intoxicating puzzle box that is international arbitration.

For many years, the mechanisms of international arbitration lay close to dormant. This was certainly the case with ICSID, the International Centre for Settlement of Investment Disputes. ICSID, a member of the World Bank Group, was designed as a venue and a set of rules for the arbitration of disputes between developing countries and their foreign investors. It was founded in 1966; but by the beginning of 1981, just nine cases had been registered.[3]

The tenth case, filed in January 1981, caught my eye, mainly because the respondent was my biggest client. The case, *Amco Asia v. Republic of Indonesia*, concerned a luxury hotel in Jakarta, the Kartika Plaza. When Suharto had come to power in 1967, one of his first acts was to nationalize various industries. The hotel, which at the time was under construction, was handed over to an instrumentality of the Indonesian army called Inkopad.[4] The case was not about that act of nationalization, however—at least not directly.

Being more adept at hostilities than hospitality, Inkopad sensibly hired an American company, Amco Asia, to develop and manage the hotel. Amco proved unequal to the task, however. In the space of a single year, they went through four general managers, including one who was fired, replaced, and then reinstated. The Kartika Plaza was not properly maintained and fell into disrepair. Amco failed to hand over money due under a profit-sharing agreement.[5] There were further allegations of financial mismanagement and even tax evasion.[6]

Exasperated, the army rescinded its management contract with Amco and replaced the company with a committee headed up by a retired general. Making the takeover perhaps more hostile than most, troops and police took up residence at the hotel, apparently with the aim of keeping the peace between the two sides.[7] Amco claimed that Indonesia had thus wrongfully deprived it of the contractual right to operate the hotel.

The case itself was small: Amco claimed only $12.5 million plus interest, which to a government is peanuts. But in the wider view, I felt there was a great deal more at stake. As soon as I saw Amco's filing, I dashed off a memo to the Indonesian ambassador in Washington analyzing the case, urging Indonesia to respond to it in a timely fashion, and setting forth the procedure for doing so.

When making business decisions, international investors take political risks into account; and one of the major ones is the possibility that the host state might take property without offering full compensation. I was concerned that Indonesia might be tempted, as a member of the Group of 77 (a coalition of developing countries), to take the stance of the UN General Assembly's 1974 Charter of Economic Rights and Duties of States, which provides only for *"appropriate* compensation" and takes "into account [the host state's] relevant laws and regulations and all circumstances that the state considers pertinent."[8]

In other words, the charter would give states carte blanche to rob foreign companies and pay them peanuts in return—the way Nigeria had done with AIG (see chapter 3). While General Assembly resolutions do not, by themselves, have the force of law (even Security Council resolutions do only if the Security Council invokes specific provisions), states sometimes argue that the charter's standard of subjective "appropriate compensation" has supplanted customary international law's more objective requirement of "prompt, adequate and effective compensation" or "full compensation."

From a host state's point of view, what is wrong with making that argument? Had Indonesia done so, it would have telegraphed to the world that it was a more politically risky place to do business and attracted less foreign investment. Avoiding such an anti-investor position would instead show that Indonesia treats investor claims in accordance with international law and, in turn, encourage future investors. Fortunately, Indonesia readily saw the wisdom of this and went forward with the usual lawyerly exchange of memorials, countermemorials, replies, rejoinders, and so forth.

In December 1983—mere days before my departure for The Hague to sit on the Iran–United States Claims Tribunal—we held a hearing in the board room of the World Bank. The witnesses from our side included one W. Max Machfud, who had been the duty manager of the Kartika Plaza when the troops and police had moved in to take it over.[9] Machfud was a graduate of Cornell University's School of Hotel Administration, one of the premier institutions of its kind in the world, and in his written witness statement (which served as his direct testimony), he had given a straightforward account of the facts, outlining the conduct of police and troops while at the hotel.

During cross-examination, however, the claimant's counsel put Amco's version of the facts to our witness. Nothing unusual there, but Mr. Machfud responded by taking an abrupt left turn from his previous account. In fact, he began agreeing with everything our opposition was saying.

W. Max Machfud thus earned the dubious distinction of being the only witness I have ever had to withdraw. At the time, I couldn't understand it. His account of the facts had been perfectly consistent up to that point, and we were sure it was true. Why would he suddenly exit the reservation? Later, a few Indonesian colleagues on the case suggested the likely reason. In Indonesian culture, maintaining personal harmony with one's surroundings to the maximum extent possible is accorded a greater value than the literal, factual truth (no doubt an asset in the hospitality industry, but less so in a courtroom). So when opposition counsel began putting forth the claimant's version of events, the manager felt compelled, as a matter of culture, to agree and preserve that harmony.

The ICSID tribunal awarded the claimant $3.2 million plus interest— about a quarter of what Amco had claimed—but the case would prove procedurally complex. While I was serving in The Hague, my White & Case colleagues had the original award annulled, essentially on the basis that the tribunal had gotten the law wrong and failed to consider Indonesia's case properly.[10]

Today, the case is best known among arbitration lawyers for being one of the first in which an arbitral award was successfully annulled. Since then, annulment has grown into an important procedural safeguard in the world of arbitration, where there usually is no formal right of appeal.

Amco resubmitted its case, and the whole thing was arbitrated all over again, with the result that, upon my return from The Hague after more than four years away, I was slotted back into the case and helped present a new set of witnesses and oral arguments to an entirely new tribunal in 1989. With all of the jurisdictional maneuvering, the challenges on the merits, and the cross-applications for annulment, the case would not finally wrap up until December 1992, almost a dozen years after it was first filed (and with a significantly smaller amount awarded against Indonesia).[11] Talk about a gift that keeps on giving!

DRILLING FOR OIL IN ALGERIA

Amco Asia was the start of my involvement with arbitration against a state. At age forty-five when the proceedings were filed—I was fifty-six when they finally juddered to a halt—I suppose I was a late bloomer; but then again, so was the field of international arbitration itself! Once I had a couple of cases under my belt, I decided I was an expert, which, given how limited international arbitration was at the time, I probably was. So I went on the speaking circuit, addressing groups of in-house counsel and others who might be interested in my services. I built my reputation and got cases that way.

My next big arbitration would see me on the side of the investor. In 1971, under the influence of Soviet Russia, Algeria had abruptly switched to a command economy. The regime nationalized the oil industry and handed all its assets to the Société Nationale de Transport et de Commercialisation des Hydrocarbures, or Sonatrach for short. Sonatrach contracted the Oklahoma-based Parker Drilling to develop some of its wells, which it did from 1976 to 1981,[12] when Sonatrach abruptly canceled the contract along with those of other foreign drillers. Parker's in-house lawyers looked to sue, and they made a road trip to interview me and others for the job. I was flattered to be considered alongside such better-known figures as Robert von Mehren of the Debevoise firm—and more flattered still to find myself hired.

Most arbitrations take place before three-person panels of senior lawyers in which one is appointed by the claimant, one by the respondent, and the third—the chair—by the other two, or by the two parties themselves (and if they can't agree, typically some arbitral institution or an independent dignitary will be appointed to name the chair). When it came time to nominate our arbitrator, I lobbied for, and got, Professor Andreas Lowenfeld of NYU Law School. I had seen him in action in *Lockheed v. Skanska,* in which he had been appointed by the other side, and I liked the measured way he handled things. A towering figure in international law, Andy had begun his career serving as State Department legal adviser under JFK and LBJ and went on to spend decades as a professor at NYU making incalculable contributions to scholarship.

Sonatrach also appointed a law professor, an Algerian one who, under the education system in Algeria, was dependent upon the state for his paycheck. A vote against Algeria in this arbitration could have brought unpleasant consequences for him. This was a huge mistake on Sonatrach's part, since the other two arbitrators were likely to see their colleague as irretrievably "captured" by Algeria and therefore would heavily discount his views. We won the case for Parker.

There is an important lesson here. Opponents of international arbitration often ask, rhetorically (or so they think) how the system can be fair when the parties can appoint whomever they want. Sonatrach's misstep here gives part of the answer: arbitrators with obvious conflicts of interest are unlikely to be listened to in deliberations. The challenge for a party is, therefore, not to find an arbitrator who will automatically agree with its case, but to appoint someone who—like the excellent Professor Lowenfeld—will command the respect of the other two.

The other part of the answer is that arbitrators can be challenged—and even removed, if the challenge succeeds—for partiality or lack of independence from the parties. In the decades since I became an arbitrator myself, I have been challenged a number of times, though usually unsuccessfully, as we will see.

The bottom line is this: you cannot just nominate your nephew and expect to get away with it (in one later case, my client wanted to appoint the CEO's brother-in-law, a notion I quickly quashed). In fact, as I often say, we arbitrators face more democracy than any other kind of judge. We are constantly up for "election," and our appointments last not for life or for a term of years, but for just one case. Arbitrations can be labyrinthine and acrimonious. Sometimes, individual arbitrators will prove to be corrupt or incompetent, just as individual judges sometimes are. But it is important to realize that the system is not inherently biased one way or the other.

CHAPTER FIVE

The Iran Connection

THE TWO KASHANIS

On September 3, 1984, I was just entering a meeting with my fellow judges of the Iran–United States Claims Tribunal when I witnessed one of the most shocking episodes of my career. Out of the blue, two Iranian judges grabbed a Swedish judge, started pummeling and strangling him, and attempted to eject him from the building by force.

I will have much more to say about this disturbing episode. For now, however, I simply wish to note the connection between the assault on the Swedish judge and the origins of the hostility between Iran and the United States. The ringleader of the attack at The Hague was Judge Mahmoud Kashani, a classic Iranian firebrand. Anti-Western agitation appears to run in the family. His father, Ayatollah Abol-Ghasem Kashani, had been a key player in the advent of Iran's quarrel with America. Before delving into the 1979 Iranian Revolution and the outpouring of litigation that resulted, it will be helpful to gain some perspective on how we got there.

Iran and the United States were not always at each other's throats.

Their enmity finds its origins in an ugly episode straight out of the bad old days of international economic relations: a military coup fomented in response to an expropriation of private property.

Starting in the early twentieth century, Iran's oil fields fell under the control of the Anglo-Iranian Oil Company (AIOC), a British private concern with close ties to its country's corridors of power. It was a humiliating arrangement, typical of the behavior of the old imperial powers. AIOC siphoned almost all the oil out of Iran for sale on the international market and kept almost all the profits. In the oil fields themselves, it practiced elements of apartheid, with drinking fountains marked "Not for Iranians."[1] But it was hard to argue with a company that enjoyed the backing of one of the world's most powerful nations.

After World War II, however, British power crumbled, and nationalist movements formed across the empire. In Iran, a largely secular politician named Mohammad Mosaddegh cobbled together a coalition around a single policy: nationalizing AIOC. In order to enjoy legitimacy among such a devout population, Mosaddegh's coalition needed a religious element, and this came courtesy of Ayatollah Abol-Ghasem Kashani, the speaker of Iran's parliament, the Majlis, and the father of my eventual colleague on the Iran–United States Claims Tribunal.

Ayatollah Kashani was a religious hardliner who wanted strict enforcement of *sharia* law, including the forced veiling of women in public. But he was hardly above politics. He led uprisings against the British during World War I and collaborated with Nazi spies during World War II.[2] Under Shah Mohammad Reza Pahlavi, installed by the British in 1941, Kashani spent time in exile and jail. Even while preaching against the West, however, behind the scenes, Kashani solicited bribes from U.S. diplomats and curried favor with the shah's advisers.[3]

In March 1951, the Iranian prime minister, who had supported a deal with AIOC, was assassinated while praying by an assailant who yelled "Long live Islam! Death to the oil company!" The assassin turned out to be a member of an extremist group with close ties to Ayatollah Kashani, and the killing was probably done on Kashani's orders.[4] Mosaddegh, leader of the nationalist coalition, seized the opportunity to gain control over parliament and steer it to nationalize AIOC. Proclaiming a new era of Iranian "self-sufficiency," Mosaddegh ordered all British employees to leave the country.[5]

The concession agreement between AIOC and Iran contained an arbitration clause, which AIOC now sought to activate. Iran, however, refused to appoint its arbitrator, which torpedoed the proceedings.[6] (Later, the Iran–United States Claims Tribunal would have a mechanism for preventing this from happening.) AIOC complained to its home government. Britain, evidently too exhausted from war to threaten stronger action with any degree of credibility, tried peaceful dispute resolution. It espoused AIOC's claim of unlawful expropriation and took Iran to the International Court of Justice, seeking to seize tankers carrying the oil it said rightfully belonged to AIOC. Mosaddegh, a lawyer trained in Switzerland,[7] represented Iran in person before the court, addressing the judges in fluent French.[8]

Despite close ties between AIOC and the British government, however, Britain's lawsuit was never likely to succeed, for the simple reason that the International Court of Justice only has jurisdiction over states and international organizations. Predictably, it found that it was not competent to adjudicate a dispute based on "nothing more than a concessionary contract between a government and a foreign corporation [which] does not regulate in any way the relations between the two governments."[9] Even the British judge voted against his own government's position (although the American judge voted in favor of it).[10]

The failure of Britain's court action, though, did nothing to ease the blockade it had imposed on Iranian oil exports—nor did it help with the fact that, with the Brits gone, the locals lacked the know-how to run the oil fields. So Mosaddegh called upon a mediator: the United States. President Harry S. Truman sent a team headed by W. Averell Harriman, one of the country's most experienced envoys. But the United States' straight-shooting diplomats were flummoxed by the mercurial Mosaddegh, whose apparent concessions one day would devolve into anti-British tirades the next.[11] One diplomatic cable from Harriman described Mosaddegh as living in a "dream world."[12]

Mosaddegh was finally brought down, and AIOC reinstated, by the unlikely alliance of Ayatollah Kashani and the Central Intelligence Agency. Speaking at a rally of the pro-Soviet Tudeh party (further evidence of his political malleability), Kashani declared "victory against British imperialism."[13] With the British apparently gone for good, the ayatollah moved on to his wider program—a fusion of politics and Islam encapsulated in a quote of his that would later inspire the revolutionaries of 1979: "Islam warns its adherents not to submit to a foreign yoke," Kashani told the crowd. "This is . . . why the imperialists are trying to confuse the minds of the people, by drawing a distinction between religion and government and politics."[14]

This kind of thinking was anathema to the secular Mosaddegh, who refused point-blank to institute Kashani's idea of *sharia*. Kashani promptly withdrew his support, and, absent any religious legitimacy, Mosaddegh's coalition began to collapse. This gave the United States an opening. The State Department and CIA urged intervention, in part on the grounds that, if the nationalization of AIOC were allowed to stand, "the example might have very grave effects on United States oil concessions in other parts of the world."[15] They urged covert action to effect regime change.

The plan received the blessing of a newly elected president, Dwight D. Eisenhower. In August 1953, the CIA executed Operation Ajax, masterminded by Kermit Roosevelt Jr., a grandson of President Theodore Roosevelt, with the objective of fomenting a coup to oust Mosaddegh. The operation included persuading the army to crush pro-Mosaddegh protests and paying a mob to march on the prime minister's office.[16] That mob included Ayatollah Kashani's numerous followers, stimulated by a ten-thousand-dollar bribe to Kashani by Kermit Roosevelt for the purpose.[17] Mosaddegh was duly overthrown and a more pro-Western government installed, with the shah restored to power.

Ayatollah Kashani, imprisoned after the coup, died a few years later; although, as we will see, his son would come back to haunt America—and me.[18]

Scholars disagree on how influential American efforts were in bringing about Mosaddegh's downfall. But more important—at least for future dealings between Iran and the United States—was how things looked to the average Iranian. It was around this time that the U.S. embassy in Tehran first attracted the nickname "nest of spies." The author Sandra Mackey calls Operation Ajax a "sore" that would "fester" before it finally "ruptured" in 1979.[19]

THE REVOLUTION

As hard as it may be to imagine today, in the decades after Operation Ajax, peaceful ties between Iran and the United States blossomed. Starting in the 1960s, U.S. multinationals moved in. The roster of companies with sizable investments in the country included the Allied and DuPont chemical companies; oil giants such as Amoco and Exxon; General Motors; and the Goodrich tire company.[20] In all, an estimated five hundred American businesses had collectively invested around $700 million in the country by 1978—the equivalent of nearly $3 billion today.[21] As a result of this vast investment, and the considerable military cooperation between the two countries, on the eve of the Iranian Revolution some forty-five thousand Americans were living in Iran.[22]

Relations burgeoned in other fields, too. At the time of the revolution, more than fifty thousand Iranian students were studying in the United States—by far the largest foreign contingent in the country.[23] In the wake of the Vietnam War, President Richard M. Nixon promulgated a foreign policy doctrine by which the United States would seek to build up allies in various regions of the world to do the security work. Iran under the shah was his chosen partner for the Gulf.

In May 1972, following his summit with Brezhnev discussed earlier, Nixon and Kissinger met with the shah in Tehran and offered him what has become known as a "blank check" for American arms: provided he had the money, he could have anything he wanted, other than nuclear weapons. The shah took up the offer, purchasing billions of dollars of armaments every year for the rest of his reign.[24] The shah knew how high the stakes were for America, bragging in an interview with *Newsweek*:

> *If you didn't have . . . a strong and capable Iran, how will you replace that? With the presence of one million American troops? Do you want several more Vietnams? In Vietnam, you had only 550,000 American boys. But the Persian armed forces have more than that. And they are not smoking grass.*[25]

Perhaps Nixon should have seen the writing on the wall when on the day of his visit to Tehran, three terrorist explosions rocked the city, one wounding an American adviser to the shah's air force.[26] But he and his successors continued to arm Iran. President Jimmy Carter, who had pledged on the campaign trail to reduce arms sales to nondemocratic states, made a major exception for the shah. In fiscal year 1978, the United States sold nearly $2.3 billion worth of arms to Iran. On July 15, 1978, despite the revolutionary upheaval, Carter greenlit the sale of $600 million more, including thirty-one F4 Phantom warplanes.[27] Six months later, almost to the day, the shah fled the country for the last time, effectively abdicating.

Three days after Ayatollah Khomeini's triumphant return to Tehran from Paris on February 1, 1979, the new government canceled practically all pending military contracts with the United States, including the purchases of over 180 airplanes, around 400 missiles, and a complete naval base at Chahbahar across the Gulf of Oman from Muscat.[28] Iran had paid hundreds of millions of dollars in advance deposits for these weapons and facilities—money left sitting in a trust account at the Pentagon, with nobody very sure what was to be done with it.

At least in the beginning, Ayatollah Khomeini professed himself unconcerned with anything as mundane as the economy. "Our people rose for Islam," he said, "not for economic infrastructure. . . . Donkeys and camels need hay. That's economic infrastructure. But human beings need Islam."[29] But the ayatollah's mastery of Koranic jurisprudence could not alter the iron laws of the market, and within weeks of the revolution, the pell-mell flight of talent and capital sent Iran's economy into a tailspin.

In a panic, the government went on an expropriation spree. On June 8, 1979, it nationalized banking (including my client, AIG, of which more soon). On June 25, it nationalized all twelve insurance companies active in Iran. Practically all industry was nationalized on July 5. (The new constitution, approved by plebiscite in December, provided for state ownership of "all major industries.")[30] Not content with this record, the following spring the Islamic Republic commenced mass land seizures.[31]

The revolution and its attendant expropriations left Americans with ties to Iran in limbo. Many individuals had seen their homes, bank accounts, or other property confiscated. U.S. businesses were owed more than $100 million for work already carried out. American banks held more than $2.3 billion in outstanding loans. The revolutionary government had made no plans to compensate anyone, and for obvious reasons there was no prospect of successfully suing in the local courts. Suit might theoretically be brought in the United States, but it was not immediately obvious that Iran had any assets in the United States to enforce against. For now, it seemed that Americans might have to eat their losses.

The United States itself, meanwhile, was cast as the "Great Satan," bent on suppressing Iran and destroying Islam. Protests erupted regularly outside the U.S. embassy in Tehran, now called a "nest of spies" by the government as well as the people. On Valentine's Day 1979, an armed militia occupied the embassy and took seventy staff hostage, killing two Iranians in the process and wounding two U.S. Marines.[32] Khomeini sent Revolutionary Guard forces to disperse the militia, blaming the attack on Iran's Communists.[33] The embassy was returned to the control of the United States.

Meanwhile, Shah Mohammad Reza, exiled and ailing, wandered from place to place. In October 1979, a group of powerful backers including Henry Kissinger and David Rockefeller persuaded President Carter to admit the shah to the United States so he could receive treatment for lymphoma in New York.[34] This decision took effect like a blowtorch to gasoline. In light of the history of Operation Ajax, the shah's admission to the United States was seen in Iran as preparation for another U.S.-supported coup.[35] On November 1, the ayatollah exhorted his supporters to "expand with all their might the attacks against the United States and Israel, so they may force the United States to return the deposed and criminal shah."[36] Three days later, another armed group overran the embassy compound once again, seizing dozens of American diplomats, consular staff, and private citizens. This time, Iranian police charged with protecting the compound melted away, letting the militias run riot.

No American who watched these events unfold is ever likely to forget them. Some of the hostages were paraded—bound, blindfolded, and with guns pointed at their heads—before a baying mob.[37] Ayatollah Khomeini lauded the seizure of "our enemies' center of espionage against our sacred Islamic movement" and announced that the occupation would continue until Carter handed over the shah, while his foreign minister stated bluntly that the hostage taking "enjoys the endorsement and support of the government."[38]

Khomeini may or may not have known about the plan to occupy the embassy (one recent study presents a "circumstantial case" that he not only knew but also instigated it);[39] but he certainly did nothing to stop it, endorsed it after the fact, and profited from it politically. This after-the-fact approval of the occupation made it an act of the Iranian state.

The inviolability of embassies is a cardinal principle; without it, peaceful international relations would be impossible. For this reason, even bitterly antagonistic states respect one another's diplomats, and only the most lawless governments would stoop as low as Iran did in 1979. As well as a humanitarian outrage, then, Iran's action was about as flagrant a breach of international law as could be imagined. The International Court of Justice decided as much, and twice ordered Iran to hand over the hostages. The United Nations Security Council passed two resolutions likewise requiring their release. But the ayatollah preferred to hold on to his most valuable bargaining chip.

GOLDWATER V. CARTER

Nine days after the hostage crisis began, I appeared before the U.S. Court of Appeals for the District of Columbia on a matter of importance to U.S. foreign policy. The case itself had nothing to do with Iran; in fact, the international drama was transpiring thousands of miles to the east, in the Taiwan Strait.

The recent history of Taiwan shows just how messy international relations can be. When Chairman Mao's Communists overran mainland China in 1949, the existing Nationalist government of Chiang Kai-Shek fled to Taiwan. From there, Chiang's Nationalists continued to claim to be the government of the whole of China. The United States, fearful of communism, recognized them as such; but this position became increasingly untenable as Mao's government consolidated its grip on the mainland.

Alongside détente with the Soviet Union, President Nixon's signature foreign policy initiative was the opening to China—meaning the People's Republic on the mainland. The opening up of relations was predicated, naturally enough, on eventually recognizing the People's Republic of China, the de facto government in Beijing, as the legitimate government of China—and on ceasing to recognize Taiwan as a state. "There is but one China and Taiwan is a part of China," as the United States formulation put it.[40] Nixon's successors continued this policy, and it fell to Jimmy Carter to bring it to fruition, in particular by terminating the cornerstone U.S.–Republic of China (Taiwan) Mutual Defense Treaty.

This was a controversial policy and, for its opponents, an opportunity to do damage to Carter's chances of reelection by claiming that the president had "abandoned" a United States ally. In September 1978, Congress wrote into a wide-ranging international security bill a provision that the executive branch "should" consult Congress before terminating the treaty. In December, Carter issued notice of termination as of the end of 1979, precisely in accordance with the terms of the treaty itself. A few days later, a group of conservative foreign policy hawks, led by Sen. Barry Goldwater, a presidential candidate in 1964, sued President Carter in the United States District Court for the District of Columbia, seeking an order enjoining him from terminating the treaty without the consent of the Senate.[41]

For these legislators, this may have been good politics; painting oneself as standing up to godless communists tended to play well. Legally, however, their claim was nonsense. The terms of the treaty expressly provided for termination in exactly the manner Carter had done it. Nothing in the Constitution required Senate approval. There is a popular misconception that the Senate is responsible for ratifying treaties; this is not so. The Senate merely gives (or withholds) its "advice and consent" to ratification. It is up to the president to decide whether or not to ratify. For a variety of reasons, presidents have decided not to ratify Senate-approved treaties down the years.[42] True, the Senate gets to advise and consent on the ratification of treaties. But advice and consent, in the form of confirmation, is also required to appoint U.S. ambassadors to foreign states; was Goldwater really saying that the president needed the Senate's permission to fire them, too?

At first, the U.S. District Court dismissed Goldwater's suit, pointing out that Congress might still approve Carter's termination of the treaty. Goldwater and his allies went back to Capitol Hill and obtained a resolution "that it is the sense of the Senate that approval of the United States Senate is required to terminate any mutual defense treaty between the United States and another nation."[43] The district court took up the claim again and on October 17, 1979—five days before the shah landed in the United States—ruled that Carter's termination of the Mutual Defense Treaty was ineffective without the approval of either both houses of Congress or two-thirds of the Senate.[44]

This judicially imposed block on a major foreign policy initiative must have come as a shock to the administration. It appears to have shocked the United States Court of Appeals for the District of Columbia Circuit, too, for it scheduled a hearing to take place less than four weeks later, deciding it would be heard en banc, meaning—as with my appeal on Miranda rights in the Drummond case almost fifteen years before—all currently sitting judges of the court would hear it at once.

I had been reading the increasingly worrying news out of Iran when I received a phone call from Arthur Rovine. A classmate of mine from Harvard Law, Arthur had worked with me in the office of the legal adviser at the State Department, where he now served as assistant legal adviser for treaty affairs. Arthur said that in his view, there was a good argument to be made based on fundamental international law principles, specifically those codified in the Vienna Convention on the Law of Treaties.

In a nutshell, only states can make treaties, and one of the fundamental tests of statehood is recognition by other states. The history of Taiwan since the 1950s had been one of steady withdrawal of recognition, including by the United Nations itself in 1971.[45] If Taiwan was no longer a state, there was no treaty, so the question before the court was moot.[46]

I was a Republican, and I was being asked to argue on behalf of a Democratic administration. I had no misgivings though, first because safeguarding presidential power should be a bipartisan concern, and second, more fundamentally, because I am in favor of the rule of law in international affairs. And from the point of view of international law, I saw a lot of merit in Arthur's argument.

Arthur went on to tell me, however, that the Justice Department, which was running the case on behalf of the government, refused to put this argument forward, feeling it had a strong case that required no bolstering from anything as abstruse as the Vienna Convention on the Law of Treaties. Arthur therefore asked me if I could find an amicus curiae and put in a brief on its behalf—the same procedure I had used to get OPEC's defense before the court in the litigation against it in California, with Antonin Scalia arguing its case before the Ninth Circuit.

I agreed and called up Professor Don Wallace of Georgetown University Law Center. Wallace was a close friend from our collaboration as successive chairs of the American Bar Association's Section of International Law, and he was now running the International Law Institute. Don signed up the institute as the principal amicus, we added him and another colleague, and I put in my brief on their behalf.

I intended to be in court for the oral argument, but as a spectator only. Counsel for amici are never called upon to argue in court unless, as in the OPEC case, a party is otherwise unrepresented. Nevertheless, the day before the hearing, the clerk of the court called me and asked whether I would be present.

"Try and stop me! Of course I'm going to be there," I replied.

"Well, I'm asking because," the clerk of the court told me, "two of the judges say they would like to ask you questions."

As far as I was concerned, this was unprecedented; but I was delighted that Arthur's and my argument was getting attention. I thanked the clerk and set about preparing.

The hearing took place on November 13, nine days after the seizure of the American hostages in Iran. The ayatollah's government had already publicly adopted the acts of the hostage takers and vowed not to compromise with the United States.

I don't remember what the questions were; but I have always operated on the theory that a good advocate will figure out how to say what needs to be said regardless. And in this case, I thought that events in Iran needed to be addressed. So, before turning to the judges' questions (whatever they were!), I began my answer along these lines:

> *Your Honors, as we are convened here today, the president of the United States is considering his response to the seizure of American hostages in Iran. One of his potential courses of action is to denounce the 1955 Treaty of Amity, Economic Relations, and Consular Rights between this country and Iran. Should Your Honors uphold the judgment of the court below, therefore, it would strike from the hands of the president of the United States a potentially potent weapon.*

While not strictly relevant, I thought this was a powerful emotional argument. The Court of Appeals judgment does not mention Iran, of course; but I think my point came across. In one memorable paragraph, the court addressed the question of mutual defense treaties in general. It wrote:

If we were to hold that under the Constitution a treaty could only be terminated by exactly the same process by which it was made, we would be locking the United States into all of its international obligations, even if the president and two-thirds of the Senate minus one firmly believed that the proper course for the United States was to terminate a treaty. Many of our treaties in force, such as mutual defense treaties, carry potentially dangerous obligations. These obligations are terminable under international law upon breach by the other party or change in circumstances that frustrates the purpose of the treaty. In many of these situations the president must take immediate action. The creation of a constitutionally obligatory role in all cases for a two-thirds consent by the Senate would give to one-third plus one of the Senate the power to deny the president the authority necessary to conduct our foreign policy in a rational and effective manner.

Those, indeed, were the stakes. The Court of Appeals decided in favor of Carter. The Supreme Court ordered the district court to dismiss the case as being nonjusticiable,[47] and the U.S.–Republic of China (Taiwan) Mutual Defense Treaty came to an end effective January 1, 1980. But *Goldwater v. Carter* would come back to haunt me in one sense— and save my bacon in another, as we will see.

THREE WOMEN, FIVE SCULPTURES, AND A TRUST ACCOUNT

Hours after I appeared in *Goldwater v. Carter* before the Court of Appeals, the president made his first big move against Iran, precipitated by Tehran's announcement that it would withdraw all funds held in U.S. banks.[48] With a handful of exceptions, he froze all property subject to U.S. jurisdiction belonging to the Iranian government, its instrumentalities, and its central bank.[49] Suddenly, all the more than three hundred

American claimants against Iran became alert to the presence of millions or even billions of dollars' worth of Iranian assets within U.S. jurisdiction, now conveniently immobile thanks to a stroke of the president's pen.

U.S. courts historically had been reluctant to get involved in claims of expropriation, because of foreign sovereign immunity and the act of state doctrine; but the Supreme Court had carved out an exception for cases where a treaty controlled the matter.[50] President Carter had not, as we have seen, denounced the 1955 U.S.–Iran Treaty of Amity, Economic Relations, and Consular Rights (it would remain in force until denounced by the Trump administration in 2018). Article 4 provided that property of U.S. or Iranian nationals "shall not be taken except for a public purpose, nor shall it be taken without prompt payment of just compensation."

In other words, when Carter froze Iranian property, the scramble for assets was on. Firms and individuals with claims against Iran hunted high and low for property within the United States on which to serve attachments—in other words, to reserve their place in line as and when they might obtain a judgment.

When the ayatollah had expropriated the insurance industry the previous summer, the victims included AIG, the multinational that had been my client since the Nigerian expropriation case in 1977 when I (lawfully) broke Louis LeFevre, their man in Lagos, out of Kirikiri Prison, out of the country, and ultimately out of baseless criminal proceedings. Now, AIG claimed to have lost some $35 million due to its expropriation by Iran. So, on the company's behalf, I now joined the scramble to attach property.

Like many others, we attached the huge trust account at the Pentagon into which the shah had paid deposits for American military hardware now never to be delivered. But we also got creative. Before the revolution, the shah's government had been building up a large collection of contemporary art to display in its museums as part of its plan to drag the country into the twentieth century. I read in the *New York Times* that some of that art had been on loan to the National Gallery in Washington, DC, and, as a result of the revolution, was still in the gallery's storage.[51]

That gave me an idea, and, alongside the shah's weapons money, we wound up attaching the painting "Woman III" by the Dutch-American artist Willem de Kooning and a five-piece sculpture by Jean Dubuffet called "La Députation."[52] The cultural-exchange community did not like the idea that art could be frozen in place for the sake of anything so petty as a lawsuit; but it is worth pointing out how much worse could have befallen these strikingly contemporary pieces had they been returned to the control of fundamentalist clerics whose version of Islam frowned on representations of nature.

In the meantime, the Justice Department attempted—twice—to have all three-hundred-plus claims against Iran consolidated in a single district court before a single judge. This might have made sense had the cases all raised essentially the same issue, but they didn't: claims related to expropriation were different from those related to unfinished construction projects, claims by individuals differed from those brought by corporations, and so on. The only party that would benefit from consolidation would be Iran. Why the Carter administration felt like doing the Islamic Republic this favor, I may never fathom. At any rate, the attorneys for the expropriation claimants honored me by picking me to argue their case against consolidation before the Joint Panel on Multidistrict Litigation in both Boston and San Francisco. On both occasions we prevailed.

Attachments in place, briefs drafted, we were all set for our court date in July 1980. At the last minute, in typically mercurial fashion, Hank Greenberg—having previously instructed me to spare no efforts in pursuing AIG's rights—decided he no longer felt like paying White & Case's (admittedly substantial) fees. So he fired us on the eve of battle and replaced us with a presumably cheaper firm. (Not for nothing has Greenberg been touted as America's worst boss.) The other firm took up our briefs (there being no time to draft new ones) and went on to win summary judgment against Iran and an order for the posting of $35 million in security pending assessment of damages.[53]

For myself and the team at White & Case, it was deeply frustrating to be denied our day in court; but I was able at least to win some credit for the result. I called up the legal publisher West and insisted that, when they reported the case, our name should be on the report. They agreed, and the record reflected our hard work.

AIG, too, would ultimately face frustration. In fact, it would wind up having to start from scratch because of negotiations halfway around the world.

THE ALGIERS ACCORDS

As useful as it was to lawyers like me, Carter's asset freeze was not primarily designed to help private parties make good their losses. It was a bargaining chip, made under sanctions legislation, designed to help balance out the bargaining chip the hostages represented for Iran.[54] The freeze helped bring the Iranians to the negotiating table; but what really lit a fire under them was a former Hollywood actor. Ronald Reagan, an avowed hardliner on foreign affairs, was making a credible bid for the presidency. Tehran feared that, if it didn't come to terms with Carter, and Reagan came to office, it would find a deal much harder to come by.

Just three days before the election, early on a Sunday morning, I received a concerned call from Davis Robinson, a friend from my State Department days, a former foreign service officer, and also a lawyer (as well as, by marriage, a member of the powerful Bush clan). Davis was then advising the Reagan-Bush campaign; he would later become the State Department legal adviser whom I approached in connection with the *Sea Oil* case described above.

Davis reminded me that the Iranian parliament, the Majlis, had just issued the terms on which it would authorize the release of the hostages. Those terms included a demand that the three-hundred-plus cases against Iran be made to disappear together with their asset attachments. Was this the October surprise of 1980? Could President Carter simply agree to the Majlis's demands, quickly bring the hostages home, and shed the political albatross around his neck?

My answer, to Davis's evident relief, was a quick "No!" Claims and attachments, I explained, are a form of property. The president could not destroy that property without making the United States liable to the American plaintiffs under the Fifth Amendment to our Constitution for the justified amounts of their claims against Iran; and the executive could not spend that kind of money without an appropriation from Congress. I was asked to put that in writing and bring it to Jim Baker at campaign headquarters. I knew Baker, having met him at the 1976 Republican National Convention (about which more below). Baker forwarded my memo to Reagan's campaign plane for the candidate's reassurance. Three days later, with no October surprise having materialized, Reagan won forty-four states and secured the presidency.

During the lame-duck period, Iran and the United States negotiated in Algiers, with the Algerian government as intermediary. The United States' delegation was led by Deputy Secretary of State Warren Christopher, who told me years later over dinner, "That's when I learned that one actually *could* survive without sleep!"

The day before Reagan's inauguration, January 19, 1981, the two sides signed the Algiers Accords. The essentials of the deal were simple: America got its hostages back, 444 days after their capture. Iran got its assets unfrozen, subject to some terms: for example, a lot of those assets were required to pay off directly all syndicated loans to Iran in which any American lender was a member of the syndicate. The three-hundred-plus cases and attachments pending against Iran in U.S. courts would be erased; but that required a constitutionally acceptable mechanism for settling those claims.

Thus the accords included as their General Principle B a mutual agreement "to terminate all litigation as between the government of each party and the nationals of the other, and to bring about the settlement and termination of all such claims through binding arbitration."[55] This would be accomplished by creating "an international arbitral tribunal (the Iran–United States Claims Tribunal) . . . for the purpose of deciding claims of nationals of the United States against Iran and claims of nationals of Iran against the United States."[56] The accords also provided for $1 billion of the unfrozen assets to be placed in escrow to be used as security for the payment of awards in favor of American claimants (not Iran or Iranian claimants). Iran was obliged to keep the escrow account at least $500 million in the black at all times.[57]

Nonetheless, for those who had been pursuing Iran through the U.S. courts, the sudden termination of their claims came as a shock to the system. AIG appealed, as did many others, arguing that in vacating domestic claims the president had exceeded his authority. For me personally, this raises an interesting counterfactual, for if White & Case had not been so unceremoniously fired by Hank Greenberg, it would have been me and my team there in the DC Circuit Court of Appeals arguing, in effect, to pull the rug out from under the Iran–United States Claims Tribunal. Would I have been appointed to the tribunal if I had fought to undermine it? I will never know.

The new administration, despite its tough stance on Iran, proved to be just as committed to the accords as its predecessor had been. Secretary of State Alexander Haig made a sworn statement to the DC Circuit Court of Appeals warning that if the judiciary were to strike down the Algiers Accords, "the whole structure of the agreements may begin to crumble, and there could be set in motion a series of actions and reactions that would have serious consequences both for the claimants and for the foreign policy of the United States."[58]

AIG lost its bid to overturn the vacation of claims; but other parties, appearing before federal appeals courts in different parts of the country, won. In situations like that, where those appellate courts disagree, it is up to the Supreme Court to resolve the discrepancies. It did so in *Dames & Moore v. Regan* (the respondent being the then–Treasury Secretary Don Regan, not the president, Ronald Reagan), deciding that the Iran–United States Claims Tribunal satisfied the Fifth Amendment's requirement for due process, thereby providing satisfactorily for the Algiers Accords' termination of the three hundred or more claims of Americans against Iran in our courts.

In oral argument at the Supreme Court, U.S. Solicitor General Rex Lee argued that the advent of the Iran–United States Claims Tribunal might "actually enhance the opportunity for claimants to recover their claims, in that the [Algiers] Agreement removes a number of jurisdictional and procedural impediments in United States courts."[59] Justice Rehnquist, writing for the court, expressed skepticism on that point; but time, and the success of the tribunal, would prove Solicitor General Lee right.

Most interesting of all, at least for an international lawyer, was the choice of substantive law. The tribunal was to operate according to well-established procedural rules laid down by the United Nations Commission on International Trade Law (UNCITRAL),[60] but the rules it would use to decide disputes were left wide open: "The tribunal shall decide all cases on the basis of respect for law, applying such choice of law rules and principles of commercial and international law as the tribunal determines to be applicable."[61]

A seat on the tribunal would therefore represent a tremendous opportunity to shape the future of international law—and in particular the law of expropriation, in which I believed passionately. Were I to be considered for an appointment, I thought I could do some good; but there was another avenue I wanted to explore first.

MY FATHER FIRED RONALD REAGAN!

Ronald Reagan, like Barry Goldwater, held views significantly to the right of my own; but he was still a Republican, and I was eager to serve. There was a potential source of awkwardness, however, in that my father—also called Charlie Brower, albeit with a middle-initial "H" instead of an "N"—held the rare distinction of having fired Reagan from his television job.

As I mentioned before, my father was an advertising executive; his own memoir was entitled, with what for him was uncharacteristic chutzpah, *Me and Other Advertising Geniuses*. Back in 1954, his agency, BBD&O, brokered a deal for Ronald Reagan to host a TV show sponsored by General Electric. Within two years, *General Electric Theater* had become America's third most popular show, with more than 25 million viewers.[62]

Each episode, Reagan would deliver a monologue, and the producers encouraged him to speak his mind, so long as he didn't stray from the brief of promoting GE products. This format worked well while Eisenhower was in the White House. Under Kennedy, however, Reagan's speeches became increasingly paranoid, antigovernment rants that compared the administration, *inter alia*, to the nascent Castro regime in Cuba. GE, already being investigated for price fixing, came under intense pressure to fire Reagan.[63]

By this time, my father had risen to become president and board chairman of BBD&O, and Ralph Cordiner, then the head of GE, prevailed on him to wield the axe. Reagan appeared in my father's office in New York City and a faintly pathetic scene ensued, with the future president (already one of the most famous men in the country, then drawing a salary of over a million dollars in today's money), weeping and pleading, "What can I do, Charlie? I can't act anymore; I can't do anything else. How can I support my family?"[64]

Apparently, though, there were no hard feelings. Years later, when Reagan was governor of California, my father found himself sitting next to Nancy Reagan at a USO event. My father introduced himself, fearing a dressing-down.

"Oh, Charlie Brower?" said the first lady. "Ronnie and I ate thanks to you for years, and we are so grateful for it." This, my father realized, was true, for his agency had brokered the deal by which Ronald Reagan became a GE spokesman.

Next was the fact that I had been a member of President Gerald Ford's strategy team at the 1976 Republican National Convention, led by Ford's chief of staff, Dick Cheney. Ford had been campaigning against Reagan when he challenged the president for the nomination. I thought Ford, a moderate, was a better president than the more extreme Reagan would have been. But this didn't seem to be a roadblock either, for Reagan hired James Baker as a senior adviser for his 1980 campaign—and later as his first White House chief of staff—despite Baker's having campaigned for

Ford *and* for another erstwhile rival, George H. W. Bush. This forgiveness seemed to apply to me, too, for as we have seen above, the Reagan-Bush campaign had turned to me for advice during the brief panic over the Majlis's "offer" to free the hostages. Reagan, of course, won the election, and I found myself appointed to his transition team at the State Department. The portents seemed good for a role in the new administration.

A few weeks after the inauguration, I got a call from a friend who was very close to the new secretary of state, Al Haig, asking me, "How would you like to be the legal adviser of the State Department?"—not "acting" this time, of course, but nominated by the president. I said I would be delighted, as I thought that to be the slot for which I clearly was most qualified. I waited for the call to an interview, but I was not summoned, though I began to hear that others had been.

Some days later I began to discover why. Max Friedersdorf, Reagan's assistant for legislative affairs, called me from the White House. I knew him from my time at State, as in the Nixon White House he had been deputy assistant to the president handling the House of Representatives side of legislative affairs. Later, he had served as consul general in Bermuda, a cushy post indeed, and when on a case in court in Bermuda I had visited him there. But now his words were: "Charlie, what the hell have you done?"

My retort: "What do you mean, Max?" *Oh my God*, I thought. *Are they seriously challenging me because I campaigned for Ford? Or worse yet, dredging up the ancient history of my father firing Reagan on behalf of GE nearly twenty years back?*

But that wasn't it. Max continued, "I have a letter here addressed to the president and signed by six Republican senators—Hatch, Helms, Humphrey, Goldwater, Laxalt, and McClure. They urge the president not to appoint you as legal adviser because you supported Carter against them on Taiwan."

So it was my appearance in *Goldwater v. Carter* that was the source of the objection. This was deeply unfair. *Goldwater v. Carter* was not a partisan case. I was standing up for the rule of law and presidential prerogative. Reagan would have made the same argument. But in politics, that is the way the game is played; and you cannot argue with six senators, particularly *those* six. Goldwater would have sufficed on his own. Humphrey and McClure, conservatives from New Hampshire and Idaho, respectively, were not as well known, but Hatch and Helms were both leading conservatives, and Laxalt had been Reagan's own campaign manager! Perhaps I should have been flattered at how much firepower was thought necessary to shoot me down.

I thanked Max for letting me know and immediately eliminated the possibility of being nominated for legal adviser. But that did not mean I could not have a political future—or, indeed, my revenge. I knew that Goldwater and the other five would not have bothered with this personally. Intuition told me that the ringleader had been a certain person, now on Goldwater's staff, with whom I had worked against the war powers legislation in the State Department.

Another detail all but confirmed my suspicions: in addition to the objection over *Goldwater v. Carter*, the letter to the president also alleged that I was "weak on the deep-sea mining aspects of the law of the sea negotiations." This was a reference to my service as chair of the Inter-Agency Task Force on the Law of the Sea when acting legal adviser, and specifically to a fight over how much protection to afford manganese nodules on the seafloor. Only a real international law nerd would know about that, and I remembered my prime suspect having been particularly agitated over the issue.

If my suspicions were correct, I had an inkling on whose behalf I had been given the hatchet—a rival candidate for the post of legal adviser. So I did two things.

First, a bit of research revealed that the competing candidate actually had testified before a congressional committee that President Carter had the legal power to terminate the Taiwan treaty (and no wonder, for as a matter of law it was utterly inarguable). In other words, this person had told Goldwater he was wrong in testimony on Capitol Hill. If I were disqualified from the post of legal adviser, having done no more than act as counsel for amici, then this person, who had flatly contradicted Goldwater and his co-claimants on the merits, certainly was too.

I then called my friend at State—the one who had asked me, "How would you like to be the legal adviser of the State Department?"—and detailed the whole story to him. He asked me to type up that information in a "non-paper" (the State Department term for an anonymous memo) and place it in his home mailbox, which I did, and am convinced that the intended use was made of it!

Second, I was concerned not to be disqualified generally and conclusively from serving in the government, in particular as I continued to harbor electoral political ambitions in my home state of New Jersey. Banking on my intuition that Goldwater would not have been personally involved in writing such a petty letter, I phoned Dean Burch, who had been Goldwater's campaign manager in his 1964 candidacy for the presidency and was still close to the senator. Dean had gone on to serve in the Nixon administration as chairman of the Federal Communications Commission and was then running Intelsat.

I had gotten to know him while working for Ford at the 1976 Republican National Convention at the Kemper Arena in Kansas City, Missouri. During the evening sessions, I would sit up in one of the skyboxes with Dean and other Republican nobility, such as Nelson Rockefeller, former Pennsylvania governor Bill Scranton, and Henry Kissinger. We all chatted with one another. It turned out that Dean's family and mine both lived in the Fort Sumner neighborhood of Bethesda, Maryland, with just one house between our two, and our daughters both attended the local public elementary school.

When I called Dean, he was immediately welcoming, and when I told him my story he immediately responded, "Barry wouldn't do a thing like that! It's a staff job!"

"Dean, you know that, and I know that, and I know who did it. I don't want, now, as a result to be totally deep-sixed for some other appointment," I said. "What I need is a second letter from the senator to the president saying that was that, but Brower is a loyal Republican, a fierce protector of American investors abroad, and should be considered for another relevant post."

Obviously, I had my eye on the Iran–United States Claims Tribunal as my plan B. The first group of American judges already had been appointed, but I thought I would be in with a shot whenever a vacancy showed up. Dean could not have been more helpful. "I'll speak with Barry," he assured me. "You draft the letter you want him to send to the president, make a date to meet with his staffer up on the Hill. Barry, I am sure, will send that letter. Let me know if you have any problem." And so it all happened, and I was rehabilitated.

The job of State Department legal adviser eventually went to the last man standing, Davis Robinson, the lawyer friend who had called me from the Reagan campaign to seek advice on the Iranian "offer" to Carter. In retrospect, I am glad it wasn't me, because of the impossible position in which Davis soon found himself.

When the International Court of Justice was established following World War II, the United States had been among the first states to accept its compulsory jurisdiction in interstate claims. As acting legal adviser, I had helped advance the Nixon administration's policy of strengthening the court and had testified on the matter before the Senate in May 1973.[65]

But the United States' commitment to the court came under strain in the early 1980s when the Reagan administration began arming the so-called Contras—opponents of the Soviet-aligned government of Nicaragua. Nicaragua responded by suing the United States at the ICJ in the spring of 1984, alleging unlawful use of force. America's defense was its alleged right to defend its allies in the region—or at any rate, it would have been. The United States first tried to avoid a hearing on the merits altogether by changing the terms of its acceptance of the court's jurisdiction before the case was due to be filed—a move that was ruled untimely. Next, it argued that the court had no jurisdiction over such politically fraught matters.

I was present for the hearing at the ICJ, where Nicaragua was represented by my old law professor Abe Chayes. As State Department legal adviser in the Kennedy administration, Abe had been responsible for the concept that Kennedy's action during the Cuban Missile Crisis in October 1962 was not a "blockade" (which could have been grounds for war) but a "quarantine." The hearing itself was undramatic—the World Court does not do drama—but the somewhat technical jurisdictional issues at stake were important for international law. More than twenty-five years later, Judge Schwebel of the United States would write that Nicaragua had perpetrated a "fraud on the court" by giving false evidence;[66] if so, it was not immediately apparent.

At any rate, the United States lost, which was bad enough; but what it did next was truly destructive. It responded to the court's unfavorable decision on jurisdiction by walking out, refusing to appear further, and withdrawing its longstanding consent to the court's compulsory jurisdiction. This series of petulant moves won us few friends internationally.

Despite having walked out at the first sign of trouble, the administration still wanted to claim that its defense was airtight. It was thus forced to posit the unattractive argument that the court itself was somehow too biased to decide the case properly. It issued a statement calling Nicaragua's suit "a blatant misuse of the Court for political and propaganda purposes," implying that the court was "determined to find in favor of Nicaragua" and had been "infected" by an alleged trend whereby "international organizations have become more and more politicized against the interests of the Western democracies," and even stating outright that presenting its case would risk U.S. national security "before a Court that includes two judges from Warsaw Pact nations."[67]

On the merits, the ICJ found in favor of Nicaragua. The United States proceeded to veto enforcement of the judgment in the Security Council, making it a judge in its own cause, about as contrary to the rule of law as it is possible to get.[68]

For internationalists like myself, this was a source of tremendous dismay. Yet Davis Robinson, as legal adviser, was forced into the impossible situation of having to choose between, on the one hand, burning one's political bridges by resigning over the matter or, on the other, enraging forever after one's international law colleagues by backing the administration's indefensible position. He chose to stay. In short, I am glad that wasn't me. I came to realize yet again that every failure of mine to get a job that I had thought I wanted was a blessing in disguise.

HEADING TO THE HAGUE

The Iran–United States Claims Tribunal, having been duly constituted, met in The Hague and spent about a year figuring out its own rules of procedure before opening up shop. Having seen its claim in federal court vacated pursuant to the Algiers Accords, AIG brought a case before the tribunal. Iran's lawyers tried to argue that the traditional requirement for "prompt, adequate, and effective" compensation for expropriation had been displaced by the watered-down standards expressed in the United Nations Charter of Economic Rights and Duties of States, which was not a legally binding document. The tribunal—thank goodness—rejected that argument.[69] Damages were set at $10 million, only about one quarter of what AIG claimed; but at least payment of that amount was guaranteed by the $1 billion security account.

As counsel, I worked on several cases before the tribunal, including one for Time Inc. in which the company eventually won essentially what it claimed; but I was careful never to appear as an advocate, lest the perceived conflicts of interest spoil my chances of an appointment to that bench when a vacancy opened. This turned out to be a good idea; much later, when I sought appointment as a commissioner of the UN Compensation Commission, my many appearances before that body would scupper my chances.

Arthur Rovine, my law school classmate and State Department lawyer who had gotten me involved in *Goldwater v. Carter*, was appointed as the first United States agent to the tribunal. In April of 1983 Arthur called me and asked if I would like to serve as a substitute member of the tribunal. I accepted and was appointed, knowing it would strengthen the possibility of my permanent appointment.

As it turned out, I need not have worried about my standing in the eyes of the Reagan administration. I quickly realized that everyone with a say in appointments to the tribunal saw my having been torpedoed for the position of State Department legal adviser as an egregious case of "the revolution devouring its children." They enthusiastically urged my appointment to the tribunal. A former partner of mine at White & Case, Ed Schmults, was deputy attorney general and put in a good word with the deputy secretary of state, with whom I had made contact and who knew the story. When I met in his office with Fred Fielding, Reagan's White House counsel (I had worked with Fred when I was at State and he was deputy White House counsel), Fred said, "Charlie, I want you to have this appointment." So in the fall of 1983 I was appointed effective January 16, 1984.

Right before I went, my immediate successor as State Department legal adviser, the Kissinger confidant and Cravath partner Carlyle E. Maw, came to dinner at my home. He gave me a *misbaha*—a set of Muslim prayer beads representing the ninety-nine names of God in Arabic.

"Where you're going," Carl said, "I think you might need these."

He was right, as we will see. But the beads did the trick; I survived the tribunal. Later, I gave them to my stepson, a British army officer who volunteered to leave his position as additional equerry to the Duke of Edinburgh at Buckingham Palace to fight in the Gulf War. He, too, returned safe and well and returned the beads to me. To this day, I carry them with me in my briefcase wherever I go, and they have not failed me yet.

CHAPTER SIX

Judging Iran, Part I

HEADING TO THE HAGUE

My permanent appointment to the Iran–United States Claims Tribunal began in mid-January 1984, but I arrived a few days early, on December 31, 1983—just in time for a New Year's Eve party hosted by one of my fellow judges, George Aldrich. I knew George and his wife, Rosemary, well from my time at State, where he had served alongside me as deputy legal adviser. So as the plane dropped through the ever-present layer of low rainclouds and touched down at Schiphol International, I was looking forward to catching up with George, as well as meeting my new colleagues.

The other American appointee, New York lawyer Howard Holtzmann, who had been chairman of the board of the American Arbitration Association, likely would be at the party together with his wife, Carol. So would the three third-country arbitrators: the Dutchman Willem Riphagen, and the Swedes Gunnar Lagergren and Nils Mangard. The three Iranians, however, certainly would not be there, being under strict instructions from Tehran not to socialize with their colleagues. This distance, alas, was to characterize my first year on the tribunal.

My predecessor, Richard Mosk, a distinguished lawyer from Los Angeles, had already departed, but his law clerk, David Caron, was still there and was to become my clerk. David picked me up from the airport in his station wagon. At the age of thirty-one, David was a veteran of the U.S. Coast Guard, where he served as a navigation and diving officer in Arctic waters. After that frigid experience, he had been a Fulbright scholar in Wales and a prize-winning law student at Berkeley. David was destined for a glittering career, and that airport transfer in his station wagon would prove to be the start of an extraordinary friendship that would last until David's tragic premature death in 2018.

I had visited The Hague once before, in July of 1966, when Oda and I left our two-year-old daughter, Rica, in the care of her grandparents in Berlin in order to spend a week touring the Netherlands, a country neither of us had visited before. On that occasion, I was particularly interested in seeing the famous Peace Palace, a neo-Renaissance building in The Hague. The home of international tribunals since before World War I, it was purpose-built with funds courtesy of the Scottish-American steel magnate Andrew Carnegie. It became the seat of the Permanent Court of Arbitration, later also of the post–World War I Permanent Court of International Justice, and eventually the United Nations' International Court of Justice following World War II. Seeing this building was a highlight of the visit for me, but the experience was overshadowed (quite literally) by the equally famous Dutch weather. In fact, it rained the entire time we were there, and we left The Hague vowing, "If we never come back, it'll be too soon!"

Eighteen years on, the climate had not improved, and the late December air was especially cold, dark, and damp. I arrived telling myself I would serve just two years, so I would only have to endure one entire winter there. As it turned out, I would spend twenty-one-and-a-half years of my life as a resident of The Hague.

For international lawyers, The Hague is Hollywood—minus the Southern California sunshine. There are many more tribunals there today; but even then, the city was home to the two most prominent: the Permanent Court of Arbitration and the International Court of Justice. As of late 1983, however, both were more or less dormant. The PCA, the body for which the Peace Palace had originally been built, had not had a case since 1935, when the Radio Corporation of America sued pre-Communist China over the setting up of a radio telegraph circuit. It would take until the 1990s to recover. The ICJ, the principal judicial organ of the United Nations, had not much on its plate either, though its docket would heat up in 1984 with the ill-starred Nicaragua case that would cause the United States to withdraw from its compulsory jurisdiction.

This meant that, when I arrived, the Iran–United States Claims Tribunal was the big show in town. To say its docket was full would be an understatement. The deadline for filing claims by nationals was January 19, 1982—one year after the Algiers Accords. Some 3,844 such claims had been filed, ranging from $63 million for expropriation of several oil rigs[1] to $160 for the unusable return leg of an Iran Air ticket (the claimant eventually obtained an award for the princely sum of $100).[2]

In claims worth less than $250,000, claimants would be represented by their respective governments. In effect, the home state would "espouse" the claim, as traditionally required in international law. Above that amount, however, parties would represent themselves. The Iran–United States Claims Tribunal, therefore, represented something new: a standing institution specifically designed to allow the nationals of one state to sue the government of another state under international law, in addition to specified types of claims that one state could pursue against the other.

Would it work? As of late 1983, that remained to be seen.

DOMINANT AND EFFECTIVE

As far as I am concerned, I arrived at the perfect time. I was not involved in the very beginning, when the tribunal spent over a year hashing out its rules and procedures; but I wouldn't have been interested in that anyhow. I would rather hear a real-world case.

Some of the rules could also be worked out by the tribunal on its own in administrative session: for example, the decision to separate into three chambers to hear claims brought by private parties. Other cases, however, had to be litigated before the entire nine-judge tribunal. These cases, called "A claims," involved the "interpretation or performance of any provision" of the Algiers Accords themselves, and they got very heated indeed. One example from before my appointment to the tribunal was case number A1, which asked: "Who gets the interest on that $1 billion security account with the Algerian Central Bank?" The answer was Iran, but it had to use the money to replenish the security account. Iran denounced the decision—but complied.

The controversy around A1 was nothing compared to that surrounding A18, the so-called Nationality Case. A significant number of claims, many of them for massive sums, had been filed against Iran by Iranian immigrants to the United States who had become naturalized U.S. citizens, and others whom Iran regarded as its own citizens. This was significant because international law traditionally does not recognize claims by nationals against their own state, seeing such claims as a matter of domestic law only. Iran therefore wanted the tribunal to treat as Iranian nationals everybody it regarded as such, so as to avoid liability. (It did not help that such dual citizens tended to be wealthy and well-connected and therefore more likely to have supported the shah.)

In violation of the Universal Declaration of Human Rights, which guarantees the right to change one's nationality, Iran made it impossible to renounce Iranian citizenship. In fact, Tehran actually *imposed* Iranian nationality on people who had never so much as set foot in the country, such as the American-born wives and children of Iranian men.[3]

Iran asked the tribunal to decide whether dual nationals could sue. After reviewing international law precedent, the full tribunal decided that the applicable standard was "dominant and effective nationality" based on ties like residence, family, and place of business. This standard was a relatively new development—the more traditional test for nationality allowed states a good deal more leeway to define who was and was not a national—but the case presented a classic example of the tribunal's freedom to apply "such principles of commercial and international law as the tribunal determines to be applicable," embodied in art. 5 of the Algiers Accords' Claims Settlement Declaration. All the judges concurred in the result—except for the three Iranians.

Having asked the question, Iran now decided it didn't like the answer. The Iranian judges penned a fiery dissent, four times longer than the award itself. In paragraph one, they dredged up Operation Ajax, the CIA's effort to support the coup against Mosaddegh in 1953. They accused the tribunal of having rendered its decision in "bad faith . . . merely to demonstrate loyalty to the United States" and the judges themselves of having acted from "political and materialistic motives." They singled out the Dutch judge, Willem Riphagen, calling him, in effect, a proxy agent of the United States. Finally, they condemned the institution of arbitration itself as "an exclusive club . . . designed to safeguard the interests of the capitalist world." (This last accusation would have a long history well beyond The Hague, and I write about it below.)

Even the Iranian prime minister, Mir-Hossein Mousavi, got involved, giving a furious speech promising "to take any legitimate action that [Iran] might deem appropriate to achieve justice." In pursuit of this aim, the prime minister said, Iran "shall pay whatever price necessary." This was a clear threat from a government that had shown itself unconcerned with the niceties of diplomatic protection, and the *Wall Street Journal* quoted one non-Iranian arbitrator as saying, "I was terrified."[4]

Because of their obvious political sensitivity, the tribunal held back claims by dual nationals until we had gone through all of the other claims by nationals of the one country against the other. But the Iranian response to the Nationality Case was, unfortunately, to set the tone for the months ahead.

STREET-FIGHTING REDUX

From the moment I took up my duties, I was working flat out. A typical hearing would last no more than a week, and my chamber was doing two per month for nine months out of the year, plus the occasional longer hearings of "A" cases before the full tribunal. Preparing for each case was like cramming for a test. The facts ranged from expropriations to breaches of contract to cases of wrongful expulsion from Iran. We cranked out awards at a rate that put other chambers to shame.

While sticking to this relentless schedule, we also had to deal with a fair bit of acrimony, courtesy (or should that be discourtesy?) of the Iranians. At one point, while back in the United States for a visit, I attended a White & Case function. One of the senior partners with whom I had worked asked me how I could give up "the joys of litigating in New York to go sit on that tribunal in The Hague with those Iranian revolutionaries?"

I replied, "Every art I learned as a brass-knuckle, street-fighting litigator in the city of New York is absolutely applicable in deliberations with my Iranian colleagues."

I was not joking. This belligerent atmosphere was the result of fierce competition for the support of the third-country judges. The Iranian members always voted for the Iranian party and were under pressure to win cases for "their" side. Those were their instructions from Tehran, and, unlike the Americans, they could be ordered to resign at any moment. We Americans were acting as judges should, and as the tribunal rules required of all nine judges, namely as independent and impartial adjudicators, as a result of which a chamber from time to time would vote unanimously against the U.S. party because the facts and the law clearly were against it. Outside of those cases, however, the third-country members, each of whom always chaired a chamber of three, would hold the casting vote.

Memoranda flew back and forth as each side vied to persuade. Sometimes, in deliberations, the Iranians would try harsher tactics, screaming insults at the Europeans, accusing them of corruption, and occasionally storming out of meetings. Iran sometimes attempted to have third-country members removed from the tribunal on frankly frivolous grounds. Arthur Rovine, the first U.S. agent to the tribunal, summed up this process when he called it "guerilla arbitration."[5]

By far the worst offenders during my first year on the tribunal were Mahmoud Kashani, the ayatollah's son and future politician, in Chamber One and Shafei Shafeiei in Chamber Two. In my Chamber Three, thankfully, the Iranian member was the stable Parviz Ansari Moin, a career civil servant at the Iranian Ministry of Justice since before the revolution.[6] Ansari became known at the tribunal as the "million-dollar man" because he refused to remit part of his tribunal salary to his government, as Iran required of him and his colleagues.

Nevertheless, Ansari never gave up, arguing the same point from different angles, while the chair of my Chamber Three, the Swedish judge Nils Mangard, never departed from his impartial and independent approach to cases. The fact is that our Chamber Three processed more cases faster than the other two, compiling a record largely unfavorable to Iran.

Early on in my time at the tribunal, Judge Ansari asked me, "Do you know what the difference is between Iranians and Americans?" Upon my plea of ignorance, he related a parable about the Iranian approach to problems. He told me that he had once surprised a would-be burglar at his home in The Hague. The burglar ran for it—out the door and then over the garden wall into the night.

"What would an American do?" he asked. His answer: "Breathe a sigh of relief and perhaps call the police."

I thought that was probably right.

"But what did I do?" Ansari continued. "I, too, immediately jumped over the garden wall and chased that man all the way down the street and did not give up the chase until I lost sight of him. Had I caught him, however, I would have beaten him senseless! That's the difference!"

As time went on, the Iranians became more and more frustrated with the tribunal. As a human matter, I understand why. From their point of view, no matter how hard they tried, Iranian respondents kept losing, losing, and losing some more. No wonder they thought the world was against them.

On the other hand, as I kept telling Ansari, this frustration was based on a misunderstanding of the tribunal's purpose. It was set up to pay legitimate American claims, of which—thanks largely to Iran's 1979 expropriation binge—there were many. Iran should have gone into the exercise expecting to have to pay out. The purpose of the tribunal, most of the time, was simply to decide how much. But our Iranian colleagues did not see it this way. Instead, their frustration only grew hotter and hotter, until it reached boiling point.

ASSAULT ON JUSTICE

I always got along well with the third-country member of my chambers, retired Swedish judge Nils Mangard. As a judge in his country's court of appeal, Mangard had spent some years in Eritrea, helping to build up its judicial system. Mangard was also one of the leading lights of another important arbitral institution, the Arbitration Institute of the Stockholm Chamber of Commerce. Since the signing of the U.S.-Soviet trade agreement (I had worked on this while at the State Department), a version of our clause "recommending" arbitration had found its way into many contracts between Western private enterprises and Communist bloc countries' state-owned foreign trade organizations.[7] As East-West trade ballooned, Sweden began to emerge as the favored neutral third country for arbitration between U.S.- and Soviet-aligned parties.

In 1973, the American Arbitration Association, the USSR Chamber of Commerce, and the Stockholm Chamber of Commerce had gotten together to produce a study designed to facilitate American and Soviet understanding of the Swedish arbitration process. Mangard had chaired that study, which was soon followed by the drafting of an "optional clause" for inclusion in commercial contracts, specifying the Arbitration Institute of the Stockholm Chamber of Commerce as the administrator of arbitrations between the parties and Stockholm as their venue.[8] By 1984, the success of the optional clause had long since made Stockholm the preeminent venue for U.S.-Soviet arbitration.

Mangard was one of the original third-country judges that both sides had agreed to, along with Gunnar Lagergren, a tribunal president and fellow Swede, and Pierre Bellet, the former president of France's highest court, Cour de Cassation. Within a year, however, Iran challenged Mangard's appointment, saying he had criticized the Islamic Republic for its numerous public executions. Mangard said he was misquoted, and the challenge was dismissed for lack of a clear accusation against Mangard—an early indication to the Iranians that the tribunal would be a judicial body, not a purely political one.[9] But thenceforward, the Iranians had it in for him. Kashani in particular insisted on calling Mangard, without any evidence, "an agent of the U.S. government."[10]

Around the tribunal, Mangard developed a reputation for being less tolerant of Iran's delaying tactics than his third-country colleagues. (Such tactics became legendary; in one later case I felt compelled to dissent from an order postponing a hearing, complaining that the tribunal had been induced to move "at a speed calculated to inspire professional envy in sloth and snail alike"—a good line, even if it didn't do much good for the claimant.)[11]

Tensions ratcheted up when the full tribunal rendered its decision in the Nationality Case on April 6, 1984. They increased again when my chamber issued one of the largest judgments against Iran yet on July 31—an award that Parviz Ansari denounced as "illegal and void."[12] I myself did not participate in either of these cases, which had been heard prior to my appointment, under art. 13(5) of the tribunal's rules. This became known as the "Mosk Rule" because it was first applied to my predecessor, Richard Mosk, who replaced me in the both cases. Still, one felt the tension rising. But there was no indication of what was to occur a little over a month later.

Almost all the tribunal's business was conducted in our individual chambers, which suited me. It meant that, most of the time, I didn't have to contend with the histrionics of judges Kashani and Shafeiei. Occasionally, however, we had to hold administrative meetings of the entire tribunal, plus the U.S. and Iranian agents and their deputies. One such meeting was held on Monday, September 3, 1984, at the tribunal's premises at Parkweg 13, a small hotel (and former maternity hospital) on a leafy street about two miles from the center of town.

I was coming down the stairs behind Mangard, Shafeiei, and Kashani, when on the ground floor the two Iranians suddenly jumped the sixty-nine-year-old Swede. Shafeiei held Mangard while Kashani punched him in the chest. Kashani then grabbed Mangard's necktie and began swinging him around. (Apart from the obvious outrage of assaulting a fellow judge, this was a significant gesture, since in Iran neckties are viewed as a symbol of Western subjugation; Iranian men don't wear them.) Kashani seemed either to be attempting to choke Mangard or eject him from the building by force.

Finally, the American agent, John Crook, his deputy, Dan Price, and Parviz Ansari—with help from my law clerk David Caron—were able to separate the men. I ran to the guard booth and shouted, "Call the police!" The guard did so, but President Lagergren forbade the police to enter the building. The tribunal is an international organization enjoying diplomatic inviolability, hence the local police are not allowed to enter without the permission of the tribunal president, which Lagergren refused to give.

In fact, to his disgrace, Lagergren refused to do anything at all. When all three American judges asked that the assailants be barred from the premises, Lagergren refused even to do that. Instead, he told Mangard to stay out of the building, disgraceful decisions that came, in part, from a misguided desire to keep Iran onside and thus preserve the tribunal. Mostly, though, Lagergren had snobbish motives. He had married into the powerful Wallenberg clan and thereby become a brother-in-law of the famous Raoul Wallenberg, the Swedish diplomat famed both for saving thousands of Hungarian Jews from Nazi concentration camps and then for his untimely disappearance and presumed death while in Soviet custody. Before joining the tribunal, Lagergren had served King Carl XVI Gustaf as marshal of the realm—the lead administrator of the monarch's household and about as prestigious as it gets short of actual royalty. As marshal of the realm, Lagergren was second in protocol behind the sovereign and therefore thought rather highly of himself. He was not about to do favors for a social lesser like Mangard.

Just three days after the attack, on September 7, Kashani not only refused to apologize for his actions but outright threatened to kill Mangard, saying, "If Mangard ever dares to enter the tribunal chamber again, either his corpse or my corpse will leave it rolling down the stairs."[13] Only then, faced with the threat of violence on a whole new level, did Lagergren suspend proceedings.

The U.S. judges, along with the third-country judges, felt Lagergren's pattern of inaction had been an outrage in itself, but his proposed "solution" to the affair was frankly breathtaking. He proposed that Mangard should meet Shafeiei (but not Kashani) in the Peace Palace, a neutral venue. There, Shafeiei (but not Kashani) would apologize, on the understanding that Mangard would resign within thirty days!

This was intolerable. George Aldrich, Howard Holtzmann, and I called on Mangard at his apartment in The Hague: "Don't resign," we advised him. "Under the circumstances, it would be bad for you and the tribunal. Go home to Stockholm for a bit." Then we assured him: "In the meantime, we have been guaranteed that the United States is about to challenge these two judges. If the challenge succeeds, you can come back safely and with your reputation and that of the tribunal intact. If by some highly unlikely chance it fails, no one in the world would blame you at all for resigning then."

Mangard did as we suggested, and sure enough, the United States issued challenges against Kashani and Shafeiei. The Islamic Republic never objected to the challenges; it simply recalled the offenders and announced the appointment of two replacement judges. The tribunal, thank goodness, interpreted this as Iran "accepting the challenges" in conformity with the tribunal's rules of procedure. The plain fact was that, for all its bombast and anti-Western rhetoric, Iran wanted the tribunal to endure. In the next chapter, I will show why.

Lagergren resigned soon after the assault, apparently having received a telephoned death threat, presumably from Iran. Mangard did resign a number of months into 1985, his reputation and the tribunal's intact, having much earlier promised his wife he would retire on his seventieth birthday. Judge Ansari, of course, remained.

For the remainder of 1984, the tribunal remained in suspended animation. Among the Americans, the mood grew downbeat. Iran had relentlessly delayed proceedings, denounced the tribunal as corrupt, threatened the judges, and now two of its three judges had physically attacked a third-country judge. It was not a good look for the tribunal— or for international arbitration more generally. As one of my U.S. colleagues told a reporter a couple of months after the attack, "I just hope we haven't dealt international arbitration a death blow."[14]

That fear would prove unfounded. In fact, for reasons that will become apparent throughout the rest of this book, international arbitration was just getting started.

CHAPTER SEVEN

Judging Iran, Part II

KASHANI'S GAMBLE FAILS

The assault against Nils Mangard had evidently been prearranged between Kashani and Shafeiei. In due course, I learned why after speaking with certain friendly Iranian staff members. Having seen how many cases Iran was losing, Kashani had concluded that the Algiers Accords had been a mistake. He had therefore aligned himself ideologically with a hardline faction in Iran that wanted to eliminate all contact with the United States—of which the tribunal was the last public vestige. For several months, Kashani had been agitating for Iran to withdraw from the tribunal altogether.

The ayatollah's government did not agree; it wanted the tribunal preserved. About a week before the attack, Tehran had apparently dispatched a high-ranking official to The Hague to tell Kashani in person to stop opposing the government on the point. In desperation, Kashani figured that if he and Shafeiei assaulted a fellow judge, Tehran would be forced to back them. The United States would never stand for it, and the resulting impasse would cause the tribunal to collapse.

Assuming this version of events is correct, Kashani miscalculated badly and, as we have seen, paid a high professional price. Having been effectively fired, along with Shafeiei, Kashani returned to Tehran and resumed his academic career. (He remained politically active. In 2001, he ran for president against the incumbent, the more reform-minded Mohammed Khatami. He garnered a whopping 0.84 percent of the vote, fourth behind Khatami, who won with 77 percent.)[1]

The tribunal reopened under new management in January 1985. Almost immediately, we resumed our relentless pace as if nothing had happened.[2] Lagergren's replacement as tribunal president was the German arbitrator Karl-Heinz Böckstiegel, in my opinion the best president we ever had. Böckstiegel worked hard to build bridges with Ansari and the two new Iranian judges—and not by caving to their demands as Lagergren had too often done. For example, Böckstiegel made clear that he empathized with what Iran was going through in the Iran-Iraq War (a shockingly bloody conflict that would ultimately kill more than one million people) by speaking movingly about Allied bombs raining down on his home during his childhood in World War II.

Michel Virally replaced Mangard as chair of my chamber. A French professor of international law, he had begun his legal career by serving in the French Zone of Occupation in Germany immediately following the war. Virally was a lovely man, but he could be stubborn. I would point out the weaknesses in his draft awards by showing him my draft dissenting opinion, saying, "Your Cartesian logic has placed you out on a limb, which I have sawed off!"

Virally would reply in his Gallic singsong, "Oh well. I do not change my mind. But perhaps I must work on the reasoning!" I was frustrated that he did not consider the possibility that different reasoning could bring a different result.

One such case was *Amoco International Finance v. Iran et al.* The facts will be familiar to anyone who has studied the nationalizations that followed the Iranian Revolution. In 1966, at the height of the shah's program of economic liberalization, Amoco and the Iranian National Petroleum Company formed a 50-50 joint venture called Khemco to set up and run a natural gas processing plant on Kharg Island, in the Persian Gulf west of Shiraz.

This it did until April 1979, when the new Islamic government announced, as in 1952, the expulsion of foreign workers from the oil fields and the buyout of non-Iranian interests by the National Petroleum Company. That July, Iran unilaterally assumed 100 percent control of Khemco. The following January, the oil industry was formally nationalized and a commission set up to "settle claims." On Christmas Eve 1980, to the surprise of nobody, this commission decided that the Khemco agreement was null and void and the compensation due was zero dollars.

Expropriation claims were among the most common types of cases brought before the tribunal. In these matters, Iran would sometimes try the dubious argument that the state had acted merely to "preserve" the property in question (a little, one supposes, like the "protective custody" used by police states to justify the indefinite detention of inconvenient persons).[3] But in the vast majority of cases, Iran had just confiscated the claimant's property.

Ultimately, the only real question was how much compensation was due the former owner. Art. 4 of the U.S.–Iran Treaty of Amity—made by Eisenhower and the shah after the latter was restored to power following Operation Ajax—provided that the property of nationals and companies of one country could not be taken by the other "except for a public purpose, nor shall it be taken without the prompt payment of just compensation." How much compensation was just in the circumstances would, in turn, depend on whether or not the taking was lawful under international law. This, then, was the legal battleground.

In *Amoco International Finance*, Virally penned an award—issued, incidentally, on Bastille Day 1987, an auspicious date for a Frenchman—built on two essential findings. First, that the expropriation was not unlawful insofar as it furthered a legitimate public purpose—namely, Iran's exercise of sovereignty over its natural resources as part of a non-discriminatory general program of nationalization.[4] Second, that the standard of compensation payable was the full "going-concern value" of the company—drawn from the famous *Chorzów Factory* case (see chapter 3) but (somehow) incorrectly excluding expected future profits.[5]

Iran had argued for a standard of partial compensation, based in part on the so-called Charter of Economic Duties and Rights of States mentioned before; so I was pleased that Virally had applied a standard of at least full compensation. Other aspects of his award I found problematic. First, the taking of half of Khemco had begun in April 1979 and been completed by July of that year—six months *before* the official nationalization of the oil industry—in clear breach of contract. Second, as any business owner knows, the only value of any "going concern" is as a generator of future profits; so if you exclude those profits from valuation, what is left, besides an absurdity worthy of Lewis Carroll?

Ansari, in accordance with his standing instructions from Tehran, refused to award one cent to an American party. In light of this, I "concurred" in Virally's judgment for the usual purpose: that of forming a majority in favor of the closest we could get to the right result. Then I entered a concurring opinion that in reality set out just how badly wrong I thought the award had gotten things. First, Iran had breached the joint venture agreement by seizing the half of Khemco it didn't already own; there was an express provision in the agreement (which the Iranian government had ratified) that annulment could happen only with Amoco's consent.[6] That made the expropriation unlawful, which in turn meant a potentially higher standard of compensation. Even if Iran didn't breach the contract, it certainly violated the Treaty of Amity, which required "just compensation" for the taking of property—something the phony Iranian claims commission had signally failed to offer.[7]

Second, "going-concern value" could only mean an enterprise's value as a potential source of profits—for what else was there? That was the plain meaning; any other interpretation would, as I wrote in my opinion, represent "both a misreading of *Chorzów Factory* and a misunderstanding of economics."[8]

When it came to *Amoco International Finance*, the right reading of *Chorzów Factory* was clear. For a lawful expropriation, you get the value of the asset at the date of the taking, as if the state had exercised

Signing of the Final Quadripartite Protocol to the Quadripartite Agreement on Berlin by the United States Secretary of State William P. Rogers (nearest one seated at the table) and (in order, right to left) Foreign Minister of the Soviet Union Andrei Gromyko, Foreign Secretary of the United Kingdom Sir Alec Douglas-Home, and Foreign Minister of the French Republic Maurice Schumann. The signing took place on June 3, 1972, in the building formerly occupied by the Allied Control Council in the American sector of Berlin. Deputy Legal Adviser Charles N. Brower, presiding, stands behind Secretary Rogers. Photograph is signed "To Charlie Brower with my warm regards and respect. William P. Rogers."

General Secretary Leonid Brezhnev and President Richard Nixon attend the signing in the United States Department of State Diplomatic Reception Rooms by Soviet Foreign Minister Gromyko and Secretary of State Rogers of Agreements on Cooperation in Agriculture, on Studies of the World Ocean, on Transportation, and a General Agreement on Contacts, Exchanges and Cooperation. Acting Legal Adviser Charles N. Brower, presiding, stands center left. (The *New York Times*, June 19, 1973)

In the East Room of the White House, President Nixon and General Secretary Brezhnev sign Basic Principles of Negotiations on Strategic Arms Limitations and Agreement on Scientific Cooperation in Peaceful Uses of Atomic Energy. To the right of President Nixon: Acting Legal Adviser Charles N. Brower, presiding, standing against portrait of George Washington; Secretary of the Interior Rogers C. B. Morton; Secretary of Labor Peter Brennan; Assistant to the President for National Security Affairs Henry A. Kissinger; White House Domestic Affairs Adviser Melvin Laird; and Counsellor to the President Anne Armstrong. (Official White House photo, June 21, 1973)

The Iran–United States Claims Tribunal in its courtroom in the Peace Palace in The Hague. From left to right: Judges P. Ansari Moin, Hamid Bahrami Ahmadi, Seyed Mohsen Mostafavi Tafreshi, Robert Briner, Karl-Heinz Böckstiegel (President), Michel Virally, Howard M. Holtzmann, George H. Aldrich, and Charles N. Brower. (Max Koot, September 3, 1985)

First meeting of President Ronald Reagan in the Oval Office with the Tower Commission. Right from the president: former Senator John Tower (Chairman), former Secretary of State and Senator Edmund Muskie, and former Assistant to President Ford for National Security Affairs General Brent Scowcroft. Deputy Special Counsellor Judge Charles N. Brower sits with his back closest to the camera. Cabinet Member as Special Counsellor to the President Ambassador David M. Abshire is absent with official leave in order to wind up his affairs as ambassador to NATO, from which post he had resigned effective January 31, 1987, prior to being appointed special counsellor to the president. (Official White House photo, January 26, 1987)

Second meeting of President Reagan in the Oval Office with the Tower Commission (seated as at the first meeting). Cabinet Member as Special Counsellor to the President Ambassador David M. Abshire this time is present (seated to the right of the president), having concluded his ambassadorship to NATO as of January 31, 1987. Deputy Special Counsellor Judge Charles N. Brower is seated to the right of the Resolute desk. (Official White House photo, February 11, 1987)

Cabinet Member as Special Counsellor to the President Ambassador David M. Abshire and Deputy Special Counsellor Judge Charles N. Brower with President Reagan in the Oval Office. Photograph signed "To Charlie Brower–With my thanks, every good wish & Very Best Regards. Ronald Reagan." (Official White House photo, February 11, 1987)

To Charlie Brower
with Respect and High Regard. —
George Bush
The White House, Feb. 20, 1987

Deputy Special Counsellor Judge Charles N. Brower chatting with Vice President George H. W. Bush in his office. Photograph signed "To Charlie Brower with Respect and High Regard. George Bush. The White House, Feb. 20, 1987." (Official White House photo)

THE WHITE HOUSE

WASHINGTON

April 7, 1987

Dear Charlie:

It is with great regret that I accept your resignation as Deputy Special Counsellor, effective April 6, 1987.

I would like to extend my deep appreciation and thanks to you for your outstanding efforts over the past three months as Deputy Special Counsellor. These few months have been especially trying ones, I know, but you have risen to the occasion and displayed the same outstanding professional skills and dedication that have always characterized your career, both public and private. I know that both Dave Abshire and I have especially valued your thoughtful and judicious counsel in the many important decisions that had to be made along the line to help expedite this entire matter.

As you resume your duties as a Judge of the Iran-United States Claims Tribunal in The Hague, you can be proud of the distinctive service you have rendered our Nation and take satisfaction in a job well done.

You have my abiding gratitude and best wishes for the future. God bless you.

Sincerely,

Ronald Reagan

The Honorable Charles N. Brower
The White House
Washington, D.C. 20500

Letter from President Reagan to Judge Charles N. Brower on the occasion of his resignation as deputy special counsellor. (April 7, 1987)

The United States and United Kingdom Agents and Counsel (Judge Charles N. Brower on right) in the Great Hall of Justice of the Peace Palace in The Hague at the opening session of *Questions of Interpretation and Application of the 1971 Montreal Convention Arising from the Aerial Incident at Lockerbie (Libyan Arab Jamahiriya v. United States of America and United Kingdom)* before the International Court of Justice in which they heard Libya's request for an order of provisional measures. (March 26, 1991)

Left to right: Professor Charles H. Brower, II, Judge Charles N. Brower, and His Excellency Mr. Jose de J. Conejo, ambassador of the Republic of Costa Rica to the Netherlands, in the Great Hall of Justice of the Peace Palace in The Hague at the opening session of the advisory proceedings in *Difference Relating to Immunity from Legal Process of a Special Rapporteur of the Commission on Human Rights* before the International Court of Justice. (Max Koot, July 12, 1998)

Photograph of the Inter-American Court of Human Rights as of January 25, 2000, including Judge *ad hoc* Charles N. Brower (upper right), convened to hear the *Trujillo Oroza* case.

First appearance of Judge Charles N. Brower (seated furthest to the right) sitting as judge *ad hoc* of the International Court of Justice in the Great Hall of Justice in the Peace Palace in The Hague, at the opening session of *Question of the Delimitation of the Continental Shelf between Nicaragua and Colombia beyond 200 Nautical Miles from the Nicaraguan Coast (Nicaragua v. Colombia)* in which the court heard Colombia's preliminary objections to jurisdiction and admissibility. (October 5, 2015)

ICJ Judges *ad hoc* Charles N. Brower and David D. Caron in Bolzaal conference room in the Peace Palace in The Hague following joint deliberations of eighteen judges in *Alleged Violations of Sovereign Rights and Maritime Spaces in the Caribbean Sea (Nicaragua v. Colombia)* and *Question of the Delimitation of the Continental Shelf between Nicaragua and Colombia beyond 200 Nautical Miles from the Nicaraguan Coast (Nicaragua v. Colombia)*.

COUR INTERNATIONALE DE JUSTICE

INTERNATIONAL COURT OF JUSTICE

PALAIS DE LA PAIX 2517 KJ LA HAYE PAYS-BAS
TÉLÉPHONE: +31 (0) 70 302 23 23
TÉLÉCOPIE: +31 (0) 70 364 99 28
ADRESSE ÉLECTR.: mail@icj-cij.org
SITE INTERNET: www.icj-cij.org

PEACE PALACE 2517 KJ THE HAGUE NETHERLANDS
TELEPHONE: +31 (0) 70 302 23 23
TELEFAX: +31 (0) 70 364 99 28
E-MAIL: mail@icj-cij.org
WEBSITE: www.icj-cij.org

5 June 2022

H.E. Judge Joan E. Donoghue
President
j.donoghue@icj-cij.org

H.E. Mr. Philippe Gautier
Registrar
ph.gautier@icj-cij.org

International Court of Justice
Peace Palace
Carnegie Plein 2
2517 KJ Den Haag

Mr. Carlos Gustavo Arrieta Padilla
Agent of the Republic of Colombia
cgarrieta@amya.com.co

Arrieta, Mantilla y Asociados (AMYA)
Carrera 7 No. 71-21, Torre B, Oficina 1601A
Bogota D.C., Colombia

Mr. Richard C. Visek
Acting Legal Adviser
VisekRC@state.gov

United States Department of State
2201 C Street, N.W.
Washington, D.C. 20520

Re: *Question of the Delimitation of the Continental Shelf between Nicaragua and Colombia beyond 200 nautical miles from the Nicaraguan Coast (Nicaragua v. Colombia)*

Certain Iranian Assets (Islamic Republic of Iran v. United States of America)

Alleged Violations of the 1955 Treaty of Amity, Economic Relations, and Consular Rights (Islamic Republic of Iran v. United States of America)

Your Excellencies and others:

As today I reach the age of 87 and thereby enter the 88th year of my life I believe that the actuarial risks to the undisturbed progress of the three contentious proceedings listed above that would be posed by my continuing to serve as Judge *ad hoc* of the International Court of Justice in them require me to resign that high office in all of them.

I note that in the first one I was appointed in 2014, and in the second and third ones in 2018. I have been privileged to sit in the third one on a Request for the Indication of Provisional Measures and in all three of them on Preliminary Objections. All three now are positioned to be heard on the merits, and the second and first ones presently are scheduled to be so heard commencing 19 September 2022 and 5 December 2022, respectively. Thus now is the time for new Judges *ad hoc* to step into all three of these cases, thereby ensuring as much as is humanly possible the smooth continuation of them all.

I am especially conscious of the singular role of a Judge *ad hoc*. As the late Sir Elihu Lauterpacht, sitting as Judge *ad hoc* in *Application of the Convention on Prevention and Punishment of the Crime of Genocide (Bosnia and Herzogovina v. Serbia and Montenegro)*, wrote at Paragraph 6. of his Separate Opinion to the Court's Order of 13 September 1993:

> . . . [C]onsistently with the duty of impartiality by which the *ad hoc* judge is bound, there is still something specific that distinguishes his role. He has, I believe, a special obligation to endeavour to ensure that, so far as is reasonable, every relevant argument in favour of the party that has appointed him has been fully appreciated in the course of collegial consideration and, ultimately, is reflected – though not necessarily accepted – in any separate or dissenting opinion that he may write. It is on that basis, and in awareness that the tragedy underlying the present proceedings imposes on me an especially grave responsibility, that I approach my task.

Thus it is especially incumbent upon me as a Judge *ad hoc* to remove myself from the scene now so as to enable the Republic of Colombia and the United States of America to appoint new Judges *ad hoc* in time to prepare for the forthcoming hearings on the merits of the three cases in which it has been my privilege to sit and thus best to ensure that those two States will enjoy in those proceedings the full and uninterrupted right to the participation of a Judge *ad hoc*.

Therefore, for the reasons stated above, and with deep gratitude for the privileges I have been afforded to serve as Judge *ad hoc* in the aforementioned proceedings, I hereby resign as Judge *ad hoc* in each of them with immediate effect.

Charles N. Brower

Charles N. Brower
Judge *ad hoc*

Letter from Judge Charles N. Brower to International Court of Justice President Judge Joan E. Donoghue and other concerned parties announcing his resignation as judge *ad hoc* from three "contentious proceedings." (June 5, 2022)

July 19, 2022

The Honorable Charles N. Brower
5600 Wisconsin Avenue
Unit 1401
Chevy Chase, Maryland 20815-4412

Dear Judge Brower:

On behalf of the Department of State, I extend my tremendous appreciation to you for the decades of service you have provided to the United States and the international community through the practice of international law. As an attorney in the Department of State and White House, as a judge of the Iran-United States Claims Tribunal, and as judge *ad hoc* of the International Court of Justice, you have left your mark on many important international legal issues.

For more than 50 years, you have dedicated your life to international law and the service of your country. You served as an assistant legal adviser, deputy legal adviser, and acting legal adviser at the Department of State. You also served as deputy special counsellor to President Ronald Reagan, during which time you and Special Counsellor David Abshire advised the administration on important legal issues, including the Iran-Contra Affair. For more than three decades, you served as a judge of the Iran-United States Claims Tribunal, adjudicating claims arising from the 1979 seizure of the U.S. Embassy in Tehran.

This is a remarkable record of service for which your nation is deeply grateful. You have served your country, the Tribunal, the International Court of Justice, and the furtherance of international law with great distinction, and my deepest thanks and best wishes go with you as you move forward in this next phase of your life.

Sincerely yours,

Antony J. Blinken

With admiration and gratitude —

Letter from Secretary of State Antony J. Blinken in acknowledgement of Judge Charles N. Brower's career in public service and international law, a "remarkable record of public service." (July 19, 2022) a legitimate right of eminent domain on that day, which necessarily includes the likely future profits a reasonable buyer would have factored into the sale price. If on the other hand the expropriation was unlawful, you get the greater of that standard or the *actual* future profits that would have accrued had you been left in possession (taking into account an unexpectedly rising market, a sudden windfall, or whatever) because, according to the law, you, not the state, ought to have been the owner that whole time.[9]

The judgment did not do Amoco much good; Virally's award controlled the compensation they received. But in the end, I had the last laugh, at least on the standard of valuation. Two years later, the majority in Chamber One (then–president Robert Briner, joined by my U.S. colleague George Aldrich) wrote in *Phillips Petroleum Co. v. Iran* that the value of "an income-producing going concern . . . cannot be determined without taking fully into account its future income-producing prospects as they would have been perceived at that time by a buyer of those interests."[10] Well, quite!

Of all the opinions I have written, my concurring opinion in *Amoco International Finance* is my most frequently cited. In fact, it has been seen as a landmark statement regarding the law of expropriation. Even today, when I sit as an arbitrator, I find attorneys citing it back to me with admiration. In its reluctance to find that a state expropriated unlawfully, the Iran–United States Claims Tribunal is far from unique. Perhaps the poster child for this reluctance is that of *Aminoil v. Kuwait*, a case in which I was involved at a later stage as an expert witness.

Kuwait had granted Aminoil (properly, American Independent Oil Company) a sixty-year concession to explore for oil, only to terminate it about thirty years in.[11] This was a pretty clear breach of the concession agreement, and the tribunal itself admitted that a "straightforward and direct reading" of the relevant terms "can lead to the conclusion that they prohibit any nationalization."[12] But the tribunal turned intellectual somersaults in order to find the expropriation lawful.[13]

As we have seen, for a lawful expropriation, claimants get only the value of the asset at the date of expropriation. The tribunal in *Aminoil* did not suggest otherwise, but it did a curious thing. In addition to the base compensation plus interest at 7.5 percent, it awarded Aminoil a "level of inflation," which it set at a compounding rate of 10 percent per annum.[14] All told, this "level of inflation" amounted to more than $50 million, on top of the base compensation of $83 million.

What was this mysterious extra amount? In short, it was disguised compensation for what the tribunal knew full well was an unlawful expropriation. A separate opinion by the claimant-appointed arbitrator, Sir Gerald Fitzmaurice, a hugely respected former judge of the ICJ, stated (albeit only by implication) that Kuwait had acted unlawfully.[15]

Kuwait duly paid up (there were whispers that the parties had agreed the result in advance). But when Aminoil's parent company, the U.S. conglomerate RJR Nabisco, filed tax returns treating the "level of inflation" as a capital gain—which would be correct if, in reality, it was compensation for the loss of the business—Uncle Sam came knocking. The Internal Revenue Service argued that the payment was income in the nature of interest, subject to a higher rate of taxation.

Before the U.S. Tax Court, RJR Nabisco called me as an expert witness, and I duly testified that the mysterious "level of inflation" was, indeed, disguised compensation to bring Aminoil up to the level to which it would have been entitled had the tribunal found the expropriation unlawful.[16]

Why would a tribunal be so touchy on the subject? Because it was worried that Kuwait might not pay. And why was that a risk? In short, politics. Governments don't want to be branded as having acted unlawfully. It drives away investors. Moreover, in this particular case, OPEC had stated a policy that nationalized Western oil companies should receive compensation for the value of the assets only—not lost profits. Kuwait would likely have resisted any award inconsistent with this policy, especially as it was the United States that had talked Kuwait into agreeing to arbitrate the dispute, a method not compelled by any contract or treaty. I testified to this effect, and the U.S. Tax Court found in favor of RJR Nabisco, primarily on the basis of my testimony, which the court found "forthright and credible."[17]

Similar logic applies in many, if not most, cases of expropriation. The last thing a tribunal wants is to damage states' faith in the system. So the reluctance to pronounce expropriations unlawful will persist.

MOSTLY CALM, WITH SCATTERED THUNDERSTORMS

Sitting on the tribunal was not without its irritations. In *Amoco International Finance*, for example, my reading was in line with previous tribunal awards—notably an interim award in *Sedco v. NIOC*, which my chamber had begun hearing under Mangard.[18] Virally was not on the panel for that case; but his failure to follow *Sedco* typified one source of frustration with the tribunal, at least for a lawyer trained in the common law system of England, the United States, and other jurisdictions: the three separate chambers hearing the cases of nationals respected no real system of precedent among them. Even on matters as elementary as costs and interest, the judgments of the three chambers of the tribunal never quite lined up.[19]

Another annoyance for me was the question of testimony by employees. Early in my tenure, Mangard raised the question whether an employee, director, or officer of a company that was party to proceedings could even testify. To a common law lawyer, that's a crazy question: who would know the facts better than somebody who works for the business? But in civil law (the other big European legal family, followed across most of the continent), the view is that such a person is likely to lie for the benefit of the company. "In my country," Mangard told me, "we would never think of putting someone to the choice between the truth and his or her employer."[20]

Most of the third-country judges showed a marked reluctance to hold Iran responsible for any wrongdoing. I think it stemmed in part from their sympathy for developing countries and in part from their desire to maintain good relations with their Iranian colleagues. Both motivations were understandable; but they occasionally led the tribunal into some frankly weird reasoning. This reluctance was a major factor underlying Virally's erroneous approach in *Amoco International Finance*, where, as we have seen, he tied himself in knots to find the expropriation lawful.

I saw it at work again in a much different context in the case of *Short v. Islamic Republic of Iran*. Alfred Short had been an executive with the aircraft manufacturer Lockheed, and he was based in Iran. As the Iranian Revolution got underway in late 1978 and early 1979, he and his family witnessed a ratcheting up of anti-American violence, culminating in firebomb attacks on the homes of American workers. In February 1979, he was evacuated from the country, and his employment with Lockheed came to an end. Short claimed for the wages he had lost as a result. Because it fell under the $250,000 threshold, this was accounted a small case, in which the State Department represented the claimant.

Short had had little choice but to leave Iran. He was constructively expelled at least as clearly as a tenant whose landlord cut off the electricity has been constructively evicted. The question was whether the regime was responsible. To me, the answer seemed clear because Ayatollah Khomeini had all but ordered the expulsion of Americans from Iran. For example, immediately upon his return to Iran on February 1, 1979, the ayatollah reiterated for the umpteenth time his "unyielding . . . hostility" toward the United States and declared that "final victory will come when all foreigners are out of the country."[21] Short was evacuated one week later.

Virally, however, threw out Alfred Short's claim because Short had been "unable . . . to identify any agent of the revolutionary movement, the actions of which compelled him to leave Iran."[22] This entirely missed the point. Short's departure, like that of around forty-five thousand other U.S. citizens who left around the same time, was precipitated by widespread violence expressly designed to chase Americans out of the country. The fact that no single organ of the revolution had specifically targeted Alfred L. W. Short was neither here nor there. In fact, as I wrote in my dissent, "It is inherent in a constructive mass expulsion that the acts effectuating it will be, in a high degree, general, unspecific, unfocused, and indirect."[23]

A much more positive experience was what has come to be known as the *International Oil Consortium* case. Following Mosaddegh's ouster in 1953, the newly reinstated shah had negotiated an agreement with the foreign "Oil Majors," including a number of American companies, to extract and refine Iranian oil in exchange for a percentage of the proceeds. The agreement faltered during the oil shocks of the early 1970s and had to be renegotiated; but its final demise came with the Iranian Revolution and the ensuing wave of nationalizations (for which, characteristically, Iran offered no compensation).

Eleven U.S. oil companies sued Iran before the tribunal, and President Lagergren consolidated all eleven claims before my chamber, Chamber Three. These cases involved large sums of money, overlapping contractual negotiations, thorny issues of law, and difficult assessments of damages. But we were able to get a handle on them. Having grouped them together, we broke down the issues involved and scheduled a common hearing to decide whether the tribunal had jurisdiction, whether Iran was, in principle, liable to the consortium members, and what elements of damages would be compensable.[24]

Seven of the oil companies settled before the hearing and obtained "awards on agreed terms" entitling them to access the security fund.[25] That left four sets of claims to be heard. Following the hearing, we issued an award determining that we did have jurisdiction and stating the basis on which Iran would be liable.[26] I had some issues with the way Virally reached this result (when did I not?), but the award proved enough to bring the remaining four cases to settlement.

Occasionally, and lamentably, the tribunal crossed the line from procedural quirks and faulty readings of the law into outright injustice. The case that stands out for me in this regard is *Avco Corp. v. Iran Aircraft Industries et al.*[27] The case itself was straightforward. Avco, a Connecticut-based manufacturer of aircraft engines, had contracted with an Iranian state-owned company that had not paid its bills. At the prehearing conference, Ansari was absent for reasons that were never satisfactorily explained, and the respondent's legal team also chose not to attend. But the conference went ahead—with Mangard and me alone.

Avco's lawyers asked us whether the chamber would need to see copies of all the unpaid invoices (there were thousands) or whether a report from an independent auditor would suffice.

Mangard, with his usual Nordic charm, said (and here I am quoting from the verbatim transcript), "I don't think we will be very, very much enthusiastic getting kilos and kilos of invoices. So I think it will but help us to use the alternative rather."[28] It would be difficult to imagine a clearer indication of how the claimant ought to proceed. Neither Ansari nor the respondent were there to object; but they were, so to speak, AWOL, having failed to explain their absence.

By the time of the merits hearing, Ansari had returned from whatever adventure he had been on, while Mangard had resigned and been replaced by Virally. Ansari did raise the absence of invoices, but neither he nor our French colleague gave the claimant any indication that the tribunal had changed its mind. In deliberations, I explained the situation to them. It was no surprise to find Ansari insisting that, in the absence of those thousands of invoices, the claimant had failed to prove part of its case; but to my shock, Virally agreed. This left the Iranian party with a net counterclaim award—in other words, Avco wound up owing *them* $1.6 million!

There was nothing I could do to resurrect Avco's original claims given that tribunal awards, like most arbitral awards, are final—there is no appeal mechanism. But the idea of Avco having to pay Iran was intolerable; and in law, as I have said before, there is more than one way to skin a cat. While awards in favor of American claimants were backed by the $1 billion security fund, Iran had to enforce its awards in the usual way. That meant going to a court with jurisdiction over the other party's assets, a process governed by the cornerstone New York Convention of 1958.

Under the convention, courts can refuse to enforce awards in only limited circumstances; but one of those grounds for refusal is that "the party against whom the award is invoked [was] unable to present his case."[29] Knowing that a court would read the exception conservatively (given that the whole purpose of the convention was to ensure the enforcement of awards almost all of the time), I tailored my opinion to this language, writing that "since Claimant did exactly what it previously was told to do by the tribunal . . . . Claimant for all practical purposes has been denied an opportunity to present its case."[30]

Sure enough, when Iran went to Connecticut to enforce the award, the federal district and appeals courts turned it down, with language taken directly from my opinion.[31] Eventually, the U.S. government had to pay Iran nonetheless because the tribunal decided in a subsequent proceeding that the United States must backstop tribunal awards that are neither paid by U.S. nationals nor enforced by courts under the New York Convention;[32] but I was proud to have helped an American claimant avoid injustice.

THE TRIBUNAL ABIDES

The Iran–United States Claims Tribunal has endured a great deal. Besides the destructive efforts of hardliners like Kashani, it has faced the Iran-Iraq War, in which the United States passed intelligence to Saddam Hussein; the election of hardline governments in Tehran; multiple crises over Iran's nuclear program; the ratcheting up of sanctions; and any number of smaller shocks to the system. Yet through all this, the tribunal has always endured. Why?

For the United States, the answer is simple: the tribunal has resulted in American claimants being compensated. Americans and U.S. companies have received well over $2.5 billion in payouts from the security account as a result of the tribunal's work.[33]

Why, though, does Iran stick with the tribunal? On a procedural level, it has been pointed out that, because the tribunal adopted (and adapted) the UNCITRAL (the United Nations Commission on International Trade Law) rules, neither side could scupper proceedings simply by withdrawing its arbitrators, similar to what Iran had done in order to stymie the arbitration brought against it by the Anglo-Iranian Oil

Company in the 1950s.[34] If that happened—as it did on at least one early occasion—the relevant chamber would simply sit as a "truncated tribunal" with just two arbitrators, neither of them Iranian. So Iran's failure to show up would do more harm than good, for not only would an award still be made; the absent side's failure to appear and argue its case could well leave the tribunal inadequately informed and hence more likely to make a mistake.

But there would have been other ways of scuttling the tribunal. For example, Iran could have refused to replenish the security account. In fact, at one point Iran tried this. The tribunal found Iran in breach of its obligations and, in successive awards, first "expected" then "requested" compliance.[35] Unlike in 1979, when it ignored the ICJ's orders and the Security Council's resolutions demanding the release of the American hostages, Iran finally complied.

Apparently, the tribunal also served as a back channel between two governments that, for more than forty years, had no official diplomatic relations. I never saw any evidence of this myself; American judges were never, and would never have been, part of any back channel. If there were one, it would likely have been done through the office of the U.S. agent (effectively the United States' principal lawyer before the tribunal). But there were other channels; for example, as I would learn through my role in the aftermath of the Iran-Contra affair, one existed between the CIA and certain Iranian officials.[36]

Partly, no doubt, Iran stuck with the tribunal because it was anxious to get to the final item on the docket: Iran's $11 billion claim (plus interest) against the United States with respect to the many unfulfilled military contracts entered into by the shah. (This still-unresolved claim is the main reason why the tribunal is still in business to this day, as we will see.) If and when the United States is finally required to pay up, Iran will reap a huge propaganda victory, as well as a fiscal windfall.

There is more to it than that, however. Fundamentally, Iran wants to be viewed as legitimate in the eyes of the world. Key to that ambition is being seen as complying with its duties under international law—especially if it can show that the United States has breached its own obligations. This is why successive Iranian governments have used the international legal forums quite extensively (as we will see when we look at the International Court of Justice); and it is a major reason why they have stuck with the Iran–United States Claims Tribunal. The fact that the tribunal is seen to confer legitimacy is good news for international law in general and for international arbitration in particular.

Of course, that fundamental commitment never stopped Iranian politicians and the Iranian arbitrators from railing against the tribunal whenever it suited them (and it frequently did). But the fact is that the tribunal has never been nearly as one-sided as they claim. From 581 tribunal awards, Iran and Iranian parties have won 210—around 36 percent.[37] (Iran has also won around 28 percent of the state-to-state claims.[38]) As a result, they have received $1 billion in payouts.[39] Not bad, considering that the point of the exercise was to enable *Americans* to claim against Iran!

Less well known, but equally notable, is that most of the payouts in both directions have been the result of settlements negotiated between U.S. and Iranian parties. Given that the two governments enjoyed no diplomatic relations during this period (indeed, they rarely stopped rattling sabers at one another), this is a remarkable achievement that underlines the utility of arbitration. From a strictly economic point of view, the incentive to settle may be the most important effect of any peaceful, reliable dispute-resolution mechanism: the "threat" of arbitration encourages each side to dispose of claims amicably rather than go to the considerable expense of paying lawyers to fight it out on their behalf.

We have already seen this in the *Oil Consortium* case, in which all eleven oil companies eventually settled their differences with Iran. The cases brought by Amoco, including *Amoco International Finance*, were also eventually settled, for a cool $500 million, and in 1990, Iran and the United States settled the remaining small claims en masse with a lump sum payment of $105 million out of the security fund.[40]

Finally, the tribunal has been a massive boon to international law. As one scholar points out, it has rendered "more than 800 reasoned decisions"—almost all of them in the twelve-year span between 1981 and 1993, a period during which the International Court of Justice issued around a dozen orders and judgments and the International Centre for Settlement of Investment Disputes (of which more soon) oversaw only a relative handful of arbitrations.[41] These decisions developed the law of international commerce, giving investors and states a stronger foundation upon which to build their relationships.

In particular, the tribunal has largely preserved the international law of expropriation from attack, confirming that full compensation is required even when the taking is lawful—thereby making it more cost-effective for companies to invest overseas, particularly in developing countries, and helping promote investment, the objective I pursued by counseling Indonesia not to assert a low standard of compensation.[42]

Finally, the experience of the Iran–United States Claims Tribunal has showed that, even in the most difficult of circumstances—where two states are at each other's throats—arbitration is capable of offering peaceful resolution of disputes between the nationals of one state and the government of the other. This would have big implications for global business—and for my career.

CHAPTER EIGHT

Iran-Contra: What Reagan Knew

AN INVITE FROM AMBASSADOR ABSHIRE

At the end of November 1986, my old friend David Abshire invited me, as he had done every year since my arrival at the tribunal, to Thanksgiving dinner at his home. David had by that time been appointed U.S. ambassador to NATO, so the dinner took place at his official residence, the stately Truman Hall near Brussels. This year dinner was special, as it doubled as a farewell of sorts. David had already resigned as ambassador effective the following January, intending to return to the Center for Strategic & International Studies (CSIS), the think tank he had cofounded years before with Adm. Arleigh Burke.

The other big topic of conversation—no surprise—was politics. About three weeks before, a Lebanese magazine called *Al-Shiraa* ("The Sail") had reported that the United States had sold weapons to Iran in return for the release of American hostages held in Lebanon by the terrorist group (and Iranian cat's-paw) Hezbollah. It seemed likely that the information had been leaked by hardliners in Tehran who, like Judge

Kashani, wanted no contact between Iran and the United States.[1] The story was soon confirmed publicly by the speaker of the Majlis.

In keeping with its hardline stance on foreign affairs, the Reagan administration had announced from the outset a policy of zero cooperation with terrorists or their state sponsors, including Iran. It expected its friends to do the same: the State Department created a program called Operation Staunch to ensure that no American ally sold arms to Iran. Yet here was this same Reagan administration selling hundreds of antitank and surface-to-air missiles to Iran, apparently in exchange for hostages. Kansas Senator Republican Bob Dole—no firebrand—publicly denounced this arrangement as rewarding terrorism.[2]

Reagan defended his administration in a speech on November 13 and followed up with a press conference on November 19. Thanks to reckless briefings by Reagan's staff, both were riddled with inaccuracies. A poll showed that just 14 percent of Americans believed Reagan—a public relations disaster for a president styled "The Great Communicator."[3]

The White House must have thought the story could not get any worse; but it did. U.S. Attorney General Edwin Meese investigated and, on the Tuesday before Thanksgiving, announced that according to his review of the White House files, the price of later arms shipments had been artificially raised and the profits redirected to the Contras, a Nicaraguan resistance group. Following the military debacle in Nicaragua—the same one that gave rise to the ICJ case where the United States walked out of the court—Congress had specifically banned the administration from supporting the Contras.

Such "high crimes" might more than suffice for Reagan's impeachment—if they could be made to stick to the president. Over the course of the next few months and years, four separate congressional committees would investigate the scandal, alongside an independent counsel and a three-man panel, the Tower Commission, convened by the president himself.

"This is going to be a bonanza for criminal defense lawyers," I exclaimed over before-dinner drinks with Dave and our ambassadors to Belgium and the European Community.

At the mention of criminal proceedings, their ears pricked up. "Oh? You think there is something to this?"

"Are you kidding?" I said. "The entire criminal defense bar in Washington is licking its chops in anticipation. Partners of Williams & Connolly for sure, and the same for their many peers."

Dave and I would be hired too, although in an altogether unexpected capacity.

WHAT THE PRESIDENT KNEW (AND WHEN HE KNEW IT)

Early in the morning on Christmas Eve—a Wednesday—my phone rang in The Hague. It was a U.S. Navy captain calling from the U.S. Embassy to NATO in Brussels. "Please hold for Ambassador Abshire."

Before my brain had a chance to wonder what on earth might necessitate such a formal summons—it was quite early—David came on the line. He told me he had received a call from Don Regan, the White House chief of staff. The administration wanted to appoint David as special counsellor to the president on the political aspects of the Iran-Contra scandal, drawing upon his years of experience navigating the thickets of Capitol Hill.

"Congratulations," I said. "What did you say?"

"I am inclined to say I will do it," David replied, "so long as it's not for more than three months. I've been away from the Center too long already," referring to CSIS, his Washington think tank. He said he had a few more conditions: cabinet rank, in order to highlight the significance of his role; unimpeded direct access to the president; and me as his deputy, if I would agree. It became clear to me that in addition to my expertise as a lawyer—not least because of the threat of criminal proceedings—he wanted me by his side as somebody he trusted who was not part of the existing White House staff.

David's plan was that he would do the job for three months and then I could step into his shoes and take over for another three months to see the job through, if necessary. Left unsaid, but only too well understood by us both, was that if things had not turned around by then, the Reagan presidency would be finished anyway.

I was flattered, of course; but I needed to think things over. In particular, the tribunal rules had no automatic provision that would allow me to take a leave of absence on such short notice and still expect to have a job when I returned. It was clear I could take only a few hours to make up my mind; the White House, naturally, wanted us there yesterday.

My first call was to my fiancée, Carmen, who would soon become my second wife, my marriage to Oda, the mother of my two children, having ended some months before I assumed my position in The Hague. We met at a café across the street from the American embassy chancery. Carmen had served as right hand to four successive U.S. ambassadors to the Netherlands, including the then-current one, and consulting with her was critical to my decision.

Of Reagan, I admit, I was no great fan. Although a Republican, he came from the opposite wing of the party, and I had worked to keep him from getting the nomination in 1976. We parted ways on several matters of substance. For example, I felt his tax policy—letting the rich off the hook in the hope that they would make jobs for the rest of us—was rightly denounced by George H. W. Bush as "voodoo economics."

But there were bigger stakes here. It was almost 1987, and the nation had not seen a completed two-term presidency since Dwight Eisenhower nearly thirty years previously. Kennedy had been assassinated; Johnson, discouraged by the quagmire of Vietnam, had declined to seek reelection; Nixon had resigned in disgrace; and Ford and Carter had been defeated at the ballot box. If Reagan were to be impeached over this, we would go yet another decade at least without a successful two-term presidency. For the sake of political stability, I felt it was important to show that it could be done.

When I explained all of this, Carmen was enthusiastic; she said I should do it, and for precisely the reasons I set out—even if it meant losing my appointment at the tribunal. As soon as I got home, I called David back and told him I was in.

Two days later, on December 26, the president called Abshire directly to thank him for agreeing to take on the role. Reagan also told David that he intended to waive executive privilege over any evidence, no matter how embarrassing. Instead, he would allow all the evidence to come out; indeed, ensuring that it did would be a key part of David's role and mine. When David told me that, I knew I had made the right decision: neither David nor I had any intention of being involved in a cover-up, and evidently the president had no intention of perpetrating one. David and I agreed, before accepting our proffered roles, that in our judgment Reagan would not be capable of doing anything criminal or even close to it.

In the meantime, I looked up the tribunal rules and found that, while I could be kicked out for failing to perform my functions, the tribunal president, after consultation with the other judges of the tribunal, could grant me leave if he determined that my absence was "due to a temporary illness or other circumstance expected to be of relatively short duration."[4] President Böckstiegel, doubtless appreciating the importance of the matter for which I was being called to the White House, was only too happy to oblige.

The United States agent to the tribunal and his bosses at the State Department were less thrilled with the idea, seeing it as a disruption to the work of the tribunal, which of course it was. But I felt this assignment was more important, and in any case, there was not a whole lot they could do about it, since I would be working directly for the president of the United States.

Don Regan, the White House chief of staff, also resisted my appointment, not relishing the idea of (as he thought of it) "Abshire bringing his own lawyer," rather than relying on the White House counsel, who of course was subordinate to Regan himself. But David (thank God) insisted, and in early January I flew back to the United States with my widowed mother, who had been staying with us in The Hague over the holidays. It was the start of a wild ride.

A FROSTY RECEPTION

The day I arrived in Washington, the 100th Congress was sworn in, with Democrats in control of both chambers for the first time since Reagan had taken office in 1981. Immediately, both the House and the Senate set about creating committees to investigate the president's involvement in Iran-Contra. Reagan himself was in the hospital recovering from prostate surgery. I didn't see him right away, but Abshire described being shocked by how "frail, pale, and thin" the president looked.[5]

Day after day, the newspapers recounted the lurid details of Iran-Contra. A *Wall Street Journal* editorial jokingly called for David's permanent appointment as "Secretary of Scandal."[6] Even before our arrival, Evans and Novak of the *Washington Post* had pronounced the Reagan presidency "dead" and "buried," thanks to the "loss of faith in the president" across his voter base.[7] As if to underline the dire straits Reagan was in, Washington had been covered by an unusually heavy snow that meant we had to be ferried around the city in four-wheel-drive vehicles.

At first, I camped out with my sister in Bethesda, Maryland, in the northern DC suburbs. After a while, however, I was politely urged by her, albeit via the intermediary of our mother's lawyer, to seek new accommodations. My sister's kids were now in college. She had been enjoying the quiet and did not appreciate my waking up at 5:00 a.m. and making noise in the kitchen. So David set me up with a room at the University Club, a few blocks up from the White House.

For our team, Abshire had chosen offices not in the West Wing but in the Old Executive Office Building on the other side of the compound. This was a deliberate decision, to avoid being seen as yet another instrument of Don Regan, whose power in government was such that he had been described—to his own evident pleasure—as America's "prime minister."[8] Predictably, the press instead excoriated us for having allowed ourselves to be marginalized—exiled to "Siberia," as one anonymous source put it.[9] Sometimes, you just can't win.

We had our work cut out for us. While the independent counsel had fifteen prosecutors and up to twenty FBI agents at his beck and call, we were a staff of just five. Reporters kept asking us, "Why doesn't the president just tell the truth?" To which the truthful answer would be, "Because he doesn't know!" National Security Adviser John Poindexter and his staff member Oliver North had orchestrated a document-shredding operation so comprehensive that nobody in the White House could tell us what had really happened. We could have subpoenaed everybody in town and still not gotten to the truth.

Abshire himself said it best:

Simply put, the White House staff did not know the truth. It was the same as the Kremlin's figures on the Soviet economy—there had been so much lying within the White House that no one could know the real truth. There had been too much shredding of documents and too much falsification of records. Truly, it was an inconceivable mess, and we were all standing on quicksand.[10]

The only possible approach was to empty the archives, get everything out in the open, and in the meantime—with utmost respect—tell the president to shut up. "The worst thing that the White House can do," I told a reporter for the *New York Times*, "is for anyone here to purport to act as judge and jury in this matter and declare in definitive form what the truth is."[11]

NO PARDONS, NO PLEADING, NO COVER-UPS, NO CLUE

A few days into our project at the White House, we met with a lawyer named Brendan Sullivan, a smooth operator from the DC superfirm Williams & Connolly. Sullivan told us he was representing Lt. Col. Oliver North, the National Security Council staffer who had been central to the Iran-Contra affair and the attempted cover-up.

North had, in fact, flown to Tehran with the first shipment of missiles, proffering gifts of chocolate cake and chromium-plated .44 magnums for the Iranian officials involved.[12] He had set up the laundering of proceeds through Swiss bank accounts for onward transmission to the Contras. He had fed documents to the White House shredders when Attorney General Meese's investigation got too close. North was elbows deep in this scandal.

Sullivan now proposed that the best thing for the president to do would be to pardon his client. It was a nice try on Sullivan's part— I would have done the same in his shoes—but a pardon for North would have been a political disaster. Besides, the request for immunity represented a fundamental misunderstanding of our role. We were not there to investigate, still less to hand out presidential pardons. Nor were we even there to act as Reagan's defense lawyers. The president had hired us to assist the various investigations in getting to the truth, and that was what we intended to do.

That said, as noted above, Abshire and I had convened early on, in private, before accepting our White House roles, to discuss whether we thought Reagan could knowingly have done wrong. Our conclusion was a firm "No!" This man, we quickly had realized, did not have a duplicitous bone in his body. When it came to Ronald Reagan, what you saw—the smile, the swagger, the sunny folksiness—was very much what you got.

While David used his trademark charm to smooth relations with the investigators, I presided over a process by which thousands of documents from many different departments and agencies would be reviewed for relevance and intelligence sensitivity. We withheld nothing from the investigators, although we did allow the general counsels for each of the main national security agencies access to the documents before they were released. Abe Sofaer, the State Department legal adviser, was especially assiduous in reviewing these, sometimes staying at the Old Executive Office Building until 4:00 a.m. reading through papers, no doubt seeking to give his boss, Secretary of State George Shultz, early warning of anything troublesome coming his way.

This work was not without its stresses. A *New York Times* profile of David set it up nicely: "What if [Abshire's] investigation turns up a

'smoking gun,' a document that could severely damage the administration he is serving?"[13] The answer, as David told the *Times* reporter,
is that we would have released it along with the rest, no matter how
much trouble it got us in. But it never came to that because there was
no smoking gun.

By the end of January, my team of reviewers had processed thousands
of documents and sent all of them to all of the investigators: the Tower
Commission, Judge Walsh, and the various congressional committees.
They must have been happy with our work, because as with my testimony on Cambodia years before, this aspect of the job made not even
a ripple in the press. Another enduring point of pride: the independent
counsel, Judge Lawrence Walsh, while pulling no punches lambast-
ing Reagan for alleged wrongdoing and his staff for making a firewall
around him to cover it up, praised David and me for our openness.[14] (It
helped that, when Brendan Sullivan challenged the constitutionality of
Walsh's appointment pursuant to the independent counsel statute, it was
we who got the president's immediate sign-off on the more constitutionally robust backup appointment of Walsh by Attorney General Ed Meese
as special counsel.)

In parallel, we set about preparing the president for his interviews
with the three-man Tower Commission he had appointed, consisting
of former Republican Senator John Tower of Texas; Democrat Senator
Edmund Muskie of Maine, a one-time presidential candidate who had
served as secretary of state in the final months of the Carter presidency;
and General Brent Scowcroft, who had been deputy national security
adviser to Nixon and national security adviser to Ford. Most White
House staffers could have died and gone to heaven if they had enjoyed
as much face time with the president as we had. In the prep sessions with
Reagan and Vice President Bush, we put the questions we thought would
be asked. Though exacting, these proceedings remained polite and civilized, just as we expected the Tower Commission to be.

Tower, Muskie, and Scowcroft interviewed the president for the first
time on January 26. In the Oval Office, the president and Tower sat in
two chairs by the fireplace, while the two other commission members

sat on one of the two sofas flanking the coffee table. I sat at the opposite end, by the Resolute Desk, facing Reagan. There was nobody sitting behind the president to whisper anything in his ear. This was Reagan's own panel, after all, and the answers had to come from him alone. Reagan put in a good performance.

The same could not be said for his second interview on February 11. The players, including myself, sat in the same positions as before. But Reagan seemed unsure of himself. In one of the prep sessions, the president had told us in no uncertain terms that, the previous August, he had been surprised to learn that the arms transfer to Iran had actually taken place. To prevent him from forgetting this important piece of information, David had drafted a memo for him, recapping the conversation and nudging the president to be consistent in his answers to the Tower Commission's questions.

During the second Tower Commission meeting, the president asked White House Counsel Peter Wallison for "the piece of paper you gave me this morning." Reagan rummaged in a drawer of the Resolute Desk, fished out David's memo, and proceeded to read aloud: "If the question comes up at the Tower Commission meeting, you might want to say you were surprised . . ."[15]

Around the room, jaws dropped. My stomach lurched. How could Reagan be so stupid? I remembered my father, who had known the president way back when, holding up his thumb and index finger in a close pincer and saying, "Ronald Reagan's brain is about this big." He was, indeed, far from an intellectual. But there was no excuse for this.

To my distinct lack of surprise, it was Abshire who figured out how to smooth things over with Tower. He had Reagan write out a personal note, by hand, apologizing to the commission and reiterating the fact that, as the note itself said, "I don't remember—period." The message was typed up on official White House letterhead; but Abshire insisted on taking the yellow legal pad containing the president's original handwriting and personally carrying it from the Oval Office directly to Tower. The senator was impressed by this show of genuine humility from the president.[16]

THE SCANDAL PLAYS OUT

Somehow, no doubt helped by his bottomless reserves of charm, Reagan recovered from his disastrous second showing before the Tower Commission. Which is not to say he enjoyed hearing their conclusions. I sat in the Roosevelt Room with the president as the commission presented their report to him. Reagan listened in silence, stone-faced and pensive, hands clasped in front of him as the Tower Commission unfolded his administration's failings.

Of course, the Reagan administration had wanted to free U.S. citizens held hostage in Lebanon. At some point, it had also decided to embark upon a strategic opening to Iran, hoping to improve relations, despite the lack of any powerful moderate faction in Iran with which to do business. Thanks to feckless management, these two policies had been allowed to devolve into what Reagan said he would never tolerate: an exchange of weapons for hostages. The Contra element seemed to have been cooked up in private among the political staff at the National Security Council, right under Reagan's nose.

Blame fell immediately on North, Poindexter, and former National Security Adviser Robert C. McFarlane, who had left office late the previous year; but White House Chief of Staff Regan, Secretary of State Shultz, and Secretary of Defense Caspar Weinberger were castigated for running a fundamentally disorderly national security process. Regan, in particular, was singled out for having presided over "chaos" at the White House, which made his subsequent firing inevitable, to the visible delight of the first lady, who had been campaigning for Regan's departure for months.

The Tower Report exonerated Reagan for funding the Contras and for the cover-up—but on the basis of culpable ignorance. Senator Tower himself told the *New York Times* that the president "clearly didn't understand the nature of this operation, who was involved, and what was happening."[17] The report criticized Reagan's management style, his naïve foreign policy, and his lack of leadership over the national security process. In particular, Reagan had sidelined the National Security Council—the same thing Kennedy did before the Bay of Pigs invasion, Johnson did during the buildup to Vietnam, and, later, George W. Bush did in the run-up to the invasion of Iraq.[18]

On March 4, Reagan addressed the nation. I was with him right beforehand in the Family Dining Room. A butler brought him a glass of water on a silver tray. Reagan picked it up, but immediately let it fall back onto the tray, almost spilling the contents. Those present wondered.

"Too hot," said the president. The butler had brought him hot water. Reagan explained this was a trick he had learned in Golden Age Hollywood: before a performance, never drink cold water—always hot. It relaxes the throat and opens the vocal cords. I use this trick to this day whenever I give a speech, and I am not shy about divulging from whom I learned it!

The trick seems to have worked, for his address to the nation was the start of Reagan's fight back.

"A few days ago," he said, "I told the American people I did not trade arms for hostages. My heart and my best intentions tell me that was true, but the facts and the evidence tell me it was not."[19] An opinion poll taken after the address showed that more than two-thirds of Americans believed that Reagan had made or would make the necessary changes to correct his mistakes.[20] Wanting to cement our gains, we scheduled a press conference for March 19. Two days before, Reagan attended the traditional St. Patrick's Day luncheon at the Irish ambassador's residence and breezed back to a prep session with David and me in the Oval Office full of the *craic*, laughing and joking with us as we took him through the outline of all that had transpired.

When he got before the press—with fifty million Americans watching at home—Reagan was back on form: breezy, charming, and unflappable. He was not quite out of the woods—Poindexter had not yet testified before Congress, and it was not yet known what he would say—but the Gipper's comeback was under way. (When Poindexter did appear before Congress, he would put the seal on the president's exoneration by testifying that "the buck stops here with me"—in other words, that he had never told Reagan about the misdeeds he and Ollie North had committed.)[21]

Abshire's original plan was for me to take over from him at the end of three months, but it was not to be. The new White House chief of staff, Howard Baker, consolidated our functions under the White

House counsel, who of course reported to him. Baker reasoned that, with Regan's departure, there was no more need for a Mr. Clean with no connection to Iran-Contra. They thus made the mistake we had worked so hard to avoid: instead of working to get everything out in the open as Reagan had ordered, they became the president's defense lawyers.

As a result, they missed things. Well into the next administration, that of Reagan's vice president, George H. W. Bush, somebody discovered Caspar Weinberger's contemporaneous notes of the Iran-Contra affair stashed in an unclassified file of the Library of Congress. Judge Walsh, still in business as independent counsel, claimed he had been lied to, indicted Weinberger for obstructing justice, and effectively accused Bush of involvement in a cover-up five days before the 1992 presidential election, which Bush lost to Bill Clinton. In Abshire's view, this debacle might have been avoided had I been there in the spring of 1987 to impress upon Weinberger and other high officials the need to release all their diaries.[22] Whether this is true or not, I cannot say; but it's an interesting counterfactual.

On March 31, Reagan threw a farewell party for Abshire, me, and our staff in the Oval Office. Abshire thanked the president for the honor of serving him, to which Reagan replied, "I'm the one to give the thanks. You didn't find me guilty!" Not our role, of course, but I appreciated the sentiment. In David's book, *Saving the Reagan Presidency*, there is a picture of Reagan raucously laughing it up with us. Again, the laughter is genuine. He was a jolly guy, always joking. Agree with him or not—and on a number of scores I certainly didn't—you could not help but like him. And after the doom and gloom of the Carter years, perhaps the best compliment to Ronald Reagan is that he made people feel good about their country again.

MOVING ON

In the circumstances, I was not upset to return to The Hague. I was happy to help get the truth about Iran-Contra out in the open, but I would not have wanted to be cast in the role of defense lawyer, the way Howard Baker would have had it.

At the tribunal, there was no letup in the pace. July 1987 turned out to be one of the busiest months in an already jam-packed career. I penned my opinions in *Amoco International Finance*, the *Short* case, and a huge case involving American members of the post-1953 Iranian Oil Consortium. I also returned to Washington to marry Carmen at St. John's Episcopal Church, Lafayette Square, opposite the White House—the fabled "Church of the Presidents."

Serving on the tribunal was a wonderfully freeing experience for a lawyer. I drew a regular salary, unbeholden to clients or fellow firm partners. My only duty was to say honestly what I thought the facts and the law were in the cases before me—an obligation I relished! At the same time, the work of the tribunal—at least, the work that most interested me—was beginning to tail off. By 1988, there were only ten cases left in my chamber that were not dual-national cases. None was worth more than ten million dollars, and none would raise my favorite legal issue, expropriation. The dual-national cases, for their part, would not grapple with any difficult issues of law, but only apply the "dominant and effective nationality" standard to varying sets of facts. The result in each case would boil down to where the claimant's house was, where their kids went to school, and so forth. To me, that would not be interesting; I wanted to engage with the law. Even after my resignation, my work for the tribunal would continue for some years under the Mosk Rule, as I had already heard seventeen cases that I would be obliged to see through to an award. Only two of these cases were ever settled.

Nevertheless, even as I wrote my resignation letter, I wondered aloud whether, in giving up job security, prestige, and a more than adequate salary, I was doing the right thing. It came down to this: while I had enjoyed living in The Hague, I did not want to expatriate myself permanently. I wanted to be able to return to the United States and attract major cases there as an international dispute resolution lawyer and—with luck—as an international arbitrator.

CHAPTER NINE

Of Parasites and Lousy Loans

INTERNATIONAL LAW EVOLVES

Reagan's presidency survived Iran-Contra, of course, and on January 20, 1989, his vice president, George H. W. Bush, was sworn in as his successor. I watched the inauguration from a prime vantage point: the terrace of the National Gallery of Art, where my old boss Jack Stevenson had been appointed board chair thanks to the longstanding connection between his firm and the Mellon family.

Watching the festivities, I felt a degree of professional pride. H. W. came to the presidency with a great deal of experience, and it seemed as if he would do a good job; but if Reagan had not come through Iran-Contra so smoothly (relatively speaking), his vice president would have had little chance.

"You should try again for State Department legal adviser," Jack told me. It was not a terrible suggestion. I liked President Bush. I had been impressed by his performance as vice president and before that as ambassador to the UN when I was at State. I thought he would be a fine foreign policy president, and I had a good chance, finally, of being appointed to the position in which I had only ever been "acting."

But that was not my path; more than ever, I wanted to pursue work in international arbitration. With that aim in mind, when I was thinking about leaving The Hague, I had looked as objectively as possible at the options available to me and concluded that White & Case still represented the best available platform: after all, I knew the firm inside and out. I knew, so to speak, where the bodies were buried.

Jim Hurlock, then the chairman of the firm, would not make it easy for me. In fact, he was still furious about my having left the first time back in 1969! As Jim told me upon my return, "You never should have gone to the State Department in the first place. If you'd stayed in New York, you could have become the premier litigator in the city."

I said, "Jim, that's as it may be. But that's not what I was looking for."

He didn't get it. When I came back with State Department, tribunal, and White House experience under my belt, he insisted on moving me down the order of seniority, telling me, "The management committee does not think your experience at the tribunal and the White House is of real advantage to the firm. So you come in one class lower in the pecking order."

This was an absurd position. How could my experience as an international judge and a prominent counsellor to the president of the United States possibly fail to advantage a firm seeking to grow its prominence in Washington, DC? Even before my tribunal and White House service, my work had been instrumental in obtaining an important client for the firm, Indonesia. What was more, I had gotten Hurlock involved in representing Indonesia by putting him on the team that I took to Jakarta in early 1977 to advise the central bank. To this day, I have no idea why Hurlock had turned so combative; but his animosity continued. "You left twice without permission!" he told me, as if I needed anyone's permission.

On a later occasion, as I arrived for a big internal meeting about international arbitration, Jim burst out at me: "You're fired!" I just stared at him. Law firms are partnerships, and one partner, even the chair of the management committee, cannot unilaterally fire another. In reality, he wouldn't try to fire me; if he had, he would have run into opposition.

Returning to my old firm was hard in other ways, too. Regardless of who I was or what I had accomplished in the meantime, nobody was going to give me my old clients back. Even Secretary Rogers had run into this problem when he returned to Arnold & Porter following his service as Eisenhower's attorney general.

Rogers warned me, "The first week, everyone is saying how happy they are to have you back, but already the next week everyone wants to know what you have done for them lately!" The loss I felt the most keenly was my biggest and longest-standing client, Indonesia, which was gone forever (the sole exception being the somehow still ongoing *Amco Asia* arbitration at ICSID, then on its second tribunal—and even then, the ever-mercurial Jim Hurlock had to order the new partner in charge to take me back as a coequal team member).

In the beginning, I did whatever cases I could lay hands on, whether or not they were in my wheelhouse. For example, a corporate law partner who in the period following my State Department years had teed me up to defeat a hostile takeover of his client, now kindly asked me to represent the same client before the U. S. Court of Appeals for the Eleventh Circuit in a federal pension regulations case.

But pretty soon I was doing almost nothing other than international arbitration. My timing was good, as it turned out, for when I returned to White & Case as of April 1, 1988, the field was on the threshold of something very big indeed.

We have already encountered the New York Arbitration Convention—the treaty that allows enforcement of arbitral awards in almost any country in the world. But how do you get disputes into arbitration in the first place? In *Amco Asia v. Indonesia* and *Parker Drilling v. Algeria,* the answer was via a term in the contract between the state and the investor. But in a contract negotiation, where the state generally holds most of the chips, it can be difficult for the investor to persuade it to remove potential disputes from its own domestic courts.

Another way of sending disputes to arbitration is via a bilateral investment treaty, or BIT, between the host state and the investor's home state. BITs typically contain a variety of protections for investors, which besides arbitration provisions may include, for example, guarantees of nondiscrimination and reassurances that their property will not be taken except for a public purpose, without discrimination, with due process and "full" (or "prompt, adequate, and effective") compensation—the standard I had convinced Indonesia to accept in *Amco Asia*.

West Germany was the pioneer when it came to BITs, partly because Bonn saw in them an opportunity to assert an independence it lacked in other areas of foreign policy. So the prototype BIT was the one West Germany made with Pakistan in 1959. Other countries were slower off the mark; the United States, for example, began pursuing BITs systematically only in 1981. The end of the Cold War triggered an explosion in BITs: whereas when the Berlin Wall fell in 1989 there were still fewer than four hundred BITs in existence, by the year 2000, there were more than eighteen hundred.[1] Today, there are nearly three thousand.[2]

International arbitration enjoyed a concomitant boom of its own. ICSID, under whose auspices *Amco Asia v. Indonesia* was arbitrated, had seen only twenty-six cases registered in the twenty-three years between its founding in 1966 and the end of the Cold War in 1989. In the twenty-one succeeding years between then and 2020, more than seven hundred cases were registered—a record fifty-eight in 2020 alone.[3]

With the building blocks of the New York Convention, ICSID, and widespread BITs in place, international arbitration was finally ready for its closeup.

In its 2021 edition, the *Global Arbitration Review* ranked White & Case no. 1 globally yet again as the premier firm for international arbitration. It recorded the situation thusly: "In the 1970s, things kicked off after Charles Brower—today a renowned arbitrator—founded an office in Washington, D.C., leading to early ICSID work (the firm has now worked on more than 100 such cases)." Indeed, the practice was a pioneer in investor-state work. Its credits include the first ICSID case against a Latin American state (*Santa Elena v. Costa Rica*); one of the largest ICSID awards on record ($877 million in *CSOB v. Slovakia*); and one of the first NAFTA cases (*Mondev v. United States*).

I was lead counsel in all three of those cases from 1988 to 2000, and I will now explore all three.

SANTA ELENA

One day in the mid-1990s, I was recommended by a mutual friend to the Costa Rican ambassador in Washington, Sonia Picado, who told me her country was having trouble importing bananas into the United States. I knew next to nothing about banana imports, but I did know that a fellow partner in my office had served as assistant secretary of commerce for import administration and would be the perfect person to handle the matter. At the same time, I gave the ambassador a warning. If Costa Rica pushed back on the banana imports issue, it could expect the United States to come after it on any and all other outstanding legal matters. I needed to know what those were so I could head them off. The ambassador mentioned two. The first was a routine sovereign immunity dispute. I put another partner on that one, too.

When she told me about the second, my eyes lit up, for it involved my favorite subject: expropriation. There was a parcel of land on the Santa Elena peninsula in Guanacaste, Costa Rica's northernmost province. It had been owned by the family of the former Nicaraguan dictator, Somoza; but they sold it off cheaply in 1970. An investment banker in New York had brought together three investors to buy the parcel. One of them, Joe Hamilton, enjoyed high-level political connections. He was reputed to have been then–Lt. George H. W. Bush's wingman in the Pacific Theater during World War II. As Hamilton recounted the story, he was the one who had directed the USS *Finback* submarine to Bush's rescue when Bush was shot down over Chichi Jima. Now, he enjoyed close ties with none other than Jesse Helms, the hardline senator whose threat to cancel American aid to Indonesia on behalf of Sea Oil I had fended off during my previous stint back at White & Case.

Hamilton and his partners wanted to chop down the trees and build golf courses, hotels, and so on, turning the place into a tourist trap. Costa Rica had other ideas. Guanacaste happens to be an area of outstanding ecological value—a field in which Costa Rica has long been a world leader—and the Santa Elena parcel was surrounded by the Area de Conservación Guanacaste, a national park. In 1978, Costa Rica took Santa Elena by decree in order to complete the national park, assessing its value at $1.9 million, which it offered to pay Hamilton and his other investors in compensation. The investors declined. Given their development plans, they asserted that the land was worth $6.4 million.[4] Now, with all the interest they said had accrued since 1978, their total claim came to more than forty million dollars. For a developing country with, at the time, fewer than four million citizens, that was a big deal.

Thus an impasse was reached. The case kicked around the Costa Rican courts for years, without much progress being made. But one big thing had now changed, courtesy of the 1994 midterms. Senator Helms was now chair of the Senate Foreign Relations Committee. Hamilton and his fellow investors thus possessed the nuclear bomb—or so they thought.

Helms continued to oppose almost all foreign aid, referring to it, with his usual level of charm, as "pouring money down foreign rat holes."[5] He would jump at any chance to block such assistance. Attentive readers may recall from the Sea Oil dispute the Hickenlooper Amendment: the law requiring the government to cut off aid to any country that expropriated American property without the required compensation, unless the dispute was sent to arbitration. That law had now been updated and was hereafter to be known as the Helms Amendment after its principal contemporary booster. Indeed, Helms had already invoked it to kill off a $175 million loan by the Inter-American Development Bank to Costa Rica.[6]

At first, it looked as if I might be able to pull the same trick I had done with Sea Oil by showing that the Helms Amendment didn't apply at all. One of the less-than-natural features present on the Santa Elena land parcel was a flat-pounded earthen airstrip. The strip was known locally as Ollie North International Airport because it had been used to land giant Lockheed C-130 Hercules cargo planes carrying weapons to be trucked over the Nicaraguan border to the Contras. What a surprise to me, years after my stint in the White House helping President Reagan successfully survive the Iran-Contra scandal and complete his full two terms, to now gaze upon Ollie North's handiwork that caused the problem in the first place!

Given this history, we investigated the possibility that the land was owned not by Hamilton et al. but by the CIA. If so, that would have helped us a great deal since the Helms Amendment applied only to U.S. citizens or majority American-owned corporations. Alas, our investigation came up empty: it seemed that Santa Elena, unlike Sea Oil, really was owned by the people who said they owned it! In other words, it was arbitration or bust. The ambassador told me that her government had already proposed an agreement to arbitrate the dispute but gotten zero traction with the American investors.

"Of course," I said. "They don't want to arbitrate. They want to blackmail you. They think they have the atomic bomb in their pocket!" I pointed out, however, that the *claimants'* agreement to arbitrate was not necessary. Costa Rica had only to consent unilaterally to arbitration and the Helms Amendment would be satisfied.

Hamilton's modus operandi, I explained, was the same as Sea Oil's: to hold the sword of Damocles over Costa Rica until they could extort more money than the land parcel was worth. I replied that we were not going to be bullied. Ambassador Picado sighed. As a city girl from San José, she didn't see what the big deal was with Santa Elena. "I don't know why it's so interesting, really," she told me. "It's cowboy country. Just rocks and stuff." Nevertheless, I thought I had better go see these "rocks and stuff" for myself.

The ambassador put me in touch with a University of Pennsylvania biology professor named Daniel Janzen. Professor Janzen was the conservation guru of Costa Rica and a leading expert on the biology of Guanacaste, where he lived for most of the year. Janzen's home, it turned out, was little more than a hut in the forest. Inside, he had strung a clothesline from the ceiling from which larval pupae hung in various stages of development. In the rafters above, Janzen's pet porcupine, Espinita, clambered about. When I asked to use the bathroom, I found an enormous bullfrog had taken up residence in the toilet bowl.

"Oh God," Janzen said. "Is he back in there again?"

As Janzen's wife, Winnie Hallwachs (an accomplished researcher in her own right) shooed the menagerie of exotic animals away, the professor and I found a safe place to sit down and talk about Santa Elena. It was a dry tropical forest, not a jungle or a rainforest, he explained—a rare biome found in only a few pockets around the world. In places, it more resembles the arid African savanna than the stereotypical Central American jungle.

Janzen underlined for me the biological importance of the region to which he and his wife had devoted their careers. With just 0.04 percent of the world's land, Costa Rica was home to 4 percent of its terrestrial and marine biodiversity; and half of that biodiversity was found in Guanacaste alone. From an ecological point of view, it was therefore imperative that Santa Elena not be turned into a luxury resort.

I thought the fact of Santa Elena's vast biodiversity might prove a good angle of attack in the eventual arbitration. I remembered the famous *Pyramids* case. Foreign investors had bought land near Egypt's ancient tombs with the intention of building a tourist resort; but in the meantime, the Egyptian government decided to crack down on commercial encroachment in the name of archaeological conservation. As part of that program, Egypt expropriated the foreign investors' land, in the process offering them compensation. The investors sued, and it greatly helped Egypt's case that the pyramids had been designated a UNESCO World Heritage Site, for it showed a legitimate public purpose in play.

"Aha!" I thought. "That's exactly what we should do here!" And I advised Costa Rica to start the process to designate the Area de Conservación Guanacaste as a World Heritage Site. In due course, UNESCO approved.

First, however, Costa Rica had to consent to arbitration of the dispute—and do so in a manner so airtight that not even Jesse Helms could deny it. In truth, Helms had done us a favor in his eponymous amendment by specifying that the arbitration should take place under ICSID rules—something to which Costa Rica could readily agree, having signed and ratified the ICSID Convention.[7] So there would be no need to invent an arbitral framework, as I had done in Sea Oil.

To ensure that nobody could argue that the government had not validly consented to arbitration, I suggested that we have it signed into a presidential decree. I met with President José María Figueres Olsen personally. Figueres was a smart guy—a West Point graduate, no less—and he got the point right away. We would have our presidential decree.

The next step was to define the dispute in such a way that they couldn't say we left anything out. Helms had done us a favor there, too. He had caused a report to be issued by the Senate Foreign Relations Committee setting out several disputes about which he was complaining. There was a page and a half about Santa Elena. We simply took that language, attached it to the decree, and pointed to it as the definition of the dispute we wanted sent to arbitration. To avoid any fights over translation, we also insisted that the decree be signed in English as well as Spanish, and both made equally authentic, to avoid any fights over translation. Figueres signed the decree. In the name of prudence, we made it conditional on the Helms Amendment actually applying to the dispute just in case the land turned out to be 51 percent owned by, say, a Greek centenarian. Stranger things had, indeed, happened.

This got the Americans' attention. We began to talk about settlement, and at first the portents seemed to augur well. The American owners invited me down to visit the Santa Elena parcel and attend a party at Hamilton's hacienda.

While I was down there, Hamilton's lawyer drove me around the property in a Jeep. It turned out the lawyer had too big of a mouth for his own good. At one point during our tour, he started musing out loud about challenging Figueres's presidential decree, saying he might do so on the grounds that the property included "natural resources of

Costa Rica," in which case, under domestic law, the Costa Rican congress would have to consent. I suddenly realized that there would be no settlement. We had to get the dispute into arbitration right away—and I knew just the thread to pull.

Back in Washington, I hurried up to Capitol Hill to meet with Senator Helms's staff—a group I called privately, and not without justification, the Brown Shirts.

"Costa Rica has bent over backward to please your boss," I told them. "They've done more than enough to convince the State Department that they're consenting to arbitration. Now it's time for the senator to do what his own amendment asks. Advise him to tell these people to agree to arbitration, or they are out of luck. If the investors take any step to get around this decree, it will be their fault, not that of Costa Rica, and the State Department will know about it."

The Brown Shirts, true to form, evinced no immediate reaction; but within a week, Hamilton et al. had agreed to arbitrate. Ultimately, my instinct had proved correct: Helms had no reason to get into a fight with the State Department over something that—as far as he and his "clients" were concerned—was only ever about money.

THE DISNEYFICATION DEFENSE

So to arbitration we went! My principal associate on the case, as on many others during my third stint at White & Case, was an exceptionally talented young lawyer, Abby Cohen Smutny. Having grown up on an Israeli kibbutz, Abby had graduated with honors from Vassar, gotten her JD from the University of Chicago, and joined White & Case in 1989. Today, she leads the firm's international arbitration practice and is rightly ranked among the finest practitioners in the field. I'm proud to say I knew her back when!

Costa Rica had appointed to the tribunal a renowned French professor of public international law, Prosper Weil. Hamilton et al. had appointed Sir Elihu Lauterpacht QC, an English barrister, Cambridge professor, and one of the giants of international law. Both were excellent choices. Eventually I persuaded the investors' counsel to accept as president of the tribunal Yves Fortier, a highly distinguished Canadian lawyer and international arbitrator, and a former ambassador of Canada to the United Nations who in October 1990 had presided over the Security Council during Saddam Hussein's invasion and occupation of Iraq. Before that he had served as counsel for Canada at the International Court of Justice in the *Gulf of Maine* case and as judge *ad hoc* of the International Court of Justice—a position to which he would return.

I cannot resist an aside involving Yves, who has become a dear friend. At one point, he called me up with an unusual request. The independence movement in his native Québec was then riding high, and to bolster their case, the separatist parties had hired a New York law firm, Rogers & Wells, to write an opinion saying that an independent Québec could enforce treaties Canada had made with the United States. This was hogwash—unsurprisingly, you generally can't just take over a treaty without giving the other party a say! Frankly, the Rogers & Wells opinion was a botch.

Yves's party, the Liberals, opposed independence, so naturally the opinion irked them. Yves asked me to draft an expert opinion in rebuttal, which I did, along with the indefatigable Abby Cohen Smutny. We shredded the Rogers & Wells opinion, showing that an independent Québec would face serious challenges in establishing relations with the United States. Yves was delighted, and I am told that the dueling opinions fueled a two-hour debate in the Québécois National Assembly (the province's legislature).

For now, though, let us return to the more hospitable climate of Costa Rica. I wanted the panel to visit Santa Elena in person. I thought they would enjoy it; they would see how stunning the landscape is; and along the way, we could underline how poor a country Costa Rica was. At our first meeting with the panel, which took place in Paris, I asked the Costa Rican foreign ministry to send their chargé d'affaires in Paris along. I felt his presence would underscore Costa Rica's status as a poor but democratic country with an intense interest in preserving the environment. The chargé came in and told the tribunal what Janzen had told me about the unique biome, the amazing biodiversity, and so on. They seemed suitably impressed.

Then Yves asked, "Is it safe?"

"Oh yes!" said the chargé d'affaires. "I mean, every once in a while there is a bit of dengue fever, but it never amounts to much."

Alas, that little revelation killed off my field trip idea. But we had other ways of convincing the tribunal! As an opening gambit, our written memorials emphasized that what the claimant sought to do was to "Disneyfy a World Heritage Site."

The substantive hearing took place over the course of a week in Washington in May 1999. As usual, I was the first to speak. On a visit to the British Museum, I had acquired a poster of the Rosetta Stone—the Egyptian tablet that finally unlocked the mysteries of hieroglyphics. I had this blown up and placed on an easel in front of the tribunal. After allowing a suitable interval to let the image sink in, I told the tribunal, "Guanacaste is the Rosetta Stone of biodiversity in this world!" A valid claim, I felt, given the statistics Janzen gave me in his jungle shack. The implication was clear: what these investors wanted was the equivalent of "Disneyfying" not just a World Heritage Site but the Rosetta Stone itself!

Daniel Janzen testified with passion and eloquence to the ecological importance of the Guanacaste region and the Santa Elena peninsula in particular. The Area de Conservación Guanacaste had not yet been formally inscribed as a World Heritage Site, but it was well on the way: experts from UNESCO had already visited and given the area a positive writeup. We made a point of having a Costa Rican diplomat testify on the country's efforts to have it so inscribed—efforts that would succeed later that year.[8]

The further proceedings were not entirely without incident, however, for one morning Professor Weil could not be present as he appeared to have a touch of the flu. When he returned, he was understandably fatigued. Professor Lauterpacht was too, because he was still recovering from coronary bypass surgery. When I proceeded to make a speech after lunch—a soporific proposition at the best of times—I saw quite clearly that both Weil and Lauterpacht had fallen asleep. I shot Yves Fortier a look and then glanced pointedly to his left and right.

"Oh!" said Fortier, looking around. "The tribunal will take a recess!"

Ultimately, as the tribunal recognized in its award, the dispute boiled down not to the ecological significance of the land, nor indeed to its touristic potential, but to how much money it was worth. Taking into account all the interest accumulated over the years, the investors had claimed a little over forty million dollars; we said the maximum amount payable was around ten million dollars.[9]

When I picked the award up from ICSID, I saw that the tribunal, affirming that Costa Rica had acted from a legitimate public purpose, had awarded the claimants exactly $16 million, including interest from its expropriation in 1978 to the 2000 award.[10] It could, in other words, have been much worse.

"Oh, this is great!" I said. And I called the first vice president of Costa Rica to tell her the good news.

"Oh, this is terrible!" she said. "We have only set aside fifteen million!"

My next call was to Daniel Janzen. While the professor was grateful for the result, when he heard about the one-million-dollar shortfall, he gave a rueful sigh.

"Yeah," he said. "They'll be asking me to raise that money." Janzen, as one would expect, was a master at drumming up donations to protect the dry tropical forest, and the Costa Ricans knew it. Evidently, he did not disappoint.

For my work on the *Santa Elena* case, Janzen told me later that he had decided to name a newly discovered species after me: *Barylypa broweri*. I wondered what magnificent beast he had deemed suitable to bear my name in perpetuity. A soaring bird of prey, perhaps? Or a hitherto unknown type of jaguar?

"It's a parasitic wasp!" Janzen told me with undisguised glee. "It devours its host from the inside out!"

"I see."

"Clearly, you're a WASP," he went on, a little gratuitously. "All good attorneys are parasites, and this one even dresses like a lawyer. In its larval form, it wears a striped suit!"

Sure enough, the official description from the American Entomological Institute describes *Barylypa broweri* as follows:

> *This elegant insect is named in honor of Charles N. Brower, in recognition of his enthusiastic and outstanding legal defense of the hundreds of thousands of species, including* Barylypa broweri, *of the Santa Elena Peninsula serpentine barrens in northwestern Costa Rica.*[11]

Not, perhaps, the conferral of immortality for which one might have hoped; but it had a certain poetry. Besides, I had my revenge. Later the same year, I invited Professor Janzen to my sixty-fifth birthday party. For probably the first time in decades, the forest dweller was forced into a tuxedo.

VELVET WARRIORS

My final arbitration was by some distance my largest by dollar value—or to be more accurate, Slovak koruna value. The former Czechoslovakia, like many Eastern Bloc countries, used its state-run foreign trade bank for political purposes, handing out dubious loans in order to curry favor with developing countries the Soviet Union wanted in its column. For example, it financed arms sales to Saddam Hussein, about whom more in the next chapter.

When the Czech and Slovak halves of the country agreed their "Velvet Divorce" in 1992, one question was what to do with the lousy loans the foreign trade bank still had on its books. It was agreed that the successor countries would fund the inevitable losses in proportion to their respective populations. The Czech Republic upheld its end of the bargain; Slovakia did not. The trade bank—whose full name, Československá Obchodní Banka A.S., I will prudently abbreviate to CSOB—hired me to pursue an arbitral claim for a truly eye-watering sum: SKK 33,724,445,229, plus interest.[12] In 1997 money, this amounted to around $1 billion,[13] at the time the largest sum ever claimed at ICSID.

Slovakia, for its part, hired a crack team from another top-drawer Wall Street firm, Shearman & Sterling, led out of the firm's Paris office by a true international law heavyweight, the late professor Emmanuel Gaillard.

The first objection Gaillard's team raised was to ICSID's jurisdiction. The BIT between the Czech and Slovak Republics provided for arbitration of disputes under the claimant's choice of ICSID or the UNCITRAL rules, and we chose ICSID.[14] But Slovakia said that the BIT was not in force because, according to its own terms, it required an additional exchange of notifications between the two foreign ministries. That exchange had, on any reasonable interpretation of the facts, simply never taken place.[15] Thus battle was joined!

Our first argument was that the extra notices were just a formality, not a requirement. But if that was the case, why bother to put them in the treaty? There is a doctrine in law that, so far as possible, legal documents are to be read so that each term carries meaning. So the tribunal did not buy that one.[16]

Second, we pointed out that, as long ago as October 1993, the Slovak government had published a notice in its official gazette reading, in relevant part, "Pursuant to Article 12, the treaty became effective on January 1, 1993."[17] International case law says that, if a state expresses a unilateral intent to be bound by a treaty, that treaty can be enforced against it. Alternatively, there is the universal legal doctrine of estoppel, according to which one party cannot back out of a unilateral statement if the other has done something costly in reliance on it. Unfortunately, the standard of proof in both cases is high; and it did not help that, in a case brought in a Czech court by a Slovak national relying on the BIT in relation to a claim to property, the legal adviser to the Czech ministry of foreign affairs had filed a statement saying that the BIT was not in force. So no sale there, either.[18]

Our third and final argument was that the contract between CSOB and the Slovak "lousy loans" vehicle had mentioned the BIT as part of its governing law. It had therefore, we said, incorporated the BIT's arbitration provisions by reference. The tribunal, thank goodness, bought this one—but only barely. It came down to the fact that, during negotiations, the phrase "after it is ratified" had been deleted from the contract.[19] That one tiny edit changed the fate of nearly one billion dollars.

Having by the skin of our teeth obtained jurisdiction, it all came down to koruna and halierov—or, if you prefer, dollars and cents. The Slovaks didn't really have a case; nevertheless, they dragged it out for as long as possible, perhaps hoping, like Mr. Micawber in *David Copperfield*, that "something will turn up."

Peter Tomka (at various times Slovakia's permanent representative to the UN and later a judge and president of the International Court of Justice) was then serving as legal adviser to the Slovak ministry of foreign affairs, and the situation evidently exasperated him almost as much as it did CSOB. Whenever I ran into him later in The Hague when he was on the ICJ, he would cry, "I've told them to settle! I've told them to settle!"

But they did not settle, and the case went on for eight years. At last, it came time for the arbitration proper, which was held in Prague, one of my favorite cities, justly famous for its architecture and musical pedigree, led by the Czech national composer Bedřich Smetana. It seems that on every corner there's a Baroque church and inside every one a daily concert at five o'clock.

By the time we were ready to examine witnesses, I was already back on the Iran–United States Claims Tribunal; but I could not resist returning for one last hurrah. When I read the statement of the Slovak Republic's expert on Czech law, I saw that he had not read the testimony of a different expert whose opinion contradicted his own in crucial ways and had appeared for Slovakia at the earlier jurisdictional hearing. Somehow, Shearman & Sterling had failed to show it to him. For a cross-examining attorney, this was a gift platter. I just had to do the cross-examination myself!

"I take it you are not familiar with the testimony of Professor So-and-So?"

At this point, he might have said, "Yes," in which case I could have asked with piquancy why it was not addressed in his witness statement. That would still have been a blow, albeit a lesser one. But to my delight, the witness said that, indeed, he had not read his counterpart's testimony. The Shearman team had messed up, big time.

"Ah!" I said. "Well, let me take you through it."

We put up slides showing the other expert's testimony; slides to which, not having been prepared, the respondent's witness had essentially no answer. It was a slaughter. It made the mighty Shearman & Sterling look like country bumpkins. It was the most fun a litigator can have: taking apart an opposing witness in cross-examination. As it was my last ever appearance as an advocate, I particularly enjoyed the triumph.

In the end, as expected, we wiped the floor with the Slovaks. The tribunal's final award came to just shy of twenty-five billion koruny—around $867 million.[20] To add insult to injury, the tribunal tacked on a ten-million-dollar contribution toward CSOB's legal costs.[21] It was ICSID's largest award to date, and in recognition of that fact, Abby Cohen Smutny and I appeared on the cover of an *American Lawyer* magazine supplement, dubbed "White & Case's Velvet Warriors."[22]

It seems Peter Tomka was right—they should have settled. But frankly, I am glad they didn't. What a way to close out my career as a litigator!

THE COMBAT ZONE

By the turn of the millennium, international law was clearly evolving in favor of investor protections, supporting the all-important flow of investment, especially to developing countries. The Charter of Economic Rights and Duties of States, with its subjective, watered-down standard of compensation for expropriation, had, more or less, been vanquished—thanks in important part to the work of the Iran–United States Claims Tribunal, which consistently held that full compensation was required. Thousands of bilateral investment treaties were in place. So were reliable mechanisms for the resolution of disputes between states and investors, in the shape of institutions like ICSID.

Pride cometh before a fall, however. My next big case would show that a pushback was underway; and this time the threat to investor protections came not from developing nations but principally from Canada and the United States.

Sometime in the late 1990s, I received a call from Yves Fortier, the Canadian lawyer-diplomat who presided over the tribunal in the *Santa Elena* case. He was by then sitting full-time as an arbitrator, so he asked if I would take on a claim by a longtime client of his, Montreal Development, or Mondev.

I said I would be delighted. Whom were they suing?

The United States.

Ah. This, I thought, *could be an issue.* It might hurt my chances of getting appointed again as a U.S. judge—a prospect I had my eye on. The State Department can be a tad oversensitive when it comes to such appointments. For example, I remembered that during the *Nicaragua v. United States* debacle before the ICJ, Keith Highet had been in the frame to serve as a consultant to the United States. It made sense: Keith had argued more cases before the ICJ than any American in history. But he wound up being blackballed. Why? Because he had represented Libya, which as usual was on America's naughty list. Never mind that it was in a technical dispute over delineation of maritime boundaries!

But a bird in the hand is worth at least one in the bush. So I accepted. (Later, the case did cause me some problems, as we will see.) The case centered around a scuzzy area of downtown Boston known locally as "the Combat Zone." Packed with strip clubs and adult bookstores, the Combat Zone was a blot on the landscape, and the City of Boston understandably wanted to be rid of it. So Boston hired Mondev to revamp the area by building, among other things, a mall, an office complex, and a hotel.[23] The first phase of demolition and construction went smoothly, but the deal fell apart in phase two. Mondev said that Boston had deliberately scuppered the deal, in part because of a certain anti-Canadian animus among city officials.[24]

Mondev was Canadian. The City of Boston was a political subdivision of the United States. Potentially, that brought into play the North American Free Trade Agreement—a massive trade deal between Mexico, Canada, and the United States that came into force in 1994. NAFTA included the now-familiar protections against expropriation: that it must be done for a public purpose, without discrimination, and on payment of full compensation.[25] In art. 1105, NAFTA added a standard of due process, entitling investors to "treatment in accordance with international law, including fair and equitable treatment and full protection and security."[26] (Ultimately, NAFTA would not avail Mondev, because it had not yet been in force when the Combat Zone deal fell apart; but that outcome was not in itself a threat to investor protections.)

We took the dispute to arbitration at ICSID. Mondev appointed James Crawford, an Australian serving as Whewell Professor of International Law at Cambridge. Crawford, who passed away in 2021 while serving as a judge of the ICJ, was famous for, among other things, resurrecting the International Law Commission's work on the responsibility of states and turning it into a landmark statement of the law. The U.S. appointee was Steve Schwebel, an American judge recently retired from the International Court of Justice, where he had served as that body's president. The president of the tribunal was Sir Ninian Stephen QC, the former governor-general of Australia, judge *ad hoc* of the ICJ, and judge of the International Tribunal for the Former Yugoslavia. The panel represented, in other words, a reassuringly high-powered bunch.

While Mondev and the United States exchanged pleadings, another tribunal in a separate NAFTA case, *Pope & Talbot v. Canada*, was deliberating on what was to be its fifth award. At a hearing on that case, Canada had argued that what NAFTA art. 1105 required was no more than the minimum standard of investor protection under customary international law—and that only "egregious" misconduct would run afoul of that standard.[27] If accepted, this argument would erase the

NAFTA standard of protection and substitute a much lower standard than the one found in most run-of-the-mill BITs!

Canada's argument was abject nonsense. The *Pope & Talbot* tribunal called it "patently absurd," which indeed it was—not least because the express intent of NAFTA was to establish especially close economic relationships among Canada, Mexico, and the United States, not a situation in which investors could lawfully be treated *worse* than they would be elsewhere in the world![28] Indeed, the standard set out in NAFTA was invented by the United States specifically to provide greater protection for investors than what was available under customary international law.[29]

That did not lay the matter to rest, however. On July 31, 2001, about four months after the *Pope & Talbot* award (and with Mondev and the United States still in the pleading phase), the NAFTA parties issued an "interpretation" of art. 1105 that purported to resurrect Canada's "patently absurd" proposition. Art. 1105, they said, did not require "treatment in addition to or beyond that which is required by the customary international law minimum standard."[30]

Mapping this "interpretation" onto the text of NAFTA, the effect of it is to insert the word "customary" and to delete the words "fair and equitable treatment and full protection and security." That is not an interpretation; that is an amendment—an amendment achieved by the back door and therefore contrary to the Constitution!

To make matters worse, the NAFTA parties, led by Canada, tried to persuade the tribunal in *Mondev* to turn back the clock by citing case law from as early as the 1920s—a time when the principal recourse for aggrieved U.S. investors was to summon the gunboats! They drew upon these ancient precedents to argue that a breach of the customary standard required "an outrage . . . bad faith . . . willful neglect of duty, or . . . an insufficiency of governmental action so far short of international standards that every reasonable and impartial man would readily recognize its insufficiency."[31] (And if nothing else, the unnecessarily gendered language in that quote betrays its decrepitude.) This ignored all the developments since, including the rise of BITs, the jurisprudence of the Iran–United States Claims Tribunal, and the advent of ICSID.

Despite all this, the tribunal found an elegant way around it—no doubt influenced by the work of Mondev's appointee, James Crawford, who in his work for the ILC had emphasized the living, developing nature of customary international law.

Fine, the tribunal said. So this is an interpretation, and we are bound to follow it. But when we look at the text of that interpretation, we see that it refers to customary international law. Customary international law is always developing. In recent years, it has been shaped by, among other things, thousands of BITs and other economic treaties, most of which themselves require the equivalent of "fair and equitable treatment and full protection and security." Whether you write it out or you incorporate it by reference to customary law, that's the standard.[32] So there!

This was a classic example of a tribunal finding a way to do the right thing. Unfortunately, the logic of the July 31 "interpretation"—and the NAFTA parties' underlying attempt to roll back investor protections—would prove a sticky threat to international investment, as we will see.

CHAPTER TEN

Suing Saddam

2.7 MILLION CLAIMS

Arbitration at ICSID and similar institutions has transformed the resolution of "one-shot" disputes between states and private parties. But from time to time, the geopolitical tectonic plates shift so significantly all at once that it makes sense to establish a special tribunal to deal with the aftermath. One such situation was the Iranian Revolution, which of course gave rise to the Iran–United States Claims Tribunal. Another, orders of magnitude more destructive, was the Gulf War.

On August 2, 1990, the Iraqi dictator Saddam Hussein invaded neighboring Kuwait on a flimsy pretext. Half of Kuwaitis were forced to flee the country (and some, including many Palestinian refugees, would never be allowed to return).[1] The economy was brought to its knees.

International law strictly prohibits aggressive war, and this was as flagrant a breach as could be imagined. Within days, the UN Security Council had imposed what amounted to a blanket trade embargo on Iraq, with narrow exceptions for humanitarian aid.[2] Iraq, of course, refused to withdraw and claimed to have annexed Kuwait as a province.

So the Security Council next authorized UN member states to "use all necessary measures" to eject Saddam's troops.[3] In UN legalese, that is code for war.

President George H. W. Bush, in his finest hour, painstakingly built an international coalition against Saddam (compare and contrast his son's headlong rush to invade Iraq a dozen years later). Coalition troops accomplished their mission in short order; but while retreating, Saddam's forces comprehensively looted Kuwait, destroying infrastructure worth an estimated $160 billion.[4] In particular, they set fire to more than seven hundred oil wells, polluting groundwater, releasing crude into the Gulf, and generally causing untold environmental damage.[5]

At the end of the conflict, having reaffirmed Iraq's liability under international law for the damage done by its unlawful invasion and occupation of Kuwait, the Security Council established a compensation fund by levying a portion of the profits on Iraqi oil. To distribute the money, it created a new body called the United Nations Compensation Commission, or UNCC.[6]

In carrying out its mission, the UNCC was required to apply relevant Security Council resolutions, "other relevant rules of international law," and (significantly) its own prior decisions.[7] This last item marked a refreshing change from the Iran–United States Claims Tribunal, which as we have seen too frequently ignored its own precedents, to my endless frustration. My old tribunal law clerk David Caron—the one who had picked me up at Amsterdam's Schiphol Airport that dark, damp night in late 1983—was appointed as a commissioner in 1996, having spent the intervening years building up a remarkable career as a professor and advocate. Part of his role was to keep the decisions of the UNCC consistent, something that, as he was painfully aware, the tribunal had often failed to do.

The UNCC, in fact, built on the lessons of the Iran–United States Claims Tribunal in a number of other important ways. In the beginning, it was staffed almost entirely by former tribunal employees—a trained and experienced group of young lawyers eager for a new challenge (and not least to exchange the dowdy surroundings of The Hague for the mountain air of Geneva). Michael Raboin, previously the deputy U.S. agent at the tribunal, was selected as the UNCC's first deputy executive director, effectively its chief operating officer, and he saw to it that the body got set up rather quickly. He and his staff did a fine job creating procedures and guidelines that allowed the commission to get through literally millions of claims with remarkable speed.

At the Iran tribunal, the default position had been that every disputed claim was to be arbitrated (albeit that in those worth less than $250,000 the relevant government took on the task of legal representation). That proved hard enough with "only" around four thousand claims filed. At one point, a couple of lawyers were drafted in to try to rationalize the small claims, but they met with little success, and the two states wound up settling 2,388 such claims en masse for a lump-sum payment.

At the UNCC, with 2.7 *million* claims filed, there was never any question of trying to arbitrate all or even most of them. Nor does justice always require such an elaborate process. So Michael Raboin and his staff created automated procedures for processing the smaller and less complicated claims, including using newly available computer technology to check information submitted to the commission and to perform statistical modeling for the appropriate level of damages.[8]

As we have seen, the Iran tribunal had elected to postpone certain claims by individuals, largely because of the controversy around the definition of nationality. Taking such divisive matters off the docket for a time helped build trust between Iran and the United States early on; but it also delayed justice for the affected claimants, some of whom, like Alfred Short and his American colleagues, had faced considerable hardship.

By contrast, the UNCC had no need to appease the Iraqis, because they had no control over its affairs. So instead, it spent its first five years processing individual claims—some 1.3 million of them in all, worth a combined $13.1 billion.[9] They included thousands of claims submitted by the UN's various refugee bodies on behalf of stateless persons (mainly Palestinian refugees who had been resident in Kuwait before Iraq's invasion and whom, shamefully, Kuwait had refused to allow back).

For the most part, the UNCC did not sit as anything resembling a court. It behaved, instead, as a claims-processing facility, more administrative than judicial. But with the biggest corporate and government claims, which it finally began considering in 1996, it did don some of the raiment of a court, including the exchange of pleadings and, in exceptionally large and complex cases, formal hearings. That was where specialist advocates like me came in. It was only a matter of time before I found myself traveling to Geneva.

CRUDE OIL, HUMAN SHIELDS

One longstanding client, the oil firm Saudi Aramco, was obviously deeply affected by the Gulf War. But could it mount a claim? Much of the company's crude had been requisitioned to quite literally fuel the fight against Saddam; but the expenses of mounting the allied response were specifically excluded from the UNCC's jurisdiction.[10] Nor could Saudi Aramco sue for lost profits, simply because it hadn't suffered any. In fact, the war (along with other factors) had driven the price of oil *up*, giving Saudi Aramco an unlooked-for windfall.

Nevertheless, the conflict had cost the company in other ways. For example, it had to secure extra insurance, fly its international staff to safety, buy gas masks and personal protective equipment for those who remained in the region (the threat of chemical attack from Saddam was perennial), purchase firefighting gear in case of attack, and repair drilling rigs damaged by mines the Iraqis planted in the Persian Gulf.[11]

Unfortunately for the client, the UNCC had announced an expansive doctrine of "set off," under which increased profits would be applied to reduce the value of other claims by the same claimant. Legally speaking (with apologies to David Caron, Michael Hwang, and my other friends on the commission), this was nonsense.

If the additional expenses had somehow *caused* the increased profits (let's say, for the sake of argument, the new gas masks allowed for more efficient oil extraction), then they might have a point. But that was not how it played out. Iraq had caused the extra expenses by invading Kuwait. At the same time, various factors had caused the oil price to rise. Without a causal connection between the two, the fact that profits happened to have gone up was irrelevant to the fact that the cost of making those sales also went up. The commission's excellent legal staff understood this point and even went so far as to hold a mock hearing on the matter to try to convince the panel of its error, to no avail.

Thus, when it came time to argue Saudi Aramco's case, we faced an uphill battle against a clutch of poorly reasoned precedents. As this was one of those "cases of extraordinary size and complexity," the panel held a hearing—albeit a relatively low-key one, in a conference room rather than a court. I represented Saudi Aramco, backed by a small team including the company's associate general counsel. The Iraqis sent no fewer than eight representatives—four officials from the state oil company, plus four darkly scowling minders whose only function, it seemed, was to look intimidating.

We turned somersaults trying to distinguish Saudi Aramco's claim from the ones that had been set off. It didn't work. The panel zeroed out all of our claims, on the basis that Saudi Aramco's increased profits were more than enough to cover its increased expenses.[12] Here, then, was the drawback to a strong system of precedent: when you set a bad one, you are stuck with it!

Another client, the Sheraton hotel chain, had better luck. Its hotels in Baghdad and the southern Iraqi port city of Basra had both been occupied by Saddam's forces. The troops evicted any remaining guests (most had sensibly fled) and used the buildings to house prisoners, including some taken hostage as "human shields"—a disgraceful practice by which Saddam kidnapped foreign nationals and kept them in strategic locations in an attempt to blackmail the coalition into leaving those locations intact.[13]

Sheraton's staff, thank God, were not mistreated, mainly because the soldiers, like any guests, needed the staff to run the buildings for them. No damage was done to the fabric of these hotels, either; but Sheraton was effectively kicked out of Iraq and deprived of the ability to manage the hotels, together with several million dollars marooned in Iraqi bank accounts that it could no longer access because of sanctions.[14]

The Sheraton in Kuwait City fared considerably worse. During the invasion, it was taken as the Iraqi military's headquarters in Kuwait.[15] That was bad enough; but when the coalition rolled in to expel Iraq from its neighbor, the hotel's manager was given one hour to get his staff out of the building. Then Saddam's soldiers moved in, stripping the building bare—they even looted the hotel's piano, carrying it back home, part of the spoils of war. Then they planted land mines throughout the building, used tanks to shoot it full of holes, and for good measure set the place on fire.[16]

We won some aspects of these claims and lost others. At the end of the day, Sheraton was able to recover around forty million dollars from Saddam's government. For me, perhaps the most interesting aspect of the Sheraton claims was getting the chance to interview some of Sheraton's staff. Even though the Iraqis had treated them relatively well, they had been through a lot. Despite this, I generally found them a remarkably resilient and cheerful bunch.

Sheraton's Lebanese-Swiss regional manager, based in Cairo, summed up the hospitality mindset for me. He told me that whenever he interviewed someone for a general manager job in any hotel he would ask them, "Why are you in this business?" And if the answer was not "Because I just love it!" they wouldn't get the job. After all, as a hotel manager, you are essentially never off the clock. Full-scale military invasions may be mercifully rare; but rowdy guests, delinquent contractors, kitchen fires, and broken pipes are a dime a dozen, and they don't care if it is 3:00 a.m. on a Sunday. If you didn't love it, you would go crazy.

A SAD DAM MESS

My largest case before the UNCC concerned the ill-starred Bekhme Dam, a construction site of epic proportions situated on the Great Zab River where it cuts a canyon through the mountains in the far north of Iraq, around twenty miles from the Turkish border.[17] Had it ever actually been built, the dam (with its triple functions of irrigation, hydroelectricity, and flood control) would have been both taller and wider than the Hoover Dam in Nevada.[18] But it was not to be.

Originally conceived in the 1970s, the project had already been placed on hold pending the conclusion of the Iran-Iraq War. Construction finally got underway after the UN-brokered ceasefire in 1988. The main contractor was Enka, a Turkish firm founded and still led at the time by Şarık Tara, an immigrant from Bosnia-Herzegovina in the former Yugoslavia.[19] The project was a 50-50 joint venture with the Bosnian company Hidrogradnja. Enka imported most of its workers from Turkey, and one of its first building projects at the site was a village with three hundred and fifty houses for the workers and their families, complete with a Turkish-style mosque on a hill.[20] Work continued until August 1990, when Saddam's troops stormed into Kuwait.

The Bekhme Dam was nowhere near Kuwait, of course; but the project succumbed to the conflict nonetheless. Turkey threw its support behind the anti-Saddam coalition, suspended trade, closed its long border with Iraq, and shut off the oil pipeline between the two countries. Enka's Turkish workers found themselves hounded by Saddam's secret police, and they understandably feared hideous reprisals. Saddam had been known to use chemical weapons against even his own people; and he was already taking foreigners hostage as human shields, like the ones imprisoned at the Sheratons in Baghdad and Basra. In fact, four employees of the U.S. firm Bechtel—which we also wound up representing in the dispute—had been kidnapped from the Bekhme Dam site for exactly this purpose.[21]

As the UNCC put it, "The workers, believing that they were trapped inside a hostile state on the verge of conflict with their home state, turned their thoughts and energies to self-preservation and escape from Iraq."[22] In other words, quite reasonably, they fled.

After the war, there would be no project to return to. When Bush's coalition finally kicked Saddam out of Kuwait the following year, the terms of the ceasefire obliged Iraqi troops to pull out of the largely Kurdish north of the country. Seeing an opening, Kurdish separatist fighters moved in, looting the site and to all intents and purposes ending the Bekhme Dam project.[23] Enka claimed at the UNCC for, among other things, the cost of evacuating its staff from Iraq, the loss of the looted materials, and the potential profits it had been denied.[24]

Abby Cohen Smutny, my supremely talented colleague and right hand on every big case I handled at the firm, starting with this one, went to work researching Enka's history and its involvement in the dam project. Her work eventually became what we called "the novel," complete with colorful characters, exotic locales, frequent peril, high-level government wrangling, and a multigenerational family saga.

The project, it quickly emerged, had never been a happy one. Its location looked like the surface of Mars and, with one access road and one telephone line, it almost could have been. Getting millions of cubic feet of concrete up there, let alone laying it, was not an easy lift—and that was before factoring in frequent shortages of vital materials. Iraqi officials squeezed Enka on price, failed to pay on time, and generally treated Enka and its fellow contractors poorly (no surprise there). Moreover, while the war with Iran had ended, the local Kurdish population's struggle against Baghdad had not. The Bekhme project represented to some eyes a giant symbol of the regime, so security was a constant worry.

At one point, Abby and our colleague Anne D. Smith hit a roadblock. On one of our trips to Istanbul, I dispatched them to sit down with Enka's executive vice president and explain to him just how we should respond to a series of interrogatories that the UNCC commissioners handling Bekhme Dam claims had put to Enka. It was a simple matter of how to present the evidence; but he flat out refused to accept their counsel.

After a frustrating day, Abby and Anne returned to our hotel, convinced that the EVP had stonewalled them because they were women—an attitude that is still disturbingly common in many parts of the world.

As lead counsel of our team, I had been working a long time with this particular gentleman, and Abby and Anne were certain he would accept the same advice if it came from me. So the next day I sat down with him myself to set him straight. And he did indeed accept the same advice from me!

On another occasion, I was sitting in the same EVP's office when he called his counterpart at Enka's partner in the Bekhme Dam consortium, Hidrogradnja. Unfortunately, Hidrogradnja was based in Sarajevo, the Bosnian capital, which at the time was under siege by Ratko Mladić's Bosnian Serbs.

"Yeah, well," I heard the Bosnian executive saying, with remarkable calm, "the windows are shot out, we have no heat, but we're here working away as best we can."

Abby, Anne, and I wound up assisting Hidrogradnja as well. Because of the ongoing siege, the only people who could go in and out of Sarajevo freely were the UN's UNPROFOR peacekeepers. Hidrogradnja's legal team told us over dinner, in a German-style Rathskeller (a beer hall traditionally located in the basement of the town hall), about how they made it to Istanbul by bribing French UNPROFOR personnel for seats on a military transport for themselves and hundreds of pounds of documents.

It was far from their worst story. Hearing their personal accounts of the Bosnian War was one of the more disturbing experiences of my life. Imagine living next door to the same family for generations, and then one day they decide that because you are Muslim you are no longer welcome, and they literally throw you into the street. That had happened to several Hidrogradnja staff.

They also told us that their CEO, in order to keep his personnel safe and avoid layoffs, was taking on replacement projects abroad. I give him credit for looking out for his people; but unfortunately, these replacement projects wound up being in Qaddafi's Libya, which unsurprisingly was proving to be a "slow pay" debtor, just like Saddam. But at least Libya wasn't (at that time) an active war zone.

In the end, Hidrogradnja did better at the UNCC than Enka. Of the latter's claim of $264 million, the UNCC panel awarded Enka "only"

$62 million. The lion's share of the shortfall was in lost profits, for which Enka received precisely zero dollars. Given all the problems that predated the invasion of Kuwait and had nothing to do with it—the remote and unforgiving geography, the unreliability of supply deliveries, the volatility of Iraqi Kurdistan, the constant bickering with Saddam's ministers, and so on—it was the panel's assessment that Enka could not have made a profit on the project, war or no war.[25] It was a disappointing result after so much toil; but such, I guess, are the vagaries of construction megaprojects.

THE UNCC'S LEGACY

Taken as a whole, the UNCC represented a milestone in the development of international justice. Its docket of close to three million cases vastly overshadowed the Iran–United States Claims Tribunal's nearly four thousand. In part, the difference reflected the massive growth in international trade and investment in the eleven years between 1979 and 1990, which meant that many more foreign nationals were caught up in the conflict. By the time it wrapped up its work, the commission had awarded over $52.4 billion to around 1.5 million victims of the conflict.[26] Its cases included a landmark claim by Kuwait for environmental damage worth over one billion dollars by itself.

The commission finished its work in 2005, whereas the Iran–United States Claims Tribunal, as we will see, is to this day wrangling its final, massive cases. The commission was able to proceed more quickly in part because Iraq, having incurred the ire of the UN Security Council and been defeated in war, was not given a choice in the matter—nor a voice on the commission—meaning that Saddam's people could not stall for time the way the Iranians have done: quite a contrast to the Mexican standoff that led to the creation of the Iran tribunal. But the commission's monumental achievement would not have been possible without the lessons of its predecessor—and a ready-made cadre of talented staff capable of applying them.

Finally, in addition to bringing a semblance of justice to the victims, the UNCC's reports created an unprecedented forensic record of the destruction and waste wrought by war—one that ought to serve as a sobering reminder to any leader thinking of pursuing a policy of aggression.

In light of its many achievements, part of me wanted to seek appointment to the UNCC; but in the end, I had handled so many cases before the body (and my advice had been informally sought by its legal staff so often) that I would have been conflicted out of sitting on it. Happily, however, that did not mean I could not sit on other tribunals! And as luck would have it, a seat on the Iran–United States Claims Tribunal was about to open up.

CHAPTER ELEVEN

Judging Iran, Part III

FRITZI AND THE AYATOLLAH

White & Case, like many firms, had a policy of mandatory retirement at age sixty-five. For me, that meant the axe would fall at the end of the year 2000. More than a year before that, the firm asked if I would stay affiliated in some capacity, which I was happy to do for five years as special counsel. But my days as a full-time advocate were coming to a close. Sitting in a rocking chair playing mahjong will never really be my style, so that meant I had to find some way to occupy myself in substantive ways.

In the spring of 2000, I received an urgent call from the State Department. Charles T. Duncan, one of the U.S. judges on the Iran–United States Claims Tribunal, had taken ill and been rushed to the hospital mere days before a scheduled hearing in a controversial "dual-national" case. Would I agree to substitute at the last minute? I did, and I soon found myself back in The Hague hearing the case of *Frederica Lincoln Riahi v. Islamic Republic of Iran* on the merits—the final claim of a national to be decided at the tribunal.

Frederica "Fritzi" Lincoln was an army brat, the daughter of Brig. Gen. George A. Lincoln, a senior military planner in both World War II and the Korean War.[1] While teaching English in Iran in the early 1970s, Frederica met her future husband, Manuchehr Riahi, a prominent conservationist who, beginning in the 1950s, had been responsible for the creation of Iran's national parks system.[2] Frederica and Manuchehr were married in Virginia in 1974 and thus, according to Iranian law, Frederica became an Iranian national.[3] As we have seen, however, the tribunal employed its own legal standard. As early as 1992, Chamber One had decided that Frederica's "dominant and effective nationality" was American (a conclusion from which, of course, the Iranian judge vigorously dissented).[4]

After Khomeini seized power in 1979, the revolutionary government issued decrees expropriating the property of certain prominent people associated with the shah. Manuchehr Riahi was one of them, but in his case the decree was applied not only against him but also against his "first-degree relatives," including his wife (and, indeed, his ex-wife).[5] Frederica had also held shares in the now-nationalized Bank of Tehran, and when she was forced out of Iran she left behind among other things an apartment under construction.[6]

Among other arguments, the Iranians said that Manuchehr, not Frederica, was the true owner of some of the property held in Frederica's name. To back up this defense, they relied upon not one but two obviously unreliable witnesses. One was a Mr. Nabavi, the managing director of one of the companies in which Frederica held shares. Nabavi's affidavit said that the shares were really the property of Manuchehr Riahi; but according to a separate report from his wife and a telephone recording of Nabavi himself, that testimony was not true. In fact, Iran had bullied Nabavi into giving false testimony by sending Revolutionary Guards to storm his home and steal his property, repeatedly interrogating him and his wife and having them evicted and fired from their jobs, rendering the family homeless and destitute. The revolutionary authorities had even stooped so low as to bar the family's children from attending school.[7]

Nabavi had at first held out against this intimidation, protesting that "we cannot sign this statement because at the top of this statement it says, 'We swear on the Koran to say the truth in the court,' and this is not the truth."[8] But they wore him down with still more threats, and at last, he had signed the false statement. How any independent and impartial judge could believe such obviously coerced testimony was to me totally unimaginable. But of course no Iranian judge of the tribunal was ever independent or impartial, and, as will be seen, the Finnish chairman of the chamber hearing the Riahi case was already known at the tribunal to be strangely, and consistently, exceedingly supportive of Iran's arguments.

The other witness was a less sympathetic character (in fact, he was an absolute bounder), but his testimony was no less coerced. An exiled member of the Iranian nobility, Abolfath Mahvi would in fact have been a royal had the shah's father not deposed his dynasty in 1925 (this minor detail did not stop Mahvi from insisting that sycophants refer to him as "prince").[9] Under the shah, he was infamous as a "five percenter," for the funds he skimmed off government contracts.[10] There was even testimony from a U.S. diplomat that Mahvi had collected ill-gotten money for the shah and been involved in procuring prostitutes for the monarch's personal enjoyment.[11] So corrupt was Mahvi that even the notoriously venal shah was forced, in 1976, to kick him out of the country.[12]

After the Iranian Revolution, Mahvi's name had been placed on a list of the "Corrupt of the Earth" (the revolutionaries were nothing if not dramatic) who were to face the firing squad if they ever set foot in Iran again. Apparently, the Iranians had ticked off this roster with efficiency, for by the time of his testimony, Mahvi believed he was the last one on the list still alive.[13] To coerce his testimony against the Riahis, Iran threatened Mahvi's daughter and grandson, who in response fled from Geneva to the United States.[14] As an added incentive, "Prince" Mahvi had a score to settle with Riahi, who had publicly called out his corruption.[15] His testimony was even more sickening than that of poor Mr. Nabavi. Whereas Nabavi at least had tried to be honest, before he was beaten down, evicted from his home, and impoverished by his tormentors, Mahvi had been corrupt for decades.

Hearing about Mahvi's corruption and the intimidation meted out to the Nabavis made me sick to my stomach. Iran should not have been allowed to get away with it. But unfortunately, the Riahi case was cursed with two of the worst judges in the history of the tribunal.

Assadollah Noori was not as bad as Kashani, but he was a hothead all the same. In deliberations, he was not averse to screaming insults in my face, provocations I was careful to disregard (as with all would-be bullies, this only made him angrier). Ultimately, however, whether they screamed or not, the Iranians could always be relied upon to vote (and vigorously dissent) in their government's interests. What really made the difference, as always, was the third-country chair of the chamber. Too bad, then, that Riahi had drawn the worst of the worst.

Bengt Broms, a Finn, was an international law professor of some repute. He had even been appointed by Finland as its judge *ad hoc* on the International Court of Justice in 1991 in a dispute it had with Denmark. For some reason, however, he seemed to be hopelessly biased in favor of Iran—so much so that we privately called him the "fourth Iranian vote." A recent data analysis supports this conclusion: of the tribunal's judgments, the average third-country judge sided with Iran 36 percent of the time, while Broms sided with Iran 67 percent of the time.[16]

Broms appeared ethically lacking in other ways, too. In his dissent in one large state-to-state case (A28, concerning Iran's eight-year failure to replenish the security account, which it had allowed to drop much lower than the $500 million minimum set by treaty), Broms revealed what had been said in deliberations, violating a fundamental precept of judicial conduct. In response, he first was chastised in writing by the president of the tribunal, who noted *"with regret* that Mr. Broms' Opinion *in a number of instances* contravenes the rule of confidentiality of the Tribunal's deliberations, as set forth in Note 2 to Article 31 [of] the Tribunal Rules."[17]

Broms was promptly challenged by the United States. The then–appointing authority for the tribunal, Judge Sir Robert Y. Jennings, a recent president of the International Court of Justice, declined to dismiss Broms outright on the ground that a judge "may be strictly and correctly impartial and independent *though massively indiscreet and forgetful of the rules.*" But Jennings nevertheless issued Broms a "yellow card," saying, "It seems right to make it clear to Judge Broms *that he should now resolve on no account to fall into this error again and to reflect that any sign of a repetition might change the balance of a decision in respect of any further challenge.*"[18]

Frederica Riahi technically prevailed in the case; but the sum she was awarded was less than a sixth of what it should have been. In fact, she was awarded the barest minimum, to which even Broms could not deny she was entitled. Meanwhile, in the award, Broms made clear his continued, inexplicable prejudice against American claimants. In addition to relying on the obviously coerced testimony of Mahvi and Nabavi, he rejected as "late filed" amendments to Riahi's statement of claim made at least three years before the hearing; refused to draw the required negative inference from Iran's repeated failure to produce evidence it had been ordered to produce; applied the higher criminal standard of proof to a civil claim; accepted a plainly fallacious argument about Iranian law; and incorrectly applied the standard set down in the dual nationality case.[19] In all, by my estimation, these errors left around $9 million in Iran's hands, money it had in effect stolen from Frederica Riahi.[20]

It was clear to me that Broms had arbitrarily predetermined this result and had worked hard to justify the lowest possible award. But what could Riahi do about it? She petitioned the full tribunal for a reconsideration, but the president said the full tribunal lacked jurisdiction and referred the matter back to Chamber One.[21] The problem with that, of course, was that Broms chaired Chamber One! So Riahi requested that Broms recuse himself from deciding on her request for reconsideration of the award—quite reasonably, one might think, since her complaints had to do with his own biased behavior!

Six months after submitting her requests to Chamber One, Riahi's counsel learned through Broms's law clerk that Chamber One "had met in deliberations on the pending Application and on the recusal request." Concluding that Broms was not recusing himself, Mrs. Riahi then challenged Broms before the appointing authority, seeking his forced removal from the case. The appointing authority, not surprisingly, found the challenge to be untimely, hence inadmissible.[22]

It is of course a cardinal rule of judicial conduct that *nemo iudex in causa sua*—"no one should be a judge in his or her own cause." But Broms, characteristically, saw no problem in his sitting in judgment over himself. And naturally, he saw no problem with the award he had rendered. In his ultimate decision proclaiming this, he even threw back in my face the polite, private letter I had sent him after the Riahi hearing ended back in 2000 congratulating him on his conduct.[23]

This was a low point for the tribunal; but by the time the Riahi award issued in 2003, the nature of the institution's work had changed utterly.

"BUT HE'S SUING US!"

It soon became clear that, sadly, Charles Duncan would not be well enough to return to the tribunal. He resigned effective the end of 2000 and would pass away from lung disease in 2004, after a remarkable career that had included, in addition to the tribunal, work on landmark desegregation cases in the District of Columbia and a stint as dean of Howard Law School.[24] That meant that an American seat was opening up—and at a critical juncture. Thanks to the mass settlement agreement, all claims of nationals below $250,000 had been removed from the tribunal; and *Riahi* itself was the last such claim worth more than $250,000. From here on out, the focus would be on the massive state-to-state disputes brought by Iran against the United States government. And when I say massive, I mean it: in one claim, B1, involving unfulfilled arms contracts concluded by the shah, Iran seeks more than twelve billion dollars in compensation.

The Iranians would be even more tenacious than usual when it came to such huge sums—especially in view of the still greater propaganda value they would carry if the United States were required to pay them.

These were weighty, legally complex cases, with a great deal of scope for argument. They would not be dealt with in panels of three judges but heard by the full tribunal of nine. To stand a chance in deliberations, the United States would need judges with deep knowledge of the issues and experience with the Iranians. Given my previous years at the tribunal, where I was also sitting as a substitute judge in *Riahi*, my name was in the frame.

But there were two problems. First, Bill Clinton was in charge, partisanship was intense, and his vice president, Al Gore, was running to succeed him. Could a Democratic administration in these circumstances appoint a Republican—one who had played a role in rescuing the conservative poster-boy Ronald Reagan?

The second problem was more situational. I learned later that when my name came up internally at the State Department, one of the deputy legal advisers had blurted out, "Charlie Brower?! But he's suing us!" Technically, this was true, as the NAFTA case of *Mondev v. United States*, discussed in a previous chapter, was still ongoing. Thankfully, however, the State Department didn't nix me outright. They gave me an opportunity to withdraw from the *Mondev* case, which I did. The client was not happy with the prospect of my turning the matter over to Abby Cohen Smutny, by then my longtime right hand, even though she would have done a terrific job. So I augmented the team with my friend Sir Arthur Watts KCMG QC, a former legal adviser of Her Majesty's Foreign and Commonwealth Office and an experienced advocate before the International Court of Justice. That resolved the issue.

Regarding optics, the ball was in the administration's court. I am told that Secretary of State Madeleine Albright tacitly approved my appointment but asked to be officially advised of my appointment by means of an "information memorandum" after the event (it being easier to ask forgiveness than permission). To avoid political blowback, the plan was to make a stealth appointment, under cover of the immediate aftermath of the 2000 presidential election. On election day itself, I was flying home from Britain, where I had been arranging a future visiting fellowship at Cambridge University. I spent the whole trip sipping champagne while praying the appointment would come through without a hitch.

The next day the news came: I was once again to be a full member of the Iran–United States Claims Tribunal, starting January 2001. Thank God! The election turned out to be even better cover than planned, as the result was so close it had to be decided for Bush in the Supreme Court. Nobody at the White House had ever been informed, and the media was not interested in writing stories about anything so trivial while epochal political struggles were unfolding in Washington. I was home free. And as it turned out, The Hague was again to be my home away from home for the next seventeen and a half years.

The nature of the work was a major contrast from my previous stint. In the 1980s, chambers of three churned through cases of nationals quickly. The schedule of two hearings per month for most months did not allow a lot of time for deliberations: we just had to get through them. Post-millennium, things are much different: all nine judges hear only one state-to-state case at a time—each Godzilla-like in its financial, factual, and legal proportions, not to mention its potential for causing political mayhem in Washington and/or Tehran.

In the course of my time at the tribunal following the millennium change, the temperature dropped slowly, and then it plunged. My Iranian colleagues—especially once all of them were swapped out midway through my lengthy second residence there—behaved more civilly. But they remain as dogged as ever. With nothing else on the schedule at any given time, there is little to keep them from dragging out the deliberations until they have made every argument they can think of in every way they can imagine. (I am reminded, once again, of Parviz Ansari's story about chasing the would-be burglar down the street and over the wall until he physically could go no farther.) Indeed, the greatest challenge for President Skubiszewski—who formerly served as Poland's first foreign minister when Lech Walesa's Solidarity had entered a coalition government—and his successors has been to coax the Iranians into ceasing their arguments so the tribunal can actually start to draft an award.

Besides, the Iranian judges enjoy at The Hague a lifestyle I imagine a legal academic or civil servant in Iran would find hard to come by. A small example: in the 1980s, all the luxury cars in the tribunal parking lot belonged to the Americans. Today, they belong to the Iranians. (In keeping with the spirit of our Dutch hosts, two of the three American judges commute exclusively by bicycle.) There is, in other words, little incentive for the Iranians to wrap up the tribunal's work anytime soon.

In addition to the B61 claim for military hardware marooned in the United States, the tribunal has as of this writing been in the middle of a number of other large and controversial cases for several years. In 2020 one of the more colorful ones produced a 691-page award in favor of Iran concerning the fate of Iranian properties ranging from antique violins, violas, cellos, and associated bows to rock-crushing machinery to archaeological artifacts excavated from the Neolithic settlement of Chogha Mish near the Iraqi border.[25]

The eight-hundred-pound gorilla among the outstanding claims is case B1—the claim of more than twelve billion dollars for unfulfilled contracts made under the Foreign Military Sales Program between the United States and the shah. In 2016, the parties settled part of B1 relating to funds left over in the shah's trust account at the Pentagon. Under the settlement, the United States agreed to pay Iran $1.7 billion; and in early 2016, a plane laden with the first four hundred million dollars, denominated in euros and Swiss francs, landed in Tehran.[26]

This was a controversial move, not least because the Obama administration appeared to link the payment to the release of American hostages; but it was important for the United States to do. That money belonged to Iran, and there was not a hundredth of a snowflake's chance in Hades that the tribunal would have held otherwise. In fact, Iran was claiming many multiples of that sum, and the longer the United States waited to pay it, the more the accrued interest would mount. But the political fallout from settling even one corner of one case demonstrates how politically delicate the tribunal's work has become.

"THE AYATOLLAH OF ARMY AVIATION"

By and large, the new Iranian judges were more knowledgeable and polite than the firebrands we had encountered early on. But there was one big exception: Assadollah Noori, whom I had encountered in the *Rihai* case. Appointed to the tribunal in 1987, Noori remained on the court well into the twenty-first century and would resort to screaming blue murder at the drop of a hat. Back in the 1980s, a United States Army major general in charge of Army helicopter forces addressed us in The Hague in a separate part of B1 involving the performance of Bell helicopters purchased and used by Iran. This separate part of B1 was being heard by the full tribunal of nine judges, including Noori. This general was straight out of Central Casting: whereas his Iranian equivalents wore civvies, he showed up in full dress uniform, his medals armor-plating his chest.

Sometime before he spoke, the Iranian representatives paid him customary compliments. When the general stood up to speak, he began: "Now that I have been proclaimed 'the ayatollah of army aviation' . . ."

Not the smartest opening gambit, to say the least. Noori went berserk, shouting: "You do not take the ayatollah's name in vain!" He was bright red, and for a moment it seemed he might vault over the bench and throttle the general. I had visions of him swinging the general around by his medals, the way Kashani had swung Mangard by his necktie. Thankfully, Noori managed to calm down before it came to fisticuffs, but it was touch-and-go.

Much later, Noori's shenanigans, like those of Kashani, proved his undoing. Under the shah, Iran had purchased billions of dollars' worth of military hardware from the United States. When the revolution took place, some of this hardware had been paid for but not delivered. In addition, some Iranian equipment was in the United States for repair or upgrade. Iran-Contra notwithstanding, the United States was not about to export weapons to the Islamic Republic of Iran; in fact, such exports were banned. So all of that matériel was frozen in place.

In case B61, heard over sixty days between September 2005 and March 2007 by all nine judges, including Noori, Iran sought delivery of a large volume of the disputed hardware—which was not going to happen—or damages of more than two billion dollars. Evidently, Noori did not like the way the wind was blowing, because on November 1, 2006, with thirty-two hearing days left, he tendered his resignation from the tribunal.[27]

His replacement arrived shortly thereafter; but he had, of course, not participated in any of the many, many hearings on B61. Under the Mosk Rule (discussed in a previous chapter), members who resign are obliged to see cases in which they had participated in merits hearings through the ensuing deliberations and issuance of the award, in order to limit disruptions to the tribunal's business. I had done this myself for years in the fifteen cases still outstanding when I left the tribunal in 1988.

A majority of the tribunal voted to force Noori to continue in office until the hearing would be over and then insisted he comply with the Mosk Rule. But Noori flat-out refused to comply, "indicat[ing] informally his dissatisfaction with [the] financial terms" set by the tribunal—in other words, he tried to extort a pay raise for himself![28] And guess who quite vocally supported Noori's demand for higher compensation than had ever been authorized for Mosk Rule duty? Yes, none other than the "fourth Iranian vote," Judge Broms!

At this point, we called his bluff. As a tribunal, we decided that Noori had "removed himself from application of the Mosk Rule as regards Case No. B61."[29] No return to The Hague, and no more money. So much for Noori and his antics.

The United States then argued, unadvisedly in my view, that case B61 should move ahead with a truncated tribunal of eight members, including just two Iranians instead of the usual three.[30] But under Skubiszewski's leadership, the tribunal decided that the case should proceed to include the new Iranian judge, who could bring himself up to speed by reading the transcripts—which the rest of us would all have to do anyway to refresh our memories in such a drawn-out case.[31] In fact, I myself drafted the tribunal's decision, as it was clear to me that it would be utterly wrong, diplomatically and practically, for the tribunal to proceed without continuing equal representation of the two states' parties. Otherwise a crisis surely would befall us.

About two weeks after the tribunal issued its award in B61 on July 17, 2009, Iran submitted to the tribunal a request for revision of that award, alleging it was based on "fundamental errors of procedure" and "manifest errors of law."[32] But the request was a lost cause. The tribunal unanimously decided to deny Iran's request for revision of the B61 award.

"Unanimous?" you say. "Can I be hearing right? The Iranians voted against their government?"

Yes, this is the only example in all of my years since 1983 of sitting on the tribunal that there ever was even one Iranian vote, let alone three, against Iran. I believe it was condoned by Tehran because President Skubiszewski had died, and his replacement, Hans van Houtte of Belgium, had made known his skepticism regarding requests for revision. This was the first matter on which he and the new Iranian judges were sitting, and the Iranians clearly calculated that it would be wise to please the new president by joining all the other judges in this exceptional manner.

From time to time, however, tensions at the tribunal still boil over. The United States at one point challenged an Iranian member who had sat on a panel outside the tribunal with the former U.S. judge Richard Mosk—a bone-headed challenge that the United States rightly lost. In the aftermath, the Iranians were looking for a way to get back at the United States, and unfortunately, I wandered into their crosshairs.

In 2010, French jurist Pierre-Marie Dupuy had been offered the tribunal presidency—replacing the deceased Skubiszewski. (The position eventually went to Belgium's Hans van Houtte.) Both governments were to write to Dupuy urging him to accept the offer. The Iranians did so, but the letter from Harold Koh, the State Department legal adviser, was delayed. Separately, I wrote to Dupuy, a dear friend with whom I had sat in an arbitration, also encouraging him to accept. Dupuy soon decided, for personal reasons, not to accept the appointment. His letter to the secretary-general gave his reasons and mentioned he was grateful for the congratulations from the Iranian government and from his friend, Judge Brower, which the secretary-general passed along to the two agents of the state parties.

"Gotcha!" the Iranians said. "Brower is acting as an agent of the U.S. government!" It was a stupid challenge, and it was soon rejected. But it did make me the only American judge ever challenged by Iran, which I wear as a badge of honor!

More than twenty years after my second appointment (and almost forty years after my first!), I am still a member of the Iran–United States Claims Tribunal, currently under the Mosk Rule. When I tell people that, the most common response is "The Iran–United States Claims Tribunal? You still exist?!" We do indeed, and we are still untangling the complex relationship between the two countries, terminated so abruptly by revolution in 1979.

Considering the tensions between the two countries since the tribunal began hearing the jumbo state-to-state claims in earnest in 2001—a period, recall, that has included, among other lowlights, successive rounds of sanctions, Ahmadinejad's saber-rattling, Bush's "Axis of Evil" speech, Iranian-sponsored attacks on U.S. troops in Iraq, the rise and collapse (and rise again?) of the P5+1 nuclear accords, and the American assassination of Qassem Soleimani—it is impressive that the Iran–United States Claims Tribunal has endured at all.

We have addressed the reasons for its startling longevity in a previous chapter. But to my mind, it would be better now for the United States to rip off the Band-Aid: reach a one-and-done settlement with Iran, take the momentary propaganda hit, and move on. Otherwise, it won't be long until these hoary old claims reach their sixth decade, and that thought is absurd. This turkey, as the Brits say, would vote for Christmas.

SAME CITY, DIFFERENT VENUE

During the life of the tribunal, Iran has also pursued the United States in litigation before another body headquartered in The Hague: the UN's principal judicial arm, the International Court of Justice. In 1988, Iran sued the United States under two international civil aviation treaties after the U.S. cruiser *Vincennes* mistakenly shot down Iran Air flight 655 over the Persian Gulf. All two hundred and ninety people on board perished. The parties eventually settled that case. In 1992, Iran again took the United States to the ICJ, this time under the 1955 Treaty of Amity, alleging damage to Iran's offshore oil platforms during the Tanker War of 1987–88. The court eventually ruled, in 2003, that the 1955 treaty had not been breached.

In 2016, Iran sued the United States once more, this time over a U.S. program that used frozen Iranian assets to pay victims of terrorism, allegedly sponsored by Iran; the case is referred to as *Certain Iranian Assets*. Joan Donoghue, the U.S. member of the court—and, from February 6, 2021, its president—had a conflict of interest, having worked on Iran sanctions while at the State Department; unlike Bengt Broms, Joan *did* see a need to recuse herself.

I was delighted when my old friend and first law clerk David Caron was appointed to replace Donoghue as judge *ad hoc*. By then David had served as a world-renowned professor of international law at Berkeley, a UNCC commissioner, dean of the Dickson Poon School of Law at King's College London, a much-sought-after arbitrator, and, as of December 2, 2015, my successor as a titular judge of the Iran–United States Claims Tribunal. In February of 2018, before the case could be heard, David suddenly fell ill and, at the age of sixty-five, died. His passing was a stunning, tragic loss—to his family and friends, to international law, and to the world.

Following the Trump administration's withdrawal from the Joint Comprehensive Plan of Action (JCPOA), i.e., the nuclear deal, Iran brought a further case against the United States at the ICJ in summer 2018, attacking the United States' reimposition of the sanctions that had been suspended by that agreement. The second case is titled *Alleged Violations of the 1955 Treaty of Amity, Economic Relations, and Consular Rights*.

I am certain that had David been alive, he would have been appointed in this case as well. Instead, I became his unwilling heir in both cases. Thus I acquired, by default, the honor of having been appointed judge *ad hoc* of the ICJ more times than any other American.[33]

Although I had contributed substantially to an ICJ submission on behalf of the Hashemite Kingdom of Jordan, my work had all been done in secret (more on that later). I had also advised Denmark in the case in which the infamous Judge Broms was appointed judge *ad hoc* by Finland, appearing as an advocate before the court only twice. The first time was in 1992, after the United States and Scotland charged two Libyans with carrying out the bombing of Pan Am flight 103 over Lockerbie in 1988 and sought their extradition. Qaddafi's government refused, claiming that it had "submitted the case to its competent authorities for the purpose of prosecution." Had this action been genuine, it would have been enough to satisfy the requirements of the Montreal Sabotage Convention— the same one I had helped negotiate twenty-one years before.

But, of course, the Libyan "prosecution" was a sham; indeed, the two suspects were most likely Libyan intelligence agents. The United States and United Kingdom pursued, and obtained, sanctions against Qaddafi at the Security Council. Libya sued both countries at the ICJ, seeking provisional measures to prevent them from taking any further action to impose sanctions. This political gesture on Libya's part had no nutritional value legally. If a state could restrain a permanent member of the Security Council from voting in that body, it would make a mockery of the whole system of international law—but it required a response.

Quite a scramble ensued. I happened to be in Moscow, attending my son Chip's wedding to his first wife, a Russian medical doctor, at the drably named (though actually quite opulent) Moscow Wedding Palace Number One. I received a call from "L," the principal deputy legal adviser of the State Department, saying that the legal adviser at State, Edwin Williamson, theretofore a partner of Sullivan & Cromwell, was unable to attend the hearing because of a family emergency. Rosalyn Higgins QC, a barrister and London School of Economics professor, would be representing the UK together with Scotland's Lord Advocate. (Three years later Rosalyn would be elected the first woman judge at the ICJ; she later became its first woman president.) Libya would be represented by Ian Brownlie QC, a barrister and the top international law professor at Oxford, as well as by Eric Suy, a former undersecretary general and legal counsel at the United Nations.

I was added to this glittering roster, "L" explained, because I would "add some class"—not least because of my history with the Montreal Sabotage Convention. (Ed Williamson was able to attend in the end, but he kindly kept me on the team.) After clearing this new assignment with White & Case (and with my UNCC client Enka, since I would have to delay our meeting in Istanbul), I addressed the ICJ for the first time on March 27, 1992. The substance was technical, entirely focused on the Montreal Convention. Libya said that the convention compelled the parties to settle their dispute solely by arbitration—not through sanctions. We didn't accept that reading; but even if it were accurate, I argued, the convention required a period of negotiation before the "invitation to arbitrate" could be issued, and the obligation to arbitrate kicked in after the passage of six months.[34] In the end, only one judge (Ni Zhengyu of China, as it happened) bought my argument.[35] But the United States and United Kingdom, quite rightly, prevailed against Libya on other grounds, and the sanctions stayed.

My second appearance was for one of my favorite state clients, Costa Rica, in a human rights case that I will discuss in a future chapter. In 2014, I had been honored by an appointment to the ICJ as judge *ad hoc*, not by the United States but by Colombia. Nicaragua and Colombia, which face each other across a southwestern corner of the Caribbean Sea, had gotten into a dispute over who held economic rights over some of those waters.

The long title of the case, *Question of the Delimitation of the Continental Shelf between Nicaragua and Colombia beyond 200 nautical miles from the Nicaraguan Coast*, betrays its extreme technicality. Bear in mind that this is the sort of thing that has frequently led to war. One study counted ninety-four "militarized attempts to settle" maritime disputes between 1900 and 2001, observing that such claims were "significantly less likely" to be settled peacefully than were territorial claims.[36] Conflict over maritime sovereignty remains a grave threat, as anyone who studies disputes in the South China or Black seas is acutely aware. So any attempt to settle such a dispute via "boring" technical legal disputation is heartily to be welcomed.

The ICJ statute says that if the court includes no judge of a party's nationality, they may appoint a judge *ad hoc* for the duration of the case.[37] Judges *ad hoc* promise to be independent and impartial, not behind-the-scenes advocates for their appointing party.[38] As one vote among sixteen or seventeen (the fifteen titular judges plus one or two judges *ad hoc*), they are unlikely by themselves to sway the result. Their purpose, rather, is to ensure that, in deliberations, the appointing party's case will be heard, understood, and considered by the other judges. (Much the same rules apply to party-appointed international arbitrators, as we will see.)

Colombia had appointed me in one of two separate but linked cases; David Caron was appointed in the other one, and all the judges in the two cases held joint deliberations on a common jurisdictional issue. Both David and I found sitting on the court every bit as dry and technical as speaking to it. In the courtroom, judges do not interrupt advocates to test their case the way they would in the United States; they remain silent until the lawyer has finished speaking, then eventually pose a smattering of questions in writing. In the deliberation chamber, judges behave in a collegiate manner. Everyone is exceedingly polite, and it is common for some of the judges to have lunch together at the Restaurant des Juges in their office annex to the Peace Palace.

This could scarcely be more different from the fissiparous atmosphere of the Iran–United States Claims Tribunal, to which David was also appointed during the course of proceedings in *Nicaragua v. Colombia*. But again, that is a good thing. Nobody should wish for states to settle their disputes in the old-fashioned way: which is to say, by force of arms. The more international disputes can be reduced to matters of law, the better. As Albert Einstein allegedly observed, "No worthy problem is ever solved on the plane of its original conception."

IRAN GETS LITIGIOUS

That brings us to the two Iranian cases against the United States that I inherited from David after his death in 2018. By then, of course, the Trump administration was in power. The White House was out for vengeance on anyone in the Republican party who had signed a so-called "never Trump" letter—and there were many among the foreign policy establishment. So to get the gig, I had to answer two questions:

1. Would I do it?
2. Did my name appear on any White House blacklist of Never-Trumpers?

I have no idea how many candidates fell at this hurdle, but my answer to the first question was straightforward and unhesitating: "I will do it for my country." As to the political question, ever since my 1983 appointment to the Iran–United States Claims Tribunal, I have thought no judge should express any views publicly on politics, a rule observed even in the fevered atmosphere of 2016. So I was in!

Lacking an elected member of the court, Iran got a judge *ad hoc* for the cases. They chose a law professor named Djamchid Momtaz, whom I have always found well-informed, thoughtful, and civilized, like his recent colleagues on the Iran–United States Claims Tribunal.

The first of the two *Iran v. United States* cases to be heard was *Alleged Violations of the 1955 Treaty of Amity, Economic Relations, and Consular Rights*, which we Americans dubbed "The Treaty of Enmity"—an instrument the United States would get around to denouncing only in October 2018. The real subject matter of the case, however, was the Joint Comprehensive Plan of Action—the nuclear deal between Iran and six major powers, including the United States. Signed in 2015, the JCPOA has as one of its principal purposes "the comprehensive lifting of . . . multilateral and national sanctions related to Iran's nuclear program." On May 8, 2018, President Trump withdrew the United States from the JCPOA and directed the immediate reimposition of those sanctions.[39] Iran sought a judgment from the ICJ compelling the United States to cancel the sanctions.

Though filed second, this case went first because Iran sought an order of provisional measures—the international law equivalent of a preliminary injunction—requiring the United States to provide various forms of humanitarian relief to the Iranian people. I joined a unanimous court in issuing the requested order, as the United States had stated to the court that under its law and regulations it already was providing the requested relief.

Thereafter, in a second hearing, the United States made five objections to the court's jurisdiction and the admissibility of Iran's case. With my agreement, the court unanimously rejected three of the United States' objections to jurisdiction. I alone, however, accepted one of its objections to jurisdiction and its objection to admissibility. I penned a Separate, Partly Concurring and Partly Dissenting, Opinion in my usual strongly worded style.

My first and simplest point was that the 1955 treaty contained an exception for "the application of measures . . . relating to fissionable materials, the radioactive byproducts thereof, or the sources thereof." I concluded that this nuclear exception was straightforward enough to apply at the preliminary stage—not least because Iran had admitted on numerous occasions, both in official statements and in the course of the proceedings before the court itself, that the relevant sanctions were indeed "nuclear related." These admissions alone should, I felt, have been enough to torpedo the case then and there.[40]

Second, I felt Iran's claim counted as an abuse of process under international law. The law on this matter is scanty; in my written opinion, I called it "the Holy Grail of international law as addressed by the Court, a storied mystery without dimensions, shape, or content."[41] The court had often spoken of "abuse of process" but had never dismissed a case on that ground. Nevertheless, if ever there were a case for its application, I felt, this was it.

Why? Simple: the JCPOA was a political document, not a legally binding one. If Iran's claim were upheld, it would become legally binding on the United States by virtue of the court's judgment. That alone, in my view, constituted an abuse of the process of the court. Such a judgment would disincentivize all states from seeking to resolve their differences via non–legally binding declarations (which, given domestic politics, could in some instances be the only means available, as indeed was the case with the JCPOA) because the other side could simply go to the ICJ and have a political statement converted into a legal obligation.[42] The resulting diminution in peaceful dispute settlement would make the world less safe. If that is not an attempted abuse of process, I am not sure what is! My fellow judges, alas, did not buy either argument, so *Alleged Violations* will go to the merits.

The other case, *Certain Iranian Assets*, arose out of United States' counterterrorism legislation. Iran has been designated a "state sponsor of terrorism" ever since Hezbollah (alleged to be an Iranian proxy) bombed the U.S. Marine barracks in Beirut, Lebanon, in 1984. Since 1996, federal law has removed sovereign immunity from any state so designated. American victims of terrorism and their families have therefore sued Iran under federal law. Iran typically does not appear in these cases, because it says it is immune; but under federal law millions of dollars have been awarded against Iran in judgments. Over the years, Congress and the executive branch have expanded the categories of Iranian assets against which the judgments can be enforced. The final straw for Iran came in 2012, when roughly two billion dollars of assets of its central bank, held at the New York Federal Reserve, were made available for distribution to claimants holding judgments against it. Iran alleges that this, too, violated the then-still-extant 1955 Treaty of Amity.

The United States said the ICJ lacked jurisdiction on three grounds and was inadmissible on two. The court granted one objection to jurisdiction, denied one objection to admissibility, and either referred the remaining objections to jurisdiction and admissibility to the merits or acknowledged them as potential defenses to the merits. I sided with my government on only one point and was joined in this view by judges from Australia, Italy, and Slovakia (the last in the person of Peter Tomka, my friend who had tried to persuade his government to settle the *CSOB* megamillions case).

I actually voted *against* the United States on four out of its five points, including its allegation of "abuse of process" and its invocation of the 1955 treaty's exception for matters having to do with "peace and security." Unlike the nuclear exception in the other case, I agreed this was too complicated to be dealt with at the preliminary phase; it would have to be argued out at the merits stage. In other words, I certainly did not behave as a "captive" of my government. The practical result is that part of that case now must proceed to the merits phase.

I, however, will not be on the bench hearing any of those cases. On the occasion of my eighty-seventh birthday last year I resigned from all three. I deemed it inappropriate, indeed unethical, given the actuarial tables, irrespective of current excellent health, to subject my appointors to the high statistical risk of my becoming incapacitated or dying with my boots on, and thereby depriving them of the uninterrupted service of their appointee during the merits phase as judge *ad hoc*. The consequences of United States Supreme Court Justice Ruth Bader Ginsburg dying at eighty-seven were fresh in my mind. I felt I would be doing my appointors a favor by making room for someone more certain to see their cases all the way through the merits to the eventual judgment. Knowledgeable colleagues hailed my decision as "done with judiciousness, responsibility and grace."

I am proud of having been the most-appointed American ever to serve as ICJ judge *ad hoc* of the only four Americans ever to be so appointed theretofore by any state. All three others were international law professors at distinguished American law schools. And I was honored in the aftermath of my resignation to receive a personal, hand-signed letter from Secretary of State Antony Blinken, which after rehearsing my half-century in public service, concluded:

> *I extend my tremendous appreciation to you for the decades of service you have provided to the United States and the international community through the practice of international law. . . . [Y]ou have left your mark on many international legal issues. This is a remarkable record of service for which your nation is deeply grateful. You have served your country . . . and the furtherance of international law with great distinction, and my*

deepest thanks and best wishes go with you as you move forward in this next phase of your life.

And under his signature Secretary Blinken, still writing with his pen, added "With admiration and gratitude."

At one point in the past, I was apparently in the frame for nomination and election by the UN General Assembly and the Security Council to the ICJ; but in retrospect, this is another of those cases in life where I am glad I did not succeed. With the volume of matters on the court's docket, a seat on the ICJ is no longer the part-time occupation it once was; on the contrary, it is today a full-time job and then some. The court has even had to change its rules to stop members accepting appointments as international arbitrators, except in rare state-to-state cases. The Iran–United States Claims Tribunal—where I continue to serve to this day—is on the other hand very much part time at this point. And that freed me up to do other work, including arguing cases before the UNCC, sitting *ad hoc* at the ICJ, and, perhaps most significant, sitting as an international arbitrator. That work is the subject of the next chapter.

CHAPTER TWELVE

International Arbitrator, Part I

CROUCHING PRESIDENT, HIDDEN WITNESS

Ever since I had learned about the burgeoning field of international arbitration decades ago, I had wanted not only to argue cases before arbitral tribunals; I had also seen myself, one day, sitting as an arbitrator. As we have seen, the cases could be huge, and the issues complex and fascinating. Best of all, as an arbitrator, like a judge, you are not beholden to a client. Your only duty is to untangle the facts and apply the law to the best of your ability. This, I thought, would be the capstone to my career.

The first problem with that ambition is the strong likelihood that as a partner of a global law firm like White & Case you will be conflicted out of most appointments, because someone somewhere in the firm will have represented one of the parties at some point. That happened to me once on account of fifteen thousand dollars the firm billed a client for a small job in Saudi Arabia. Another proffered appointment cratered when it turned out that, unbeknownst to anyone in the firm involved in international arbitration, another partner had advised a bank that had been approached to finance the case for one of the parties. For this reason alone, I had to turn down something like 95 percent of potential arbitral appointments while I was still a partner at White & Case.

Worse still, the firm disliked such appointments because your activity as an arbitrator might wind up conflicting corporate partners out of substantial future business. I remember receiving a highly unpleasant phone call to this effect from a corporate partner. The respondent in a case where I'd been appointed by the claimant was the Thai manufacturer of ceiling fan slats—a portfolio company of Lehman Brothers, a client of the firm. I wound up having to resign from that arbitral panel, and this was *after* I had left the firm's conflicts system!

Finally, firms don't like partners sitting as arbitrators. They become lone rangers—meaning the firm doesn't get to send out platoons of associates in their wake. Every hour you spend as an arbitrator is an hour for which the firm doesn't get to bill a lot of associate time. The argument my fellow arbitration partners would make to the firm was that having experience on the other side of the bench enables us to market our services as counsel more successfully because we understood arbitration from every angle. Similarly, we were touting the fact that we represented both corporate claimants investing abroad and host countries alike. I thought that was a good argument. But overcoming the firm's objections proved an uphill battle, and I managed to sit on only a handful of panels while still a partner.

One such case did achieve notoriety, although not for the reasons I might have wished. Instead, *Vacuum Salt Products v. Ghana* has become known for two quirks: a no-show president and a disappearing witness.

Vacuum Salt was founded in Ghana by Gerassimos Panagiotopulos, a Greek national who had fled there when Greece was invaded during World War II.[1] The business grew until, in 1992, it was (allegedly) expropriated by the Ghanaian government.[2] The problem for Mr. Panagiotopulos was that he had already sold most of the shares to local Ghanaian interests; only 20 percent remained in his hands.[3] ICSID tribunals only had jurisdiction over disputes between one contracting state and the national of another contracting state. The issue was whether

Vacuum Salt, being only 20 percent foreign owned, qualified under this provision. (In the end, it did not.)

Vacuum Salt appointed me. Ghana appointed Kamal Hossain, a Bangladeshi who had been a prime mover in his country's struggle for independence from Pakistan and later served as its foreign minister. (As if this were not enough, Hossain held a doctorate in international law from Oxford.)[4] To preside over the Vacuum Salt ICSID arbitral tribunal, I recommended Sir Robert Jennings, then serving as ICJ president. The venue was to be the Peace Palace in The Hague, the same building where the ICJ itself sits.

At the time, there was controversy over whether it was proper for ICJ judges to sit as arbitrators on the side. In a case between France and Australia, one of the lawyers had famously castigated the judges for allowing lucrative arbitrations to distract them from their work on the court. There was a measure of jealousy involved, too, for whereas some judges made piles of money as arbitrators, others were never asked to serve in that capacity. The practice was finally done away with in 2018, when the court's docket had become so full that side gigs had grown impractical.[5]

When the court's registrar, Eduardo Valencia-Ospina, got wind of Robbie Jennings's appointment to preside over the Vacuum Salt ICSID arbitral tribunal, he urged Jennings to resign from that tribunal. Valencia-Ospina believed the spectacle of the ICJ president chairing a relatively minor ICSID arbitration down the hall would diminish the court. Robbie told me he wanted to resign.

While I understood Valencia-Ospina's concern, I didn't think it would be a good idea for Robbie to resign outright from the Vacuum Salt ICSID arbitration, especially as the tribunal had been asked to order time-sensitive provisional measures to halt procedures already ongoing in Ghana. If Robbie were to resign from that ICSID arbitration, it would throw everything into disarray and reflect poorly on Robbie, on ICSID, and on the ICJ. Nobody would win.

I took him to dinner in The Hague to hash out a compromise. We decided that he would remain as president of the tribunal but inform the parties of his "unavailability" to attend hearings. That way, he would avoid messing up the arbitration while not appearing publicly as tribunal president. As a side benefit, this made me the acting president under the ICSID rules because I was appointed first.

The disappearing witness was the company secretary of Vacuum Salt, Leone de Graft. In an unusual move, she had provided written statements to both sides. In the event, neither saw fit to call her to give oral testimony, but the tribunal wanted to hear from her. At the start of the hearing, we had her flown out to The Hague and set her up in a hotel. On day one, she arrived promptly, only to be told we were not ready for her. The second day, it was the same story. When we finally were ready to hear de Graft's testimony, she was nowhere to be found.

For help finding the disappearing witness, I paid a visit to the secretary-general of the Permanent Court of Arbitration, P.J.H. Jonkman, a Dutch diplomat whom I knew well. Jonkman had served as his country's ambassador to the UK and, before that, grand master of the royal household. In other words, he had all the right contacts to locate anyone in the Netherlands.

We found de Graft in a fleabag hotel in the wrong part of town. Kamal and I showed up at her room at seven in the morning and expressed concern for her whereabouts (we thought this would play better with her than annoyance at her abscondment). We had breakfast together and accompanied her to the Peace Palace to give her testimony, which in the end turned out to be, in a word, useless. Evidently there was a reason why neither side had bothered to call her as a witness!

"THE REIGNING KING"

After I left White & Case, my work as an arbitrator exploded. At the height of my practice, I worked on around twenty-five cases in every two-year period—averaging more than one per month! That was comparable to my caseload at the Iran–United States Claims

Tribunal—except that, as an independent arbitrator, I did not enjoy the support of the full bureaucracy that the tribunal possesses. In recognition of my diligent industry, in 2013 *American Lawyer* magazine anointed me "the reigning king of international arbitrators." I can't say I was thrilled by the autocratic implications of that title, but it was nice to get the acknowledgement!

So I consider myself qualified to opine on the state and future of international arbitration. Unfortunately, I can't talk in any detail about the bulk of my cases, because confidentiality still veils many of them. For the most part, I strongly believe the veil should be lifted, and to some extent it is dissipating, though slowly, as we will see. The cases I discuss below have all been made public by one means or another.

Fundamentally, international arbitration is a means of protecting investors against the risks of doing business overseas. That is why arbitration clauses are often found in bilateral investment treaties (BITs) as well as in multilateral treaties such as NAFTA, its successor USMCA, and the Energy Charter Treaty, alongside safeguards against expropriation and other kinds of mistreatment. In many countries—and most often in the ones that need investment the most—local courts cannot be relied upon to dispense justice swiftly or impartially. Even in places where justice is efficient and independent, the government is capable of changing the law to the detriment of investors. This happened, for example, to the Swedish nuclear energy firm Vattenfall doing business in Germany, as we will see.

When the going gets tough, there is little political cost to treating foreigners poorly. In fact, there is potentially a great deal to gain, as we saw with the expropriation of AIG Nigeria by the Obasanjo regime in the 1970s. But even when states act honorably, their motivations are too often fundamentally different from those of private parties, because they include much stronger doses of politics, public opinion, national security, economic management, and so on. And states have many more levers they can pull to make investors' lives difficult.

One of my early arbitrations illustrates well why such protection is necessary.

THE "STRATEGIC REQUIREMENTS" OF MR. ORBÁN

Like most countries suddenly released from Soviet-sponsored oppression after the fall of the Berlin Wall, Hungary in the 1990s witnessed an economic miracle. As part of its wholesale modernization program, the government hired the Cypriot offshoot of a Canadian architecture firm, ADC, to renovate the Budapest airport, build a new terminal, and operate the airport. This worked smoothly for a while, until the notorious Viktor Orbán was elected to his first term as prime minister in 1998. As with many authoritarians, Orbán sought to strengthen state power via strategic expropriation of profitable industries.[6] With passenger numbers rising at a meteoric rate and Budapest becoming a hub for travel around eastern Europe and beyond, the new government began licking its chops. In December 2001, it nationalized the airport by legislation, citing "strategic requirements of the state," together with a vague and unconvincing reference to European Union convergence criteria (Hungary would eventually join the EU in 2004, with the airport back in private hands).[7] Predictably, Hungary offered ADC no compensation.

The hearing took place in London in January 2006. Two witnesses from the Orbán government openly lied, claiming not to have known about the planned nationalization until the final legislation was adopted—despite being in charge of the entity created to carry out the nationalization![8]

When it came to the law, Hungary claimed a vague "right to regulate," which would have made having a BIT nonsense in the first place. As we put it in the award, "It is one thing to say that an investor shall conduct its business in compliance with the host state's domestic laws and regulations. It is quite another to imply that the investor must also be ready to accept whatever the host state decides to do to it."[9] Hungary even had the gall to try arguing that its agreement with ADC—the one Hungary had signed and from which it had drawn benefits for years—had been unlawful under Hungarian law![10]

Hungary had no case. The Orbán regime had breached nearly every investor protection. It never articulated a convincing public interest, nor did it afford due process. It singled out ADC for discrimination, offered no compensation, and generally acted unreasonably, unfairly, inequitably, and "with callous disregard of the Claimants' contractual and financial rights."[11]

The upshot: not only had Hungary expropriated ADC's investment, but it had done so unlawfully. The applicable BIT, like most treaties of its kind, gave the standard of compensation only for a lawful expropriation, leaving customary international law to govern here. That meant we fell back on the *Chorzów Factory* case, which says that if the value of the investment goes up between the expropriation and the date of the award, the claimant gets the higher value.

In most cases prior to *ADC v. Hungary*, the difference between these two standards had been almost academic, because state interference typically spells doom for the value of any commercial asset. But since Orbán took over the airport, footfall there had nearly doubled and was still rising. The airline trade association, the IATA, was projecting Hungary as the third-fastest-growing market in the world during much of that period.[12] The valuation, therefore, would have to be done at the date of the award.[13] And because the case was public, we had a chance to put on record a precedent for how to perform such a valuation. All told, we awarded ADC some $83.8 million—a sum that, in view of Hungary's desultory approach throughout, included ADC's costs of the proceedings.[14]

NOT-OK-DOW

Investments can have their plugs pulled for less pernicious reasons, too. In late 2008, the Michigan-based Dow Chemical Company signed a contract with the petrochemical arm of the Kuwaiti government to form K-Dow, a 50-50 joint venture that would have been the world's largest manufacturer of polyethylene, a plastic used in everything from grocery bags to bullet-proof vests.[15] Dow wanted to divest itself so far as possible of what was a commodity business, subject to the up-and-down swings of all commodities markets, and instead to increase production of specialty chemicals. For its part, Kuwait saw itself gaining market share via commodity production.

To uphold its end of the bargain, Dow bought Rohm & Haas, a 15,400-employee specialty chemical company based in Philadelphia, for $15.7 billion. The catch was that Dow had outside financing for only around half that price; the remainder was to come from the K-Dow deal.[16] But exactly one month after signing the contract to form K-Dow, the Kuwaiti government, facing an embarrassing revolt in parliament, backed out on the eve of the closing.[17] With a $7.5 billion hole in its balance sheet and already reeling from the 2008 financial crisis, Dow Chemical—a 111-year-old Fortune 100 company with around 46,000 employees at the time, thousands of them in its home state of Michigan—was left flirting with bankruptcy.[18]

Dow started proceedings against Kuwait, based not on any BIT but on the joint venture agreement itself. As it happened, Shearman & Sterling represented Dow—the same team I had beaten so soundly in the *CSOB* "Czech megamillions" case years before. In what must be accounted one of the sincerest acts of flattery I have ever received, the Shearman & Sterling team appointed me to the tribunal in *Dow Chemical v. Kuwait*. The hearing took place in London, and the other two members were distinguished English lawyers: Kenneth Rokison QC, as tribunal president, and Lord Hoffmann, the South African–born recently retired second senior law lord.

It was clear that Kuwait had breached the agreement; the only question was the level of damages. We issued an award that made *CSOB v. Slovakia* look like a county court slip-and-fall case, awarding Dow some $2.161 billion in damages plus $318 million in interest and costs (the parties eventually agreed that Kuwait would pay just the principal, which it proceeded to do).[19] This peaceful post-award agreement came about because the two parties had other, ongoing business relations that they desired to maintain. Thus, while K-Dow may have been strangled in the crib, Dow and Kuwait remained fast friends: indeed, as of this writing they are still in at least one joint venture together, a company called Equate with the tagline "Partners in Success."[20]

ARGENTINA COMES UNPEGGED

Sometimes, a state's motives are more understandable, but its actions no less harmful to investors. Back in 2000 and 2001, while I was wrapping up my career as an advocate and hanging out my arbitrator's shingle, Argentina seemed to be imploding. During the 1990s, the country had liberalized its economy. It privatized many state-owned businesses; clamped down on tax evasion; lowered trade tariffs; signed dozens of BITs with various countries; and created a new currency, the peso, with its value pegged to the U.S. dollar at a one-to-one ratio in order to encourage exports and investment.[21]

This worked well. Investment poured in, and in less than a decade, Argentina's GDP more than doubled.[22] But starting in the third quarter of 1998, the Asian financial crisis spread via Brazil to Argentina, causing a recession that was to last for the next four years.[23] On May 29, 2000, Argentina's new president, Fernando de la Rúa, announced spending cuts of $1 billion. The same day, twenty thousand demonstrators took to the streets. The protests only escalated from there, eventually turning into riots in which dozens of people died.

Spending cuts are invariably unpopular. Indeed, unwillingness to make them is one of the reasons governments get into dire fiscal straits in the first place. But if you want to enact cuts that people will actually accept, expropriating foreigners is one of the few ways to do it. So in such circumstances it is no surprise to find big-time international investors in the crosshairs. The result was a flood of international claims against Argentina. In addition to the two claims discussed in detail below, the cases on which I sat as an arbitrator included one brought by a Spanish phone company,[24] one by a German highway builder,[25] and one by an Italian operator of water and sewerage systems.[26] But the first case I heard against Argentina showed in dramatic terms the differences between states and private companies.

In 1996, during its economic revolution, Argentina requested bids for an integrated system to keep track of immigration, to issue personal ID cards to Argentine citizens and residents, and to administer elections. The German company Siemens won the bid, but in February 2000, shortly after the de la Rúa government took power—and with the IMF all but certain to require deep spending cuts as a condition of its assistance—the contract was suspended, never to be reinstated.[27] After more than a year of wrangling, the Siemens contract was terminated by presidential decree in May 2001.[28]

There was, of course, a BIT in place between Argentina and Germany containing all the usual terms requiring investor protection. But Argentina said it had terminated the contract simply because Siemens had failed to perform. On that basis, the government argued it was acting merely as an ordinary commercial party to a contract and not in its capacity as a state. Commercial parties don't incur liability under international law—only states do. Argentina said the BIT did not apply.[29]

Had the facts been in Argentina's favor, this might have been a decent argument. As my fellow arbitrators and I wrote in the eventual award in *Siemens v. Argentina*: "for the behavior of the state . . . to be considered a breach of an investment treaty, [it] must be beyond that which an ordinary contracting party could adopt and involve state interference with the operation of the contract. . . . For the state to incur international responsibility . . . it must use its public authority."[30]

From the point of view of traditional public international law, however, Argentina's argument was unusual for a state to make. Typically, a state would want to argue always that it acted *qua* state, because that could entitle it to sovereign immunity. But in the era of BITs, states have willingly sacrificed immunity in order to attract investment. Thus we see the opposite phenomenon: a state claiming not to be a state. O brave new world!

The facts were not, however, in Argentina's favor. In reality, it was abundantly clear that the decree terminating the contract was part of Argentina's effort to rein in public spending and shore up its economy. An ordinary contracting party neither worries about nor has the power to do these things.[31] We decided unanimously that Argentina was liable for expropriating Siemens's investment.[32] Not only did the Argentine government cancel contracts during the crisis, but in early 2002, de la Rúa's successor, President Eduardo Duhalde, also unpegged the Argentine peso from the dollar, devalued the currency, and required that all debts be denominated in pesos. That move instantly wiped out most of the value of remaining foreign investments, which of course had invariably been denominated in dollars.

Another case on which I sat involved this unpegging policy. Daimler Finance AG was a German-based offshoot of the car manufacturer then known as DaimlerChrysler (it's now back to plain old Daimler). Daimler Finance had entered the auto loan business in Argentina in 1995, encouraged by economic reforms, including in particular the peso-dollar peg and the accompanying right to issue leases and loans denominated in dollars, thus protecting their value.[33]

The business proved profitable—right up to the point when the peso was unpegged and dollar-denominated contracts were compulsorily converted into pesos in a process called *pesification*. With its loans now essentially worthless, Daimler Finance went pretty much bankrupt overnight.[34] The company issued a claim that came before a panel consisting of myself, Pierre-Marie Dupuy (the French professor whose refusal of the presidency of the Iran–United States Claims Tribunal would later indirectly produce the Iranian challenge against me; see chapter 11), and a Spanish law professor, Domingo Bello Janeiro, with whom I had sat in the *Siemens* case.

During the proceedings, the fired former chief executive of Daimler Finance in Argentina turned coat and gave evidence on behalf of Argentina instead. Incensed by this, the company's associate general counsel appeared at the hearing and testified that the turncoat had tried to blackmail the company for a five-million-dollar payout. He was asked in cross-examination, "Did you go to the Argentine authorities?"

"No," he said. "Not then."

Daimler's advocate in the arbitration didn't pick up on that word, "then." But I did.

From the bench, I asked, "Did there come a time when you did involve the authorities?"

"Oh yes!" said the general counsel. It turned out that, smelling a rat when being blackmailed for five million dollars, they had brought in a forensic accountant who discovered that the turncoat had embezzled some three hundred thousand dollars from the company, of which fact the Argentine authorities were indeed notified. This theft, of course, discredited the witness somewhat.

In the end, though, that revelation didn't help Daimler much, because for technical reasons Argentina won the arbitration. The BIT between Germany and Argentina said that any dispute had to be litigated in front of the local courts for at least eighteen months before it could be referred to arbitration. The BIT also contained, however, a "most favored nation" clause that said, in essence, German investors doing business in Argentina (and Argentine ones doing business in Germany) had to be treated no worse than investors of any other nationality.

Daimler could point to BITs Argentina had signed with other countries (Chile, for example) that omitted the eighteen-month domestic litigation requirement. Fewer hoops to jump through was more favorable treatment, at least in my book. So Daimler should have been able to avail itself of the more favorable clause in the Chilean treaty. Eleven public awards had been issued dealing with this exact issue, and nine of them had come to the same conclusion. Indeed, one of those awards was *Siemens*, with a panel of two-thirds the same makeup, in the shape of myself and Professor Bello Janeiro.[35] *Stare decisis*, as we common lawyers say, "stand by that which has been decided." It is a counsel of consistency.

But Professor Bello Janeiro evidently had undergone a change of heart—indeed, he stated as much in his separate opinion.[36] He and Professor Dupuy read the "most favored nation" clause in a bizarrely restrictive way. Instead of just reading the plain words as they appeared on the page, they conjured up an additional requirement of "affirmative evidence" of consent to arbitration on the part of a state, which they said was missing in this case.[37] This, to my mind, was tortured reasoning, and I said so in one of my trademark blistering dissents, writing that the majority's conclusion was "profoundly wrong," the product of "substantial confusion," resting on "weak reeds."[38]

Pierre-Marie Dupuy, a seasoned pro, did not flinch at my criticism, viewing it as part of the normal way arbitrators operate. Indeed, two years later, Dupuy described me in print as "a gentleman in the truest sense of the word . . . an affable colleague, a generous mentor, a loyal friend, a worthy adversary." He specifically cited the *Daimler* case as an example of our close friendship despite divergent views.[39] And the feeling is, of course, mutual. Professor Bello Janeiro did not feel the same way. He took personal umbrage at my pointing out the inconsistency between his views in *Siemens* and *Daimler*.

"Oh my God," Dupuy said to me some time after my dissent was published. "I've got my hands full with this guy."

"What do you mean?"

"He feels his honor has been impugned. It's like he wants to fight a duel with you or something!"

Thankfully, Pierre-Marie was able to calm the professor down before he confronted me; but evidently the legal fraternity took a dim view of Bello Janeiro's inconsistency, because to my knowledge he has never been appointed in another case.

"I DISSENT!"

Of course, my dissent in the *Daimler* case is far from the only one I have written.

Across the common law world, dissenting opinions are a well-known tradition. In the United States, for example, many people who have never approached the bench nevertheless count themselves connoisseurs of the piquant dissents of, say, Ruth Bader Ginsburg or my late friend Antonin Scalia.

Arbitrators, however, come from many different legal traditions, and in the civil law world—which includes almost all of Latin America and most of Europe outside the British Isles—dissents are not typically a feature of judicial practice. Some civil law–trained arbitrators never dissent, maintaining a strict policy of *nemine dissentiente* in order (they say) to maintain the collegiality and integrity of the arbitral tribunal.

Albert Jan van den Berg, who has been my colleague on a number of panels, is one. Albert Jan has written that "a dissent . . . should be issued in extreme cases only. Surprise and comment should be reserved for those cases where serious procedural misconduct or a violation of fundamental principles occurs; for example, where an arbitrator commits fraud."[40]

The problem with his view is that, as we saw at the Iran–United States Claims Tribunal, the number of instances of "serious procedural misconduct" or violations of "fundamental principles" pales in comparison to the number of times the majority simply gets the law wrong or applies it incorrectly to the facts. When I dissent, it is usually because I believe my interpretation is correct and that of the majority is not. Albert Jan may call this "intellectual exhibitionism."[41] I call it principled. As arbitrators, it's our job to apply the law to the facts to the best of our ability. Where we disagree, we ought to say so.

Moreover, the party that appointed me deserves to know that I wasn't asleep at the switch, blindly going along with whatever the majority said. This doesn't mean I am an advocate for that party—that kind of conduct is wrong and will get you fired, as we will see below. It just means they shouldn't have any reason to think they made a bad decision in appointing me.

When the award is to be made public, a dissent becomes even more important, because it puts on record the interpretation of the law that, by definition, I consider correct. It shows that the views in the award were not unanimously held, which in turn helps to diminish the precedential weight of the majority award. Albert Jan claims that dissents are rarely cited in subsequent awards. That may be so, but that alone is no excuse for not trying to get other arbitrators in other cases to listen to one's sincerely held views and perhaps be persuaded to emulate them.

Perhaps most important, when a serious irregularity could bring injustice to one of the parties, I consider it part of the purpose of my dissent to help domestic courts understand any annulment challenge. Again, Albert Jan disagrees, writing that "a dissent should not be a platform for preparing for annulment. If there is something wrong with either the award or the procedure leading to it, the award itself and the record of the arbitration should suffice for applying for annulment."[42]

It would be nice if we could always rely on this precept. But we can't. We have already seen this in the *Avco* case before the Iran–United States Claims Tribunal. The claimant had been told it could submit an auditor's report in lieu of receipts, only for Chamber Three (which in the meantime had come under new management) to renege on this commitment at the hearing—depriving Avco of part of its claim and resulting in a net award in favor of Iran.[43] This rug pull visited injustice on the claimant, so I wanted to do my best to see that Iran would be unable to enforce the award. I copied chunks of the transcript into my dissent to make sure that the federal district court in Connecticut was able to understand what had happened. And Iran, quite appropriately, lost its enforcement action.

CHALLENGING TIMES

Arbitrators are subject to more democracy than any other kind of judge. We are constantly up for "election," because we are appointed not for life or a term of years but for each case individually. Even then, our appointments are not secure, because there is always a system for challenging an arbitrator. As it happens, the first-ever challenge to an ICSID arbitrator was mounted by me in 1982, acting on behalf of Indonesia in the *Amco Asia* case. Since then, I myself (like most veteran arbitrators) have been challenged several times. And occasionally, these challenges have succeeded. Hoist, perhaps, on my own petard.

A case in point is *Perenco v. Ecuador*. Starting in 2007, Ecuador's new president, the Chavez-esque Rafael Correa, began to nationalize foreign oil companies, as he had promised on the campaign trail. Little or no compensation was offered, so a flurry of arbitration ensued. The Correa regime responded by denouncing Ecuador's BITs, pulling out of ICSID, and announcing that it would not comply with arbitral awards. Predictably enough, foreign investment in Ecuador took a nose-dive; but Correa's actions did not affect claims already filed.

I was appointed in one of these, an ICSID case. While the case was in its early stages, I gave an interview to *Metropolitan Corporate Counsel* magazine, which asked me what I thought were the biggest threats facing international arbitration. I answered, honestly, that among the main challenges was the behavior of "recalcitrant host countries" like Ecuador, whose actions were putting international investment in jeopardy.[44] That didn't sit well with Correa's people, who accused me of bias against them. Ecuador challenged me on that basis. The first thing I did, as always, was to ask the appointing party's counsel whether they wanted me to resign. Sometimes their clients do, simply to avoid the expense of having to defend against a challenge. Perenco didn't want me to resign, however. In fact, they defended my appointment with some vigor.

Under the ICSID Convention, challenges are to be decided on the basis of the convention standards by the other two arbitrators, or, if they cannot agree, by the president of the World Bank. Counsel for Perenco, however, had been persuaded by Ecuador's in-house counsel to agree instead that any challenge would be decided by the secretary-general of the Permanent Court of Arbitration, applying the International Bar Association's Guidelines on Conflicts of Interest in International Arbitration. That agreement was, of course, utterly inconsistent with the ICSID Convention, but the secretary-general of the PCA acted nonetheless. Under those IBA Guidelines, there was no need to find that I was actually biased or subjectively intended the meaning Ecuador ascribed to my words; and in fact, the secretary-general specifically found that I *didn't* mean them that way. But it was enough to show an "appearance of bias" according to a "reasonable interpretation" of my words—and the secretary-general found that Ecuador's interpretation was a reasonable one. Although that decision had no authority in an ICSID case, counsel to Perenco ultimately decided to protect an eventual award in Perenco's favor by sticking with the deal he had made and asking me to resign, which I did. I was replaced by a distinguished English arbitrator and friend, Neil Kaplan.[45]

Perenco still got an award in its favor, albeit tempered by Ecuador's successful counterclaim of fifty-five million dollars to remedy environmental damage the company had caused.[46] In the meantime, Correa continued to rail against Western oil companies—while secretly negotiating with the Chinese to permit drilling in Ecuador's Yasuní National Park.[47] Similarly, in *Vale v. BSG Resources*, a fight over ill-gotten mining rights in Guinea, the standard was "justifiable doubts" as to my independence or impartiality. After my appointment as tribunal chairman by the two coarbitrators, I had spoken about the case at a conference. I had stuck to the publicly reported facts; but the appointing authority (the London Court of International Arbitration) faulted me for not affixing qualifications to my remarks, such as "'it has been reported that' or 'as is public knowledge, allegations have been made that.'"[48]

Again, mea culpa. When your place of work is a battlefield, you will occasionally get shot. Still, at least I fared better than the head of BSG, Beny Steinmetz, who in 2021 received a five-year jail term for fraud, plus a fine of $56.5 million.[49]

There is such a thing as overzealous use of challenges, however. This scorched-earth approach, which ultimately benefits no one, was on full display in another case in which I sat, *Vantage Deepwater v. Petrobras*. Vantage, an American company, had provided an ultra-deep-water drilling ship to the Brazilian national oil and gas company Petrobras. The arrangement had fallen apart, and Vantage blamed Petrobras. Rusty Park, a fantastic arbitrator, chaired the tribunal. Petrobras appointed one James Gaitis.

The first challenge took place before the hearing. Petrobras challenged me on the basis that one of my former law clerks, Epaminontas Triantafilou, was (and still is) a partner with Quinn Emanuel, Vantage's law firm. Petrobras pointed out, inter alia, that Epaminontas was one of four coeditors of a book dedicated to me and that I had invited him and his wife to Thanksgiving dinner.[50] Never mind that he was based in a different office (indeed, in a different country—the UK), or that he had naught to do with this client or this case. This challenge was, in short, much ado about nothing, and the American Arbitration Association dismissed it in a sentence.

But Petrobras had me in their crosshairs—and in Texas, that's a bad place to be. The hearing took place over three weeks in Houston. Throughout the proceedings, Petrobras stationed a staff member by the bench to take pictures of me with an iPhone and try to show that I was not paying attention. (Later, they claimed I had been snoring but, thankfully, were unable to adduce audio to evidence this.)

The second challenge alleged I spent too long questioning a witness—one Sr. Padilha. As the only eyewitness implicating Vantage in alleged corruption, Padilha had gotten his sentence suspended as long as he kept cooperating with the Brazilian government, including in this proceeding. Moreover, while giving evidence via video link, he could be heard whispering to his Brazilian lawyers—a definite no-no because of the risk of witness coaching. Both Rusty Park and I had to tell him to knock it off.[51]

In these circumstances, I felt that some additional probing was more than warranted; and indeed, the transcripts showed all three arbitrators—not just me—questioning Padilha.[52] So that challenge, too, went nowhere.

The third challenge said that I had been caught visiting the Quinn Emanuel offices, located in the same building as the arbitration. I'd been getting a coffee from Starbucks.

The fourth challenge came about because I said things under my breath while counsel for Petrobras engaged in particularly repetitive and annoying questioning of witnesses. I am alleged to have said, "that's ridiculous," "come on," "already talked about," and "asked and answered," although I only remember the last of these. Petrobras also accused me of making "a variety of mocking noises," whatever that means.[53]

The fifth challenge stemmed from a rather ugly episode. Steve Schwebel, a former ICJ president, appeared as an expert witness for Vantage Deepwater. Eighty-eight years old at the time, Steve had suffered a serious fall the previous day. Gaitis went on the attack. At one point, he put Petrobras's reading of a critical provision of the parties' contract to Steve (no doubt if I had done the same thing in reverse, Petrobras would have added a sixth challenge to my rap sheet). Steve should probably have stuck to his guns, but he was in a delicate state following his fall. "I'd have to think about that," he said.

Gaitis barked, "But that's the way it reads!"

This outburst was utterly inappropriate. Arbitrators are not meant to prejudge cases. "You said that's the way this reads," I said to Gaitis. "Is that a final conclusion on your part, before the hearing is over and we've deliberated the case?"

"No, Charlie," Gaitis snapped. "I think if you read these provisions, I think they're plainly written and that's what they say. I think I'm farther away from a final conclusion in this hearing than you are, sir. So that's a question that really was very inappropriate on your part."[54] Petrobras challenged *me* on this basis! They said I had engaged in a "gratuitous effort at rehabilitation" of Steve as a witness, using "soft and encouraging questioning."[55]

None of these challenges went anywhere, and Rusty Park and I issued an award in favor of Vantage.[56] Gaitis dissented, of course, but his "dissent" was just a paragraph, citing various annulment provisions of the federal Arbitration Act—including, bafflingly, section 10(a)(1), which applies to awards "procured by corruption, fraud, or undue means."[57] This was a transparent (and frankly quite lazy) attempt to set up a motion to annul the award.

My name was featured heavily in Petrobras's motion before the federal courts in Texas. They repeated most of the allegations mentioned above and indeed added some more, saying that I had "usurped" Rusty Park's role as chair (on one occasion I reminded him that one of the witnesses had to leave early), and that I had hurt the defense counsel's feelings by being rude to them.[58] They also attempted to bolster their case by alleging my "past record of partiality," although the only successful challenges they could point to were the two mentioned above, *Perenco* and *Vale*—out of the dozens and dozens of arbitrations in which I had sat.[59]

The district court was having none of it, and its decision was upheld on appeal.[60] When Petrobras lost on appeal, it petitioned for an en banc hearing. This was rejected, as not a single judge of the appellate court indicated interest in such a hearing. Petrobras's petition to the Supreme Court for a writ of *certiorari* also was quickly dismissed. So Vantage got its roughly $660 million award enforced and I was "exonerated." Not without some unwelcome publicity, mind you, although as an arbitrator that rather comes with the territory.

In my experience, for the most part, arbitrators are not biased. The few who are (or appear to be) can easily be challenged and for that reason tend not to get too many more appointments. In fact, I believe that the whole system of international arbitration works rather well. But that is not to say that it cannot still be improved—as we will see in the next chapter.

CHAPTER THIRTEEN

International Arbitrator, Part II

"LEGAL VULTURES"?

"By signing investment treaties and agreeing to arbitration, states have indeed accepted to be sued by the Devil in Hell."[1] So wrote a Dutch activist group in a 2012 report on international arbitration entitled *Profiting from Injustice*. According to the report, bilateral investment treaties had "ensnared hundreds of countries" in a system that was "business-biased."[2] This idea that BITs impair state freedom is a core thesis of the Columbia Center on Sustainable Investment, which publishes frequently on the subject.[3]

Individual arbitrators come in for criticism, too. The Dutch report included an "Elite Fifteen" of international arbitrators. (I was slightly put out to be ranked number two, behind Brigitte Stern of France.)[4] We were called "legal vultures," condemned for displaying "an inherent pro-corporate bias" and all but accused of being in favor of war, human rights violations, and economic collapse because these things are supposedly good for business.[5]

They are not alone. The former press secretary to Lyndon Johnson and longtime PBS host Bill Moyers, otherwise a sensible and thoughtful person, famously attacked NAFTA's Chapter 11 in a broadcast entitled "Trading Democracy," opining that "corporations have stretched [it] to undermine environmental decisions[,] the decisions of local communities[,] even the verdict of an American jury . . . in secret tribunals."[6]

Even as exalted a figure as Sen. Elizabeth Warren has jumped on this bandwagon, publishing a *Washington Post* op-ed in which she called arbitral tribunals "rigged pseudo-courts" and claimed that the same people "go back and forth between representing corporations one day and sitting in judgment the next" (any partner of a global law firm who has repeatedly been conflicted out of accepting arbitral appointments is likely to raise an eyebrow here).[7]

Let me not mince words: it is all nonsense. Senator Warren ought to know this. Not only was she a tenured professor specializing in bankruptcy law at Harvard Law School, but she was once paid in the region of ninety thousand dollars to appear as an expert witness in a NAFTA arbitration.[8]

First, BITs do not in any meaningful sense impair the freedom of states—any more than anyone's freedom is impaired by their bank's insistence that they keep up with their mortgage payments. They agreed to pay—it's in the contract. In the same way, states agree to abide by their treaties. *Pacta sunt servanda*, as the legal Latin puts it: agreements must be kept. Otherwise, the system breaks down.

It is true that big corporations have power—that much is plain to see. But so do states. As a small example: a few years ago, I sat in an arbitration between Shell and Exxon on one side and the wholly state-owned Nigerian National Petroleum Corporation on the other. As required by the freely negotiated agreement between the parties, the arbitration took place in Abuja under Nigerian arbitration law and rules and thus was subject to review by Nigerian courts. The Nigerian capital was so dangerous for foreigners that we were accompanied to and from the airport by armed guards. Needless to say, Shell and Exxon would never have accepted to arbitrate in Nigeria, under Nigerian arbitration law, subject to judicial review by Nigerian courts had the two companies not needed Nigerian oil at least as much, if not more so, than Nigeria needed them to exploit it. Moreover, unlike private parties, states can generally denounce treaties without long-term consequences. And as we will see in the next chapter, states get a wide margin of freedom to regulate in the public interest under the international law doctrine of "police powers."

Second, the system of international arbitration is demonstrably *not* biased. There are statistics to prove it. As of this writing, a database maintained by the UN Conference on Trade and Development cata- logued 740 concluded international investment arbitrations. Of these, states had won 274 (37 percent), investors 212 (29 percent). The rest were settled or dealt with in other ways.[9] ICSID's statistics show similar proportions, with 31 percent of investor claims upheld and 35 percent dismissed or declined on jurisdictional grounds.[10]

It is worth noting that the "system" (if one can call it that) that existed prior to the rise of investment treaties was massively biased in favor of states, which could essentially treat investors as poorly as they liked—until a bigger dog entered the arena. I have seen this kind of bad behavior first- hand: recall the repeated detentions visited on AIG's manager in Nigeria, for example. But this kind of conduct hurts investment; states have come to realize that and constructed a more peaceful alternative.

What about me personally? Am I inherently "pro-investor"? It is true that I have been appointed largely by investors; but this is largely an artifact of having spent much of my early career working for a big law firm. The people who knew and trusted me from those days, and later appointed me as a party-appointed arbitrator, tended to be other Amer- ican lawyers in large firms, whose clients tended to be big companies investing abroad. But I have worked for, and been appointed by, states, too. We have already seen my work for Indonesia and Costa Rica, and we will cover my work for Jordan and Bolivia in the next chapter. Nor do I consider myself a captive of the party that appointed me; a review of my CV indicates that I have voted against the party that appointed me 30 percent of the time—a figure in line with the above statistics on prevailing parties.

In other words, I am not pro-investor. I am not pro-state. I am pro-investment. Responsible investors are not going to invest if they don't enjoy reasonable protections. This is why the system of BITs and peaceful dispute settlement exists. Of course, anticorporate rhetoric (some of it well deserved) plays well with a certain component of Western electorates. But popularity alone does not make a claim true. We must avoid a situation where blaming corporations gives prominent voices carte blanche to say whatever they want without regard for the facts. Being antibusiness is not a smart economic strategy—especially for the low-income countries that stand to suffer the most from any decline in investment inflows.

REAL-LIFE CHALLENGES

That is not to say that the current system is perfect. On the contrary, the state of international arbitration today presents several challenges.

First, the system has been too secretive. Under most arbitral frameworks, everything is kept confidential by default—pleadings, hearings, witness statements, and awards. The main problem with this is that it damages arbitration's perceived legitimacy—and opens the door to conspiracy theories like the ones repeated by Senator Warren, Bill Moyers, and others. Of course, limited confidentiality is sometimes justified. Notably, trade secrets deserve protection—Coca-Cola, for example, should not be forced to reveal the formula for Coke in open court. This could be handled, as it is in domestic courts, with redactions and closed-door portions of otherwise open hearings.

There are other circumstances that might justify some measure of confidentiality. For example, at one hearing in the *ADC v. Hungary* case discussed in a previous chapter, a witness from Viktor Orbán's authoritarian Fidesz Party demanded the transcript of another Hungarian witness's oral testimony in order to "obtain satisfaction" against him for contradicting him. It was a naked political threat (unsurprisingly, given the bullying style of Fidesz). We declined to release the transcript.[11]

Subject to such protections, I believe everything should be made public—and not just because I want to see the release of all my opinions, which I consider treasures of literacy and logic! International arbitrations involve big issues as well as big sums of money. People deserve to know how such important matters are being decided. In addition, the broader the public release of awards and opinions, the greater the volume of precedents available to guide other tribunals.

On this issue, matters do seem to be moving in the right direction. The present high-water mark for transparency came in one case of mine, *Vattenfall v. Germany*, an arbitration under the multilateral Energy Charter Treaty that questioned Germany's accelerated phasing out of nuclear power following the Fukushima disaster.[12] Counsel for Germany pushed to make everything public—radically so—and the other side agreed. Our hearings were even streamed live online for all to see. Readers who suffer from a bad case of insomnia can watch them in their entirety on the ICSID website, or even on YouTube.[13]

These are positive developments. We ought to be able to show we are not hiding anything. And we should proceed always according to Lord Hewart's famous dictum: ". . . justice should not only be done, but should manifestly and undoubtedly be seen to be done."[14]

The second problem is related: international arbitration is crying out for a doctrine of precedent. Gabrielle Kaufmann-Kohler, a Swiss arbitrator with whom I've had the pleasure of sitting a number of times, inserts a boilerplate paragraph into all of the awards by tribunals over which she has presided:

The Tribunal considers that it is not bound by previous decisions. At the same time, it is of the opinion that it must pay due consideration to earlier decisions of international tribunals. It believes that, subject to compelling contrary grounds, it has a duty to adopt solutions established in a series of consistent cases. It also believes that, subject to the specifics of a given treaty and of the circumstances of the actual case, it has a duty to seek to contribute to the harmonious development of investment law and thereby to meet the legitimate expectations of the community of states and investors towards certainty of the rule of law.[15]

I have a great deal of sympathy with this view. The purpose of any legal system is to provide a measure of predictability and stability in dispute resolution. This is especially important in international law, where the alternative has too often been direct conflict between states. The sometimes wild inconsistency between awards at the Iran–United States Claims Tribunal shows the need for stronger precedent, as do the four cases based on the Argentina-Germany BIT, each of which managed to interpret the exact same text in different ways—and that was with me appointed in three of them and Professor Bello Janeiro in two!

Greater transparency could remedy this problem by making more awards and opinions available for consultation. However, a word of caution is in order. As Ralph Waldo Emerson wrote, "A foolish consistency is the hobgoblin of little minds."[16] I would probably not go as far as he does two sentences down, when he counsels his self-reliant readers to "speak what you think now in hard words, and tomorrow speak what tomorrow thinks in hard words again, though it contradict everything you said today." But the point is made: if you get a bad precedent, you don't want to be locked into following it (or else having to turn somersaults trying to distinguish the case before you).

In truth, precedent is difficult to implement, unless one is prepared to formalize the arbitral "judiciary" to an extent that, as I explain in the final chapter of this book, I do not think is wise. Insofar as that precedent comes at the expense of investors and states having equal stakes in the system via appointment rights, I don't think it will be worth it.

Third, the system has historically been geared toward allowing investors to sue states—not the other way around. This, too, is less of a problem than it has been in the past. For example, we have already seen how Ecuador won a huge counterclaim for environmental damage in the *Perenco* case. Whether states can initiate claims depends on the language in the treaty or contract. In ICSID cases, for example, it is possible for a state or state-owned entity to initiate arbitration against a foreign investor, as occurred in *TANESCO v. IPTL*, in which I was appointed as arbitrator by the wholly state-owned Tanzania Electric Supply Company Limited claiming against the respondent Malaysian investor in a power purchase agreement. Elsewhere, particularly in newer BITs, moves are being made to grant states and state-owned entities increased rights in this area.

In the case of *Foresti v. South Africa*, in which I was appointed by the investor, we were able to take a step toward greater participation in international arbitral proceedings. As we will see in the next chapter, the claim involved South Africa's Black Economic Empowerment policies vis-à-vis the mining industry. Four human rights and environmental NGOs applied to participate in the case as nondisputing parties—in effect, amici curiae. We decided unanimously—over the objections of the investor that appointed me—to give the NGOs access to the pleadings and witness statements and allow them to make submissions to the panel. We also invited the NGOs and the parties to comment on the fairness and efficacy of the procedure we adopted, with a view to including these comments in a section of the eventual award.[17]

The *Foresti* case was discontinued before the hearings on the merits were due to take place, so we did not get a chance to test this novel procedure. But we did at least manage to get this precedent in favor of openness in the books. Our decision reflected a wider trend toward permitting amici where they can add something useful that does not duplicate arguments the parties will address anyway. (In *Foresti*, as we will see, those arguments concerned the important human rights and environmental impact of Black Economic Empowerment.)

Finally, there is a distinct lack of geographic diversity among arbitrators. Most of the best-known repeat appointees hail from Europe or North America. This reflects a bigger problem in the international legal profession: an undersupply of senior lawyers from developing countries. This, too, is getting better, though slowly. Another small example: in the past, my law clerks—young, promising lawyers—hailed exclusively from the developed world. But one of my most recent—and most talented—Pem Chhoden Tshering, a member of the Bar of England and

Wales as well as that of New York State, hails from the Himalayan nation of Bhutan and is now an associate of Sidley & Austin—and, perhaps, a future arbitrator!

In this regard, I take heart also from the rising number of women arbitrators over the past few decades. When I started in arbitration, there simply weren't any. Today, there are many, some among the best in the business, including the aforementioned Brigitte Stern and Gabrielle Kaufmann-Kohler as well as Judith Gill QC and Wendy Miles QC of my own Twenty Essex Chambers, and Lucy Reed, Juliet Blanch, and Jean Kalicki of Arbitration Chambers.

Greater transparency and diversity are the future of international arbitration, and I welcome both developments. The next frontier is the harmonization of international investment law with human rights—and that is the subject of the next chapter.

CHAPTER FOURTEEN

Human Rights

PARALLEL LIVES

In the fall of 2019, I attended a fundraising gala for the American Society of International Law, held in the opulent surroundings of the Frick Collection, a Manhattan mansion originally built as the home of the robber baron Henry Clay Frick. The actor George Clooney was there that night, sporting a gray mountain-man beard; but the real star of the evening was his wife, the Beirut-born British barrister Amal Clooney (née Alamuddin). She was being honored for her work on behalf of victims of genocide, terrorism, media censorship, and other human rights violations.[1]

I had donated enough to the society to get myself and two assistants into the VIP reception. I approached Amal, who looked gorgeous as always, and introduced myself.

"Oh!" she responded immediately with a smile. "Everyone in international law knows Charlie Brower!" It was like receiving a papal blessing! I could not keep the grin off my face. Most important of all, perhaps, my young colleagues were suitably impressed with my celebrity connections.

Amal Clooney is one of the most prominent avatars of a development in international law parallel to—and at least as important as—the international investment law that has been my bread and butter for so many years. Since the Universal Declaration of Human Rights was adopted by the UN in 1948, the field has been evolving to include more global and regional treaties, tribunals, and case law as well as a system of special rapporteurs mandated by the UN Human Rights Council or the UN Commission on Human Rights to report on specific countries or issues.

COSTA RICA

I do have some experience of this parallel field. As noted in a previous chapter, one of my ICJ appearances was in a human rights case. Param Cumaraswamy, a Malaysian appointed by the UN Commission on Human Rights as special rapporteur on the independence of judges and lawyers, had spoken out publicly against certain Malaysian business interests for serially manipulating his country's justice system.[2] Cumaraswamy was then promptly slapped with a series of defamation lawsuits in Malaysia, seeking damages totaling $112 million—a steep sum for an unsalaried UN special rapporteur, or indeed a salaried one.[3]

Cumaraswamy pointed out that, as a UN rapporteur, he was immune from suit. Unfortunately for him, he had been right all along about the Malaysian courts—they were in the pocket of his persecutors. Despite repeated protests from the UN, including to the prime minister of Malaysia, their courts denied Cumaraswamy's immunity. The Federal Court of Malaysia derided the special rapporteur as an "unpaid, part-time provider of information," ignoring the fact that his immunity was spelled out in an international convention to which Malaysia was a party.[4]

The UN dispatched no less a personage than my Canadian friend Yves Fortier, a former Canadian ambassador to the UN who had presided over the Security Council when it resolved to expel Saddam Hussein from

Kuwait in 1990, to convince the Malaysian government to refer the matter to the ICJ. Unfortunately, despite two trips to Kuala Lumpur, Yves was unsuccessful; but the case came to the court instead via a request from the UN's Economic and Social Council for an advisory opinion.[5]

At the time, I was representing Costa Rica in international matters, including the Santa Elena arbitration. As a state party to the ICJ statute, and also because it was a party to the convention that gave Cumaraswamy and other special rapporteurs their immunity, Costa Rica was entitled to participate in the *Immunity* case.[6] I strongly recommended that the Costa Rican government exercise this right, for two reasons.

Costa Rica was known internationally for two things: conservation (as in the *Santa Elena* case) and human rights (as in this one). The country was an early and enthusiastic champion of human rights conventions, from the 1948 Universal Declaration of Human Rights onward. San José, the capital, was the venue for the negotiation of the American Convention on Human Rights in the late 1960s and today plays host to a number of important human rights bodies, including the Inter-American Court of Human Rights (on which I have also sat as judge *ad hoc*—more on that below). This advisory proceeding represented an opportunity for Costa Rica to burnish further its reputation as one of the world's foremost defenders of human rights.

At the same time, I also was aware that, aside from a brief appearance in 1986 that was soon discontinued, Costa Rica had never been a party to a proceeding before the court. But looming disputes with Nicaragua over the San Juan River, which forms much of the border between them, could very well bring Costa Rica before the court in the foreseeable future. So the *Immunity* case was a chance for Costa Rica to get in some practice and strike up a rapport with the court. It seems I was prescient, as since then, the two countries have been before the court in three disputes over use of the San Juan River and two additional contentious cases to resolve maritime and land border disputes.

Given the importance of the issue, I offered to represent Costa Rica in the *Immunity* case for expenses only, no fees. Costa Rica thus became the only state appearing at the hearing, other than Malaysia itself, from outside the United States and Europe. By this time, my son, Chip, had become the Croft Visiting Assistant Professor of International Law at the University of Mississippi School of Law. I made Chip my copilot, and we developed our written submission together, to include a strong statement on the vital importance of international human rights monitoring, not just to Costa Rica, but to all people worldwide.[7]

When I appeared before the court, on the first day of proceedings, the arguments were largely technical, as ICJ arguments typically are. In this case, they concerned interpretation of the Convention on the Privileges and Immunities of the United Nations.[8] I noted that Cumaraswamy, the special rapporteur himself, was present in court and seemed remarkably calm considering the potential consequences for him and his profession. Such is the steely determination required of an international human rights defender.

Malaysia was represented by my late friend Sir Elihu Lauterpacht QC, a giant of international law, so it was an especially sweet victory when the court upheld Cumaraswamy's immunity with only a single dissent.[9]

BOLIVIA

The court issued its opinion in the *Immunity* case in 1999, and later that same year, I was appointed by another Latin American state, Bolivia, to sit as a judge *ad hoc* of the Inter-American Court of Human Rights.

Between 1969 and 1978, Bolivia suffered under five successive military dictators. The last of these, Col. Hugo Bánzer Suárez, aka El Petiso ("Shorty"), was by some accounts the most repressive of the lot, and he reigned the longest, from 1971 until 1978.[10] Bánzer was so suspicious of campus politics that he closed all of Bolivia's universities for an entire year.[11] More infamously, his regime "disappeared" dozens of people, among them several student activists. One of them was twenty-one-year-old José Carlos Trujillo Oroza, who was arrested in the first few months of Bánzer's rule. When his mother, Antonia Gladys Oroza de Solón

Romero, was allowed to visit José Carlos in prison, she could tell from his wounds that he had been tortured.[12] A few days later, he vanished, murdered under mysterious circumstances by Bánzer's security forces.[13]

Gladys Oroza never gave up the search for her son's body; and she soon became an advocate for other families of the disappeared. The Bolivian state tried to intimidate her. She was fired from her job at the national teacher training college, beaten and robbed, and saw her husband exiled.[14] But she never gave up. Twenty-one years after her son's disappearance, with democracy finally established in Bolivia, Gladys Oroza filed a complaint with the Inter-American Commission on Human Rights, an organ of the Organization of American States (OAS).[15] The commission, in line with its usual procedure, investigated and referred the matter to its sister organ of the OAS, the Inter-American Court of Human Rights. Bolivia appointed me as judge *ad hoc* in the case.

Why me? A senior official of the Bolivian government contacted an old friend of his, a former *procurador* (attorney general) of Costa Rica with whom I had worked extensively, namely Fabián Volio Echeverria, and asked him to represent Bolivia in the case. Fabian advised his friend that Bolivia should not appoint a Bolivian, or in fact any Latin American. He recommended instead that in order for the judge *ad hoc* to have maximum credibility Bolivia should appoint someone from another continent with a positive global reputation as an international jurist. That turned out to be me.

It stands to Bolivia's credit that, from the start, it accepted responsibility for José Carlos's disappearance—the more so because, beginning in 1997, the president of the country (elected, this time) was once again none other than Hugo Bánzer Suárez, who had evidently mended his dictatorial ways to some extent in the interim.[16] Before the proceedings began, Bolivia had offered Ms. Oroza substantial monetary compensation— some $40,000, at a time when Bolivia's per capita GDP was just over $1,600 per year.[17] But money was not what this still-grieving mother sought. She wanted to know how and by whose hand her son had died and to find his remains so that he could be properly buried.

Bolivia had opened an "administrative investigation," but it had achieved little. By the state's own admission, the investigation had only "determined some of the facts and identified certain persons who might be guilty."[18] The Bolivian authorities resisted opening a full investigation—ostensibly on various grounds, but the holdup was most likely politically motivated.

We held a hearing in September 2001 at the Inter-American Court's seat in San José, Costa Rica. Gladys Oroza, then seventy-five years old, appeared in person and gave moving testimony about the physical and mental wounds inflicted on her son and about her thirty-year struggle for justice.[19] It was a humbling experience to hear about her determination in the face of overwhelming tyranny.

As we wrote in our eventual judgment on reparations and costs, Bolivia's failure to investigate was not only a violation of its obligations to provide justice: "The continued denial of the truth about the fate of a disappeared person is a form of cruel, inhuman, and degrading treatment for the close family." Moreover, "the delivery of the mortal remains in cases of detained-disappeared persons is, in itself, an act of justice and reparation."[20]

We ordered Bolivia to investigate, identify, and punish the perpetrators; to take all necessary measures to locate and deliver the remains of the victim; to make forced disappearance a distinct crime in domestic law (as it was obliged to do under human rights conventions it had ratified); and to pay almost $400,000 in monetary compensation to Gladys Oroza and other family members of the victim.[21]

The foreign investment cases I am more used to hearing typically involve only money—albeit massive sums thereof. Sitting on the Inter-American Court of Human Rights opened my eyes to the very different stakes in human rights cases. There is no doubt in my mind that, if they had to choose between $400,000 or a successfully completed investigation to establish what truly had happened to José Carlos, Gladys Oroza and the family would have chosen the truth over the money every time.

THE WALL

My best-known human rights case was one I could take part in only *sub rosa*, given my position as a U.S.-appointed titular judge of the Iran–United States Claims Tribunal at the time. This was the ICJ's advisory opinion on the Israeli wall through the West Bank, in which I assisted the neighboring country of Jordan.

I had first represented Jordan back in the 1980s, when Royal Jordanian Airlines was fined by the U.S. Department of Transportation for selling tickets to Beirut at a time when such sales were prohibited by U.S. law, due, as I recall, to the ongoing civil war in Lebanon. Thereafter, my work for Jordan largely concerned the legal position of Palestinian refugees in Jordan, who make up some 40 percent of the country's population. I have always been proud of this work because I feel deeply for the Palestinians, who have been handed a raw deal in a number of respects.

In 2001, at the behest of Jack O'Connell, a former CIA station chief in Amman turned personal lawyer to the ruling family, I worked on proposals for a claims settlement program for Palestinian Jordanians who had been evicted from what is now Israel. I introduced Jack and the Jordanians to the collaborator on the project I had chosen, Sir Arthur Watts KCMG QC of my Twenty Essex Chambers in London. He had been the legal adviser of Her Majesty's Foreign and Commonwealth Office and was a well-received advocate before the International Court of Justice. Of course, the Jordanians quickly grew to love him. Later, I helped Jordan figure out how Palestinian Jordanians with investments in Kuwait could register claims with the UN Compensation Commission—the complication there being that Kuwaiti law had required them to invest under the auspices of local partners. I later worked with a different collaborator to produce a legal opinion for King Abdullah on the status of Palestinian refugees.

Israel's lawful eastern border was established in a series of 1949 armistice agreements between that country and its Arab neighbors. It was called the "Green Line" because of its color on contemporary maps.[22] In 2002 and 2003, however, during the second intifada, Israel began constructing a barrier—sometimes a concrete wall, sometimes a barbed-wire fence laden with high-tech sensors—through the West Bank, supposedly for self-defense against terrorist attacks.

This barrier did not always follow the Green Line, however, but made frequent deep excursions into Palestinian territory to embrace Israeli settlements, which themselves have been repeatedly declared unlawful under international law.[23] While there were gates in the wall, they opened infrequently and did not follow the Israeli government's own published schedule. Some 14.5 percent of the Palestinian West Bank lay inside the Israeli barrier, and its existence cut more than 400,000 Palestinians off from markets, clinics, schools, and even water sources. In some cases, the barrier bisected individual farm holdings, rendering large swathes of land essentially uncultivable.[24]

It was clear to me and many others that these measures went well beyond what was necessary for self-defense; in reality, the wall was part of an attempt by the hardline government of Ariel Sharon to annex those parts of the West Bank that contained the illegal settlements. In December 2003, a few months after the first sections of the barrier went up, the UN General Assembly exercised its power to request an advisory opinion on the matter from the International Court of Justice. Jordan of course had a deep interest in the proceedings, and Jack O'Connell asked me to help draft their submissions.

The problem with this was that I was once again sitting as a titular member on the Iran–United States Claims Tribunal. It was no secret that the administration of George W. Bush would support Israel to the hilt. Unlike my Iranian colleagues, I was not controlled by my home government; but it would cause significant embarrassment to the State Department should my name be associated publicly with the case. Therefore I quietly approached the then–legal adviser of the department, who tacitly approved my participation, so long as it stayed behind the scenes.

Sir Arthur Watts joined the team, led by Prince Zeid Ra'ad al Hussein—a member of the Hashemite royal family and a prominent Jordanian diplomat then serving as president of the Assembly of States Parties to the Rome Statute that established the International Criminal

Court (and who later served as UN High Commissioner for Human Rights). Prince Zeid and Arthur would become Jordan's lead advocates in the hearings.[25] We based our argument on some of the most fundamental precepts of international law—including the prohibitions on annexation and on the threat or use of force, the right of self-determination, and the obligations of occupying powers under the Fourth Geneva Convention—as well as on multiple human rights conventions, including the International Covenant on Civil and Political Rights.[26]

The existence of the barrier, we argued, seriously impaired human rights, including the freedom of movement and to choose one's residence and the rights to food, education, and health care.[27] We also found support in the international law of expropriation, citing among other authorities the *Amoco International Finance* case in which I had sat on the Iran–United States Claims Tribunal.[28] Thus we proved that the protection against unlawful taking of property is not just for mega-corporations!

In July 2004, the ICJ concluded that the wall was unjustified by military exigency or self-defense. In fact, it was unlawful as a de facto attempted annexation, a violation of the Fourth Geneva Convention, and a transgression of multiple human rights conventions to which Israel was party. An important part of the victory was the court's holding that human rights law continued to apply everywhere—even in occupied territory that was subject to the Fourth Geneva Convention—rejecting the old canard *inter arma silent leges* (in war, law is silent).[29]

In this instance, the court couldn't order anyone to do anything—this was, after all, only an advisory opinion—but it did call upon Israel to stop construction of the barrier, dismantle the sections already built, return the land requisitioned, and pay reparations.[30] Israel, however, has continued with construction apace, and in 2020 Benjamin Netanyahu even proposed formal annexation of some occupied land.[31] Evidently, we still have some way to go before all states can be made to respect international law.

SOUTH AFRICA

Increasingly, I see the commercial and human rights sides of international law as complementing each other. To some, this may seem a counterintuitive proposition—but why not? After all, the aim of both is (or ought to be) ultimately the betterment of humankind. Historically, prosperity and the growth of a commercial middle class has been the surest route to lasting democracy and respect for individuals.

A convergence of the two spheres has been in the cards for a number of years; and in 2009 and 2010, it looked as if I might get to sit in the case that finally brought them together: *Foresti v. South Africa*.

Apartheid is a crime of historic proportions, and its effects reverberate today; for example, nearly two-thirds of Black South Africans live below the poverty line, compared to 1 percent of Whites.[32] The South African Constitution expressly authorizes affirmative action to address these inequalities.[33] On this basis, the government has pursued a policy of Black Economic Empowerment.

South Africa's mining industry was one of the wellsprings of apartheid; practices in the mines, where small groups of skilled Whites oversaw huge numbers of unskilled Blacks from the late nineteenth century onward, inspired a wider system of racist policies formalized in the 1940s and 1950s.[34] Since the end of apartheid, therefore, the industry has been a particular focus for Black Economic Empowerment. In 2004, a new law imposed ownership requirements on mining companies operating in South Africa, which would henceforward be obliged to transfer 26 percent of their shares to Historically Disadvantaged South Africans.[35]

The Forestis, an Italian family of stonemasons that owned a quarrying business in the Johannesburg suburbs, objected to the new law. They mined what is called "dimensional stone," granite and the like, that then is, by a process known as "beneficiation," formed into end products such as gravestones, architectural components, and so forth. They were a closely held family firm, not a huge company, and they said they could not afford to comply with the requirement to divest themselves of 26 percent of their shares. As Italians whose company was organized under the law of Luxembourg, the Forestis had the right to claim against South Africa under the applicable BITs. This they did, arguing that the law constituted an indirect expropriation of part of their investment in South Africa.[36]

Under international law, states enjoy broad police powers, neatly summarized by the *Restatement (Third) of the Foreign Relations Law of the United States*: "A state is not responsible for loss of property or for other economic disadvantage resulting from bona fide general taxation, regulation, forfeiture for crime, or other action of the kind that is commonly accepted as within the police power of states, if it is not discriminatory."[37]

Was the 26 percent law a justified exercise of these powers? Or was it an infringement on the rights of foreign investors?

The applicable BITs, read alongside the relevant ICSID rules, required us to decide the case with reference to South African law and international law, as well as the provisions of the BITs themselves. So the South African constitution would come into play, as would international human rights law—specifically, the scope of a state's right to address historic human rights violations via what is known in the United States as affirmative action. As noted in the previous chapter, we allowed a group of NGOs to participate in the case in order to help us untangle the complexities of international and domestic law on the subject.

It would have been a fascinating case, to say the very least. But before we could get to a hearing, the parties had negotiated a solution. The South African authorities allowed the Foresti family to reduce the percentage of their shares they were required to alienate to a level at which the Forestis were willing to give them to trusted Black South African employees who had been working with the firm for ages. On their part, the Forestis undertook to employ a number of Historically Disadvantaged South Africans to perform "beneficiation" of the mined stone, which theretofore had been done by others or elsewhere, thereby increasing for South Africa the number of those employed whom its legislation was designed to help.

Given this negotiated solution, the convergence of human rights and commercial law will have to await another arbitration; but I am confident that it will happen sooner rather than later.

EVERYTHING THAT RISES MUST CONVERGE

As I hope the contents of this book have shown, I am 1,000 percent in favor of human rights, and I want to see them taken into account by arbitral tribunals. The same goes for the environment, about which I was passionate even before the *Santa Elena* case for Costa Rica. The good news is that there is no need to change the system in order to bring about this long-overdue convergence, for the doctrine of police powers already exists.

The limits of police powers will likely be tested soon, with a wave of claims around governmental responses to the Covid-19 pandemic. Clearly, measures to protect public health against a deadly virus fall well within "action of the kind that is commonly accepted as within the police power of states." But were these measures in all cases applied proportionately, with due process, and in a nondiscriminatory fashion?

In a mock arbitration in November 2021, I was faced with exactly this question in a hypothetical case involving the *Star Wars* planets of Alderaan, Bespin, and Corellia. It seemed to me that the claimant, in arguing against proportionality and so on, had a hard row to hoe. But the real answer will have to await real cases. That, like so much in international commercial law, remains to be seen.

CHAPTER FIFTEEN

The Future

EXTENDING THE EMPIRE OF LAW

For my eighty-sixth birthday, my son gave me an original photograph of the famed American statesman Elihu Root. Root had inscribed it: "For Philip C. Jessup with respect and affection." Jessup, Root's protégé and biographer, later served as a senior American diplomat and, in the 1960s, a judge of the International Court of Justice.

Like the scale model of the CSS *Alabama*, also a treasured present from Chip, the picture was a thoughtful gift from one international lawyer to another. As secretary of war, secretary of state, and finally a U.S. senator between 1899 and 1915, Root served at the height of "gunboat diplomacy"—the ugly practice of forcing weaker states to accept trade terms at cannon-point. Theodore Roosevelt, president from 1901 to 1909, was a leading proponent.

Secretary Root, however, had a more peaceful vision—one in which states settled their differences judicially. He became the architect of the Central American Court of Justice, the International Joint Commission for the settlement of border disputes between the United States and

Canada, and some forty arbitration treaties between the United States and other nations. In 1912 Root won the Nobel Peace Prize "for bringing about better understanding between the countries of North and South America and initiating important arbitration agreements between the United States and other countries."[1]

In his Nobel lecture, Root quoted the preamble to the Hague Convention of 1899, in which the state parties professed themselves "desirous of extending the empire of law" and "convinced that the permanent institution of a Court of Arbitration, accessible to all . . . will contribute effectively to this result." Root's hope for the future, he said, was that "when an international controversy arises, the first reaction is not to consider war but to consider peaceful litigation."[2]

That goal has not yet been fully realized, of course; perhaps it never will be. But thanks in large part to the twin systems of free trade and dispute-resolution mechanisms, we are closer to Root's vision than ever.

Noel Maurer, in his economic history *The Empire Trap*, draws a telling comparison between two investment disputes, separated by 107 years. In 1900, Venezuelan troops forcibly ejected American asphalt companies. The McKinley administration responded by dispatching three U.S. warships to the scene. Only by deft political maneuvering was the government of President Cipriano Castro able to avoid a shooting war.[3]

Castro's equivalents in other countries fared less well. Between 1900 and 1965, as Maurer shows, trade and investment disputes prompted U.S. intervention in the Dominican Republic, Nicaragua, Haiti, Liberia, Mexico, Bolivia, Iran, Guatemala, Cuba, Sri Lanka, Indonesia, and other countries. American responses ranged from sanctions and aid cuts to CIA-sponsored coups and outright invasions.[4]

During the George W. Bush administration, in 2007, things had evidently changed. In that year, Venezuela under Hugo Chávez announced the confiscation of U.S. oil and telecom assets. Maurer picks up what happened next:

> *The administration limited itself to an anodyne announcement that it expected "fair and quick compensation." Despite*

repeated provocations by the Venezuelan government, including a threat to expel the U.S. ambassador, the United States stuck to that line. No sanctions were implied or threatened. Nor did the affected companies lobby Congress or try to mobilize political pressure.[5]

What, exactly, had changed? The main factor was the rise of international arbitration charted throughout this book. Instead of pushing for intervention, the expropriated U.S. companies pursued their claims through arbitrations at the ICC and ICSID, winning just short of one billion dollars—an amount that was significantly limited thanks to canny moves by Venezuela when negotiating the relevant contracts. Chávez indulged in his usual anti-American posturing, but his government paid up.[6]

Such is the power of international justice.

For commercial lawyers, international law used to be the poor relation. It certainly was in the late 1950s, when I decided that taking more than one course in the subject at law school would make me look like a weirdo when applying for jobs at major law firms! As recently as 1983, when I started at the Iran–United States Claims Tribunal, the international legal establishment in The Hague was relieved to have us there, because we injected some life into the place. That year, only one case was filed with the International Court of Justice (a border dispute between Mali and Burkina Faso), and not a single judgment was issued.[7] The Permanent Court of Arbitration, established by the 1899 Hague Convention that Elihu Root so admired, was moribund. Outside The Hague, the picture was similar. For example, in the decade leading up to 1983, ICSID had registered just thirteen cases.[8]

Today, things are different. The Permanent Court of Arbitration is busier than ever and has a huge staff, while the ICJ's schedule has become so packed that it has had to ban its members generally from sitting as arbitrators. Arbitral bodies like ICSID collectively oversee hundreds of arbitrations between states and private parties.

There is, of course, still no "sheriff" at the international level to keep states in line. But people don't refrain from running red lights because they think they'll get caught—they do so because otherwise they might get killed! The more traffic, the more incentive there is for drivers to abide by the rules of the road. In an interconnected world, by the same token, most states want to comply because they see that it is in their interest to do so. They may lose individual cases, but the value of an orderly dispute-resolution system far outweighs these setbacks. If international relations are a prisoner's dilemma, international law is the iterative solution—the more times you run the game, the more sensible cooperation becomes.

Exceptions exist. Russia and China, for example, are frequently criticized for refusing to participate in major cases. But they are outliers. Most states, even powerful ones, usually participate in international justice in good faith. And even Russia and China participate sometimes (generally when the stakes are either low or very high indeed): for example, as of this writing I have on my docket a BIT case stemming from the Russian takeover of the Crimea.

Another welcome development in international law: Americans have gotten better at it! Aggression, bickering, and potshots at the other side might impress a jury in Manhattan; but they are unlikely to garner much sympathy from an arbitral panel of three European law professors. That kind of behavior is much less common today, as are incidents like that of the California attorney who told the Iran–United States Tribunal, including three continental Europeans and three Farsi-speaking Iranians listening through simultaneous translation, "We want the whole enchilada!"

With these positive developments in place, is the trajectory for international law plain sailing from here on out? Not quite. In fact, a worrying backlash appears to be growing against Investor-State Dispute Settlement, or ISDS.

A DEMOLITION DERBY

"For the EU, ISDS is dead." So said a fact sheet issued in 2017 by the European Union itself.[9] And there is good reason to believe the rhetoric. The EU is one of the most reckless participants in what I have called a "demolition derby" looking to destroy international arbitration as we know it.[10]

As we have seen again and again in this book, states—even poor ones—have vastly more power than private parties. They can forcibly expropriate investors. Impose surprise "taxes." Change the law in a discriminatory fashion. There is little inherent incentive for states to treat foreigners fairly. In fact, when the chips are down, the incentives are likely to run in precisely the opposite direction.

The present system seeks to redress the balance in three ways: First, by removing disputes from the domestic courts. Second, by allowing each disputant to appoint an arbitrator to sit alongside a tribunal president in whose selection the contesting parties have an equal role. Third, by affording investors protection against discrimination and unlawful expropriation.

The EU has chosen to strike against the second of these pillars. It has proposed to establish a permanent investment court—with all fifteen of its judges appointed by states. I call it "the fifteen-headed hydra."[11] Reportedly, the European Union did not bother to consult the arbitration community before putting together the proposal for this polycephalous abomination.[12] If it succeeds in establishing the court, which currently is being negotiated in Working Group III of the United Nations Commission on International Trade Law (UNCITRAL), it will do so in the face of near-universal opposition from the investor side, for the court would remove a key protection and drive up the cost of investment. But the EU pushes on regardless, writing the court into its trade agreements, first with Canada and then Vietnam,[13] and compelling all twenty-seven of its member states to support the hydra in the UNCITRAL negotiations.

Nor is the EU alone among powerful developed economies in holding such an attitude. In recent years, Canada and the United States have struck at pillar number three—investor protections. We have already seen how the NAFTA countries, led by the United States, attempted to "interpret" such rights out of the agreement. Thankfully, as we have seen, the tribunal in *Mondev* found a way around it. Subsequent panels—including some on which I served—have done the same.[14]

This has not stopped similar attempts at destruction. For example, the new U.S. model BIT, adopted in 2012, would give the United States and its respective treaty partner, acting together, the right to "interpret" investor-state disputes out of existence. This is scarcely likely to incentivize American investment overseas; but, shockingly, that all too recently was part of my government's intention. A few years ago, a high-ranking U.S. trade official told me point-blank that the administration in which he was serving did not want arbitration provisions in BITs or trade agreements because they made it too easy for Americans to invest in developing countries instead of in the good old U.S. of A! That kind of economic nativism ought to have no place in today's world—and yet, that was the case.

This sort of thing is bad enough for capital-exporting countries, which if they succeed will only push up the cost of doing business with them, to the detriment of all. But the developing world has entered drivers in the demolition derby, too, and their target has been the first pillar—the right to arbitrate outside the domestic courts.

We have already seen how, in 2007, Bolivia under Evo Morales withdrew from the ICSID Convention, becoming the first member state to do so. It would not be the last. Ecuador did the same in 2009, followed by Venezuela in 2012.[15] These same three states have also denounced (an international law term meaning "terminated") BITs with individual investment partners, as have Indonesia, South Africa, and others. But two developing countries stand out for their extreme reactions to arbitral losses.

In the case of *White Industries v. India*, I was appointed by the claimant, an Australian company. India appointed Christopher Lau SC, a distinguished Singaporean arbitrator. Bill Rowley QC, a longtime chair of the London Court of International Arbitration, presided over the tribunal. In 2011, we unanimously ruled against India, holding that the country's courts had failed to afford White Industries its treaty right to "effective means of asserting claims and enforcing rights" with respect to an ICC award it had earlier obtained.[16]

India responded by going berserk, blasting out fifty-eight notices terminating BITs outright and twenty-five proposals for "interpretations" that would effectively erase investors' rights to enjoy "fair and equitable treatment" and to settle their disputes via arbitration.[17]

Ecuador may represent the most extreme case. With typical understatement, former president Rafael Correa described ICSID, a technical and administrative dispute-resolution institution that since 1966 has been a member of the World Bank Group, as a symbol of "colonialism" and "slavery."[18] Under Correa's leadership, the country adopted a new constitution that imposes an outright ban on arbitration clauses and other ISDS agreements. To chair a new commission on ISDS, the Correa government chose Cecelia Olivet, the Uruguayan co-author of *Profiting from Injustice*, the 2012 report that made lurid and unsubstantiated claims about arbitration and arbitrators, including myself. To nobody's surprise, Olivet's 668-page report on behalf of the Correa regime recommended a new round of denunciations of BITs, forcing yet more investors back on Ecuador's domestic courts—hardly models of celerity or impartiality.[19] (Faced with a mass exodus of investment, Correa's successor has reversed course, as we will see.)

For developing countries dependent on inflows of capital from overseas, these moves are tantamount to economic suicide. In October 2017, amid the Trump administration's war on trade agreements, some 230 law professors, adherents of the "law and economics" school of legal scholarship, sent an open letter to the president urging him to take a stand against ISDS provisions in NAFTA. If U.S. businesses wanted to invest overseas, these academics suggested, the answer was simple: "purchase risk insurance or look for safer jurisdictions."[20] This letter inadvertently betrays the double iniquity of the current crusade against ISDS. "Looking for safer jurisdictions" means declining to invest in the poorest countries that need these inflows the most. Meanwhile, only the biggest and best-heeled corporations will have the resources to purchase risk insurance—or to negotiate their own, sweeter deals with host governments.[21] In both cases, the little guys will suffer disproportionately.

Moreover, attacks on ISDS almost invariably reintroduce an unwelcome measure of politics into international dispute settlement. Take the EU's hydra-headed investment court. Just five of the fifteen seats are to be appointed by the EU's twenty-seven member countries, which thus will fight tooth and nail over them, in the process doubtless forming internal blocs and alliances in favor of this or that candidate. They will seek to appoint political loyalists over technical experts, with a resulting diminution in the quality of the court's decisions.[22]

Nor are these the worst potential consequences of weakening ISDS. Without the option of a reliable method for resolving disputes judicially, we may even see a return to state-to-state confrontation over trade and investment disputes.

Maurer cites Brazil as an example of what may lie in store should this happen. Brazil does not do BITs (it has negotiated a few, but only two are in force as of this writing) and is not a member of ICSID. It has, instead, found less savory means of handling its problems. In 2006 and 2007, when Bolivia nationalized Brazilian natural gas and refining assets, the government of Luiz Inácio Lula da Silva caved under Brazil's domestic media and popular pressure and rattled the saber, first by threatening an embargo and then by openly contemplating support for secessionist governors in Bolivia's eastern provinces.[23] Bolivia was forced to back down. That is but a foretaste of the destabilization that could result from a decline in ISDS.

There are signs that states may be awakening to the danger. The EU's hydra has hit roadblocks, in particular in the shape of the European Court of Justice's decision that such courts cannot be established by the EU institutions unilaterally but require the consent of every member state.[24] Since the fall of Rafael Correa in 2017, Ecuador has rowed back from its extreme anti-BIT stance. It has proposed new negotiations on BITs with fifteen countries, and its propaganda now highlights the fact that, via the existing arbitral mechanisms, Ecuador actually avoided

83 percent of the damages claimed against it in the decade following 2008. In 2017, the new Ecuadorian trade minister admitted: "In order to secure private direct investment, we must have BITs."[25]

There is, in other words, hope.

ARBITRAMENT OF THE SWORD

After more than sixty years as an attorney, a judge, and an arbitrator, how do I view my career? First, I don't see myself as ever having had a job! When asked to list my pastimes, I say that my work *is* my hobby; I am the living embodiment of the old saying that if you love what you do, you will never work a day in your life. The fact that I got paid to do what I loved is the cherry on top.

At any rate, it seems I must have done something right, for as of this writing I have amassed six lifetime achievement awards (or their equivalents), including the American Society of International Law's Manley O. Hudson Medal for "pre-eminent scholarship and achievement in international law . . . without regard to nationality."

I am immensely proud of the contribution I have made to the development of a working system of international dispute settlement. Law matters. Law gives order to life. And in the international arena, order means peace. Thus, I end this account where I began—indeed, where modern international arbitration itself arguably began—with the case of the CSS *Alabama*. By the time the panel issued its substantial award, the British political winds had brought to power Prime Minister William Ewart Gladstone, one of his country's foremost statesmen. Gladstone was no fan of the award, but he recognized that his government's paying it was a necessary part of being a good global citizen.

In Parliament, the prime minister spoke sagely:

> *Although I may think the sentence was harsh in its extent, and unjust in its basis, I regard the fine imposed on this country as*

dust in the balance compared with the moral value of the example set when these two great nations of England and America— which are among the most fiery and the most jealous in the world with regard to anything that touches national honour— went in peace and concord before a judicial tribunal rather than resort to the arbitrament of the sword.[26]

Words to live by.

Notes

INTRODUCTION: THE WORLD THAT SUES TOGETHER HEWS TOGETHER

1. Thomas Bingham, "The *Alabama* Claims Arbitration," *International & Comparative Law Quarterly* 54, no. 1 (Jan 2005): 2, n7.

2. Bingham, "*Alabama* Claims Arbitration," 8.

3. William S. Dudley, "CSS *Alabama*: Lost and Found," *U.S. Naval History and Heritage Command,* May 13, 2020, https://www.history.navy.mil/research/underwater-archaeology/sites-and-projects/ship-wrecksites/css-alabama/css-alabama-lost-and-found.html.

4. J. Bradford DeLong, "Estimating World GDP, One Million BC–Present," May 24, 1998, http://holtz.org/Library/Social%20Science/Economics/Estimating%20World%20GDP%20by%20DeLong/Estimating%20World%20GDP.htm.

5. Bingham, "*Alabama* Claims Arbitration," 19.

6. Bingham, "*Alabama* Claims Arbitration," 22.

7. Congressional Budget Office, "The Federal Budget in 2019: An Infographic," April 15, 2020, https://www.cbo.gov/publication/56324.

8. Roy Jenkins, *Gladstone: A Biography* (New York: Random House, 1997), chap. 21.

9. Thomas Hobbes, *De Cive* (1642), preface.

10. Noel Maurer, *The Empire Trap: The Rise and Fall of U.S. Intervention to Protect American Property Overseas, 1893–2013* (Princeton University Press, 2013).

11. Raphael Semmes, *Memoirs of Service Afloat During the War Between the States* (Baltimore: Kelly, Piet & Co., 1868), chap. 34, p. 282.

12. Bingham, "*Alabama* Claims Arbitration," 24.

13. Communiqué No. 16/1 (May 9, 2016), Office of the Secretary-General of the Iran–United States Claims Tribunal, http://www.iusct.net/General%20Documents/Communique%2016.1%20(9%20May%202016).pdf.

CHAPTER ONE: STREET-FIGHTING MAN

1. U.S. v. Nelson Cornelious Drummond, 354 F.2d 132 (2d Cir. 1965).

2. Herbert Brean, "A Master Rogue Unmasked," *LIFE*, July 20, 1959, 19–24.

3. Arthur L. Liman, *Lawyer: A Life of Counsel and Controversy* (New York: PublicAffairs, 1998), 50.

4. Homer Bigart, "Birrell Ends Exile of 7 Years; Financier Fled U.S. During S.E.C. Study in October, 1957; Lived in Cuba Under Regime of Batista and Then in Brazil," *New York Times*, April 24, 1964, https://www.nytimes.com/1964/04/24/archives/birrell-ends-exile-of-7-years-financier-fled-us-during-sec-study-in.html.

5. Brean, "Master Rogue," 19–24.

6. Brean, "Master Rogue," 19–24.

7. Bigart, "Birrell Ends Exile."

8. Bigart, "Birrell Ends Exile."

9. Liman, *Lawyer*, 52.

10. "Birrell Is Guilty in Stock Selling," *New York Times*, December 29, 1967.

11. Rahimtoola v. The Nizam of Hyderabad, [1958] A.C. 379 at 418.

CHAPTER TWO: MIGHT MAKES RIGHT

1. Chronik der Mauer, "Chronicle," https://www.chronik-der-mauer.de/en/chronicle/_year1961/_month8/?language=en&month=8&moc=1&year=1961&opennid=182291&filter=1&dokument=0&audio=0&video=0&foto=0.

2. Martin Hillenbrand, *Fragments of Our Time: Memoirs of a Diplomat* (Athens: University of Georgia Press, 1998), 282.

3. C. J. Schuler, "History of the Berlin Wall Through Maps," *Here 360*, November 6, 2014, https://360.here.com/2014/11/06/fall-wall-missing-pieces/.

4. Honoré Catudal, "Steinstücken: The Politics of a Berlin Exclave," *World Affairs* 134, no. 1 (1971): 58.

5. Catudal, "Steinstücken," 59, n45.

6. Ellen Lentz, "The Talk of Steinstücken," *New York Times*, December 11, 1971.

7. Judgement of the International Military Tribunal, September 30 and October 1, 1946 (section "Judgement: Hess"), https://avalon.law.yale.edu/imt/judhess.asp.

8. "Report of Commission to Examine Defendant Hess," November 17, 1945, https://avalon.law.yale.edu/imt/v1-28.asp.

9. Hillenbrand, *Fragments of Our Time*, 285–93.

10. U. Alexis Johnson, *The Right Hand of Power* (Englewood Cliffs, NJ: Prentice-Hall, 1984), 560.

11. Patricia Sullivan, "Robert Mardian; Attorney Caught Up in Watergate Scandal," *Washington Post*, July 21, 2006, https://www.washingtonpost.com/politics/robert-mardian-attorney-caught-up-in-watergate-scandal/2012/05/31/gJQARJ6vFV_story.html.

12. Martin Weil, "J. Fred Buzhardt Dies," *Washington Post*, December 17, 1978, https://www.washingtonpost.com/archive/local/1978/12/17/j-fred-buzhardt-dies /0ffd34e0-8b33-445c-8c7b-71678d46b2e8/.

13. Murrey Marder, "Senators Worried by Cambodia Crisis," *Washington Post*, April 13, 1971.

14. CBS News, *Face the Nation*, April 15, 1973, transcript.

CHAPTER THREE: RUG PULLS, INVESTMENTS, AND SHAKEDOWNS

1. David C. Berliner, "Frelinghuysen: Moderate Republican," *New York Times*, June 3, 1973.

2. Brown-Forman Distillers Corp. v. Matthews, 435 F. Supp. 5 (W.D. Ky. 1976) at 8.

3. Brown-Forman Distillers Corp. v. Matthews, at n1.

4. Alfonso A. Narvaez, "Judge James Gordon Dies at 71; Imposed a Landmark Busing Plan," *New York Times*, February 13, 1990, https://www.nytimes.com /1990/02/13/obituaries/judge-james-gordon-dies-at-71-imposed-a-landmark -busing-plan.html.

5. Brown-Forman Distillers Corp. v. Matthews, at 12, 16 (italics in original).

6. Robert W. Benson, "B.A.T.F.? F.D.A.? Is Jurisdiction Exclusive or Concurrent?" *American Bar Association Journal* 64, no. 10 (October 1978): 1596.

7. Robert W. Benson, "Will the Real F.D.A. Please Be Allowed to Stand Up?" *American Bar Association Journal* 64, no. 6 (June 1978): 907.

8. Benson, "B.A.T.F.?", 1596.

9. Maurer, *Empire Trap*, 387.

10. Graham Hovey, "Nigeria's Arrest of an American Threatens to Mar Visit by Carter," *New York Times*, March 29, 1978; Hovey, "Nigeria Rearrests U.S. Executive Shortly Before Carter's Arrival," *New York Times*, April 1, 1978.

11. General Assembly Resolution 3281 (XXIX), art. 2(c).

12. General Assembly Resolution 3281 (XXIX), preamble.

13. Hovey, "Nigeria's Arrest."

14. Cable, October 31, 1977. More information available at Wikileaks, keyword search "Charles N. Brower."

15. Hovey, "Nigeria's Arrest."

16. Date based on reporting in "American Is Released on Bail by Nigerians," *New York Times*, March 31, 1978.

17. Louis Achi, "F. R. A. Williams Is Dead," *This Day*, March 27, 2005, https ://www.laits.utexas.edu/africa/ads/538.html.

18. Graham Hovey, "Nigeria Rearrests U.S. Executive Shortly Before Carter's Arrival," *New York Times*, April 1, 1978.

19. Cable, April 6, 1978.

20. Robert B. Semple, "Nixon and Tanaka Announce Plans to Cut U.S. Deficit," *New York Times*, September 2, 1972, https://www.nytimes.com/1972/09/02 /archives/nixon-and-tanaka-announce-plans-to-cut-us-deficit-japan-buying.html.

21. Atomic Heritage Foundation, s.v. "Oak Ridge, TN," https://www.atomic heritage.org/location/oak-ridge-tn.

22. Charles N. Brower, "Litigation of Sovereign Immunity Before a State Administrative Body and the Department of State: The Japanese Uranium Tax Case," *American Journal of International Law* 71, no. 3 (July 1977): 438–60.

23. "Abner Linwood Holton (1923–2021)," Department of State, https://history .state.gov/departmenthistory/people/holton-abner-linwood.

24. Thomas O'Toole, "Japanese Resist Tennessee Tax on $175 Million Pile of Uranium," *Washington Post*, September 25, 1975.

25. Maurer, *Empire Trap*, 314, 327–36.

26. Maurer, *Empire Trap*, 314, 339–40.

27. Maurer, *Empire Trap*, 339–43.

28. Jeff Gerth, "Seeking Testimony in Pipeline Case: Immunity Given to a Secretive Swiss," *New York Times*, March 6, 1988, https://www.nytimes.com/1988/03/06/ world/seeking-testimony-in-pipeline-case-immunity-given-to-a-secretive-swiss.html.

29. *Encyclopedia Britannica*, s.v. "Sukarno," https://www.britannica.com /biography/Sukarno.

30. Claudia Luther, "A. Andrew Hauk, 91; Federal Judge Whose Comments Raised Some Hackles," *Los Angeles Times*, November 12, 2004, https://www.latimes .com/archives/la-xpm-2004-nov-12-me-hauk12-story.html.

CHAPTER FOUR: HOW TO SUE A STATE

1. John Y. Gotanda, "Awarding Interest in International Arbitration," *American Journal of International Law* 90, no. 1 (January 1996): 51.

2. Charles N. Brower, "Investomercial Arbitration: Whence Cometh It? What Is It? Whither Goeth It?" *Arbitration* 80, no. 2 (2014).

3. ICSID, "The ICSID Caseload—Statistics," issue 2021–1 (2021), https://icsid .worldbank.org/sites/default/files/publications/The%20ICSID%20Caseload%20 Statistics%20%282021-1%20Edition%29%20ENG.pdf.

4. Amco Asia Corp. et al. v. Republic of Indonesia, ICSID Arbitration No. 81/1, Award dated May 31, 1990, paras. 2–12.

5. Amco Asia Corp. et al. v. Republic of Indonesia, ICSID Arbitration No. 81/1, Award dated November 20, 1984, paras. 83–88, 112.

6. Amco Asia Corp. et al. v. Republic of Indonesia, November 20, 1984, para. 117.

7. Amco Asia Corp. et al. v. Republic of Indonesia, November 20, 1984 paras. 89, 92, 101.

8. GA Res. 3281(xxix), UN GAOR, 29th Sess., Supp. No. 31 (1974), 50, art. 2(c) (emphasis added).

9. Amco Asia Corp. et al. v. Republic of Indonesia, November 20, 1984, para. 6.

10. Amco Asia Corp. et al. v. Republic of Indonesia, ICSID Arbitration No. 81/1, Ad Hoc Committee Decision on the Application for Annulment, May 16, 1986, para. 4.

11. See procedural history for Amco v. Indonesia at https://jusmundi.com/en /document/decision/en-amco-asia-corporation-and-others-v-republic-of-indonesia -decision-on-the-applications-for-annulment-of-the-1990-award-and-the-1990 -supplemental-award-thursday-17th-december-1992.

12. "Petroleum Reserve Deals at $8.5 Million," *The Oklahoman*, March 4, 1986, https://www.oklahoman.com/article/2139735/petroleum-reserve-deals-at-85 -million.

CHAPTER FIVE: THE IRAN CONNECTION

1. Sandra Mackey, *The Iranians: Persia, Islam, and the Soul of a Nation* (New York: Penguin, 1996), 193–94.

2. Mackey, *The Iranians*, 196–97.

3. Ray Takeyh, *The Last Shah: America, Iran, and the Fall of the Pahlavi Dynasty* (New Haven, CT: Yale University Press, 2021), 74, 94.

4. Takeyh, *Last Shah*, 64.

5. Mackey, *The Iranians*, 199–200.

6. Wayne Mapp, *The Iran–United States Claims Tribunal: The First Ten Years, 1981–1991* (Manchester, UK: Manchester University Press, 1993), 42.

7. *Encyclopaedia Britannica*, s.v. "Mohammad Mosaddegh," https://www .britannica.com/biography/Mohammad-Mosaddegh.

8. Anglo-Iranian Oil Co. Case, Judgment of July 22, 1952, 94, https://www.icj-cij .org/public/files/case-related/16/016-19520722-JUD-01-00-EN.pdf.

9. Anglo-Iranian Oil Co. Case, 112, https://www.icj-cij.org/public/files/case-related /16/016-19520722-JUD-01-00-EN.pdf.

10. "World Court Bars Ruling on Iran Oil," *New York Times*, July 23, 1952, https://archive.nytimes.com/www.nytimes.com/library/world/mideast/072352 iran-world.html.

11. Mackey, *The Iranians*, 202; Takeyh, *Last Shah*, 72–73.

12. Takeyh, *Last Shah*, 74.

13. Takeyh, *Last Shah*, 82.

14. Mackey, *The Iranians*, 197–98.

15. Maurer, *Empire Trap*, 304–05.

16. Mackey, *The Iranians*, 206.

17. Stephen Kinzer, *All The Shah's Men: An American Coup and the Roots of Middle East Terror* (New York: Wiley, 2003), 177–178.

18. Takeyh, *Last Shah*, 124.

19. Mackey, *The Iranians*, 208.

20. Mackey, *The Iranians*, 250; Kate Gillespie, "U.S. Corporations and Iran at the Hague," *Middle East Journal* 44, no. 1 (Winter 1990): 19–20.

21. Gillespie, "U.S. Corporations and Iran," 19.

22. William Branigin, "Iran Canceling U.S. Arms Sales Worth Billions," *Washington Post*, February 4, 1979, https://www.washingtonpost.com/archive/politics/1979/02/04/iran-canceling-us-arms-sales-worth-billions/ba4263e2-9ac0-410d-90e2-19876b28727d/.

23. Daniel Thomas Potts, "Iran and America: A Forgotten Friendship," *The Conversation*, July 31, 2018, https://theconversation.com/iran-and-america-a-forgotten-friendship-99350.

24. Robert W. Murray and Stephen McGlinchey, "The Reluctant Realist: Jimmy Carter and Iran," in *Realism in Practice: An Appraisal*, ed. by J. R. Avgustin, Davide Orsi, Max Nurnus (E-IR publishers, 2018).

25. Mackey, *The Iranians*, 250.

26. Robert B. Semple Jr., "Bomb Rocks Site in Iran Just Before Visit by Nixon," *New York Times*, June 1, 1972.

27. "Carter Said to Approve Huge Arms Sale to Iran," *New York Times*, July 16, 1978, https://www.nytimes.com/1978/07/16/archives/carter-said-to-approve-huge-arms-sale-to-iran.html.

28. Branigin, "Iran Canceling U.S. Arms Sales Worth Billions."

29. Takeyh, *Last Shah*, 252.

30. Mapp, *Iran–United States Claims Tribunal*, 4.

31. Mackey, *The Iranians*, 340–42.

32. Nicholas Gage, "Armed Iranians Rush U.S. Embassy; Khomeini's Forces Free Staff of 100," *New York Times*, February 15, 1979.

33. Gage, "Armed Iranians."

34. David D. Kirkpatrick, "How a Chase Bank Chairman Helped the Deposed Shah of Iran Enter the U.S.," *New York Times*, December 29, 2019, https://www.nytimes.com/2019/12/29/world/middleeast/shah-iran-chase-papers.html.

35. Mackey, *The Iranians*, 294.

36. ICJ, *Diplomatic and Consular Staff in Tehran*, Judgment of May 24, 1980, para. 59.

37. ICJ, *Diplomatic and Consular Staff in Tehran*, para. 23.

38. ICJ, *Diplomatic and Consular Staff in Tehran*, paras. 26, 70, 73.

39. Takeyh, *Last Shah*, 254–55.

40. U.S. Department of State, "Joint Statement Following Discussions with Leaders of the People's Republic of China," February 27, 1972, https://history.state.gov/historicaldocuments/frus1969-76v17/d203; "Address by President Carter to the Nation," December 15, 1978, https://history.state.gov/historicaldocuments/frus1977-80v01/d104.

41. Goldwater v. Carter, 617 F.2d 697, https://casetext.com/case/goldwater-v-carter-2.

42. Congressional Research Service, "Treaties and Other International Agreements: The Role of the United States Senate," January 2001, 152–53.

43. Quoted in Goldwater v. Carter, 617 F.2d 697, https://casetext.com/case /goldwater-v-carter-2.

44. Goldwater v. Carter.

45. Sigrid Winkler, "Taiwan's UN Dilemma: To Be or Not to Be," Brookings Institution, June 20, 2012, https://www.brookings.edu/opinions/taiwans-un -dilemma-to-be-or-not-to-be/.

46. Details of the argument summarized in Goldwater v. Carter, fn2.

47. Goldwater v. Carter, 444 U.S. 996 (1979), https://www.oyez.org/cases/1979/79 -856.

48. Mapp, *Iran–United States Claims Tribunal*, 6.

49. Executive Order 12170 (November 14, 1979), https://www.archives.gov/federal -register/codification/executive-order/12170.html.

50. Banco Nacional de Cuba v. Sabbatino, 376 U.S. 398 (1964), https://www.oyez .org/cases/1963/16.

51. "Iran Says U.S. Museums Hold Its Art," *New York Times*, December 12, 1979, https://www.nytimes.com/1979/12/12/archives/iran-says-us-museums-hold-its -art-doesnt-want-to-sell.html.

52. Laura A. Kiernan, "Iran-Owned Art Held Here," *Washington Post*, December 20, 1979, https://www.washingtonpost.com/archive/politics/1979/12/20/iran -owned-art-held-here/40e3849b-6ae2-484a-a724-c587fa1fd480/.

53. American Intern. Group v. Islamic Republic of Iran, 493 F. Supp. 522 (D.D.C. 1980), https://law.justia.com/cases/federal/district-courts/FSupp/493/522/1557756/.

54. Congressional Research Service, "The International Emergency Economic Powers Act: Origins, Evolution, and Use," July 14, 2020.

55. General Declaration, General Principle B.

56. Claims Settlement Declaration, art. II(1).

57. General Declaration, paras. 7, 10.

58. American International Group, Inc., et al. v. Islamic Republic of Iran, et al. 657 F.2d 430 (D.C. Cir. 1981), https://law.justia.com/cases/federal/appellate-courts /F2/657/430/395493/.

59. Dames & Moore v. Regan, 453 U.S. 654 (1981) at 687.

60. Claims Settlement Declaration, art. III(2).

61. Claims Settlement Declaration, art. V.

62. Thomas Kellner, "Lights, Electricity, Action: When Ronald Reagan Hosted 'General Electric Theater'," GE, February 17, 2019, https://www.ge.com/news /reports/ronald-reagan-ge.

63. Edmund Morris, *Dutch: A Memoir of Ronald Reagan* (New York: Random House, 1999), 320.

64. Morris, *Dutch*, 321 (based on interviews with my brother and my mother).

65. Strengthening the International Court of Justice: Hearings before the Committee on Foreign Relations, United States Senate, 93rd Congress, May 10 & 11, 1973, Statement of Charles N. Brower (May 10, 1973), 94.

66. Stephen M. Schwebel, "Celebrating a Fraud on the Court," *American Journal of International Law* 106, no. 1 (January 2012): 102.

67. U.S. Statement on Withdrawal from Case Before the World Court, January 19, 1985, https://www.nytimes.com/1985/01/19/world/text-of-us-statement-on -withdrawal-from-case-before-the-world-court.html.

68. Keith Highet, "Between a Rock and a Hard Place—The United States, the International Court, and the Nicaragua Case," *The International Lawyer* 21, no. 4 (Fall 1987): 1094–95.

69. AIG v. Iran, IUSCT, Award No. 93-2-3 (December 7, 1983), para. 54, https ://jusmundi.com/en/document/decision/en-american-international-group-inc -and-american-life-insurance-company-v-islamic-republic-of-iran-and-central -insurance-of-iran-bimeh-markazi-iran-award-award-no-93-2-3-wednesday-7th -december-1983.

CHAPTER SIX: JUDGING IRAN, PART I

1. Sedco, Inc. v. National Iranian Oil Company and The Islamic Republic of Iran, IUSCT Case Nos. 128 and 129, https://jusmundi.com/en/document/decision /en-sedco-inc-v-national-iranian-oil-company-and-the-islamic-republic-of-iran -award-award-no-309-129-3-tuesday-7th-july-1987.

2. Noah A. Baygell v. The Islamic Republic of Iran, IUSCT Case No. 10212, https://jusmundi.com/en/document/decision/en-noah-a-baygell-v-the-islamic -republic-of-iran-award-award-no-231-10212-2-friday-2nd-may-1986.

3. Islamic Republic of Iran v. United States of America, IUSCT Case No. A-18, Decision, paras. 1, 30.

4. Stewart and Truell, "U.S. Firms Win Some, Lose Some at Tribunal Arbitrating $5 Billion in Claims Against Iran," *Wall Street Journal*, November 15, 1984.

5. *Proceedings of the Annual Meeting (American Society of International Law)* 105 (2011): 220.

6. Ronald Reagan, "Message to the Congress Reporting on Developments Concerning the Declaration of a National Emergency with Respect to Iran," November 4, 1983, https://www.reaganlibrary.gov/archives/speech/message -congress-reporting-developments-concerning-declaration-national-emergency-3.

7. Howard M. Holtzmann, "Dispute Resolution Procedures in East-West Trade," *International Lawyer* 13, no. 2 (Spring 1979): 236.

8. Holtzmann, "Dispute Resolution," 241, 244–45.

9. Mapp, *Iran–United States Claims Tribunal*, 44–48.

10. Stewart and Truell, "U.S. Firms Win Some."

11. Ford Aerospace & Communications Corp. v. Air Force of Iran, IUSCT Case No. 159, Dissent of Judge Brower, June 24, 1985.

12. Stewart and Truell, "U.S. Firms Win Some"; R. J. Reynolds Tobacco Company v. The Government of the Islamic Republic of Iran and Iranian Tobacco Company (ITC), IUSCT Case No. 35, Award, https://jusmundi.com/en/document/decision /en-r-j-reynolds-tobacco-company-v-the-government-of-the-islamic-republic-of -iran-and-iranian-tobacco-company-itc-partial-award-award-no-145-35-3-friday -8th-june-1984#decision_4036.

13. "AROUND THE WORLD; Iranian Judge Threatens a Swede at The Hague," *New York Times*, September 7, 1984.

14. Stewart and Truell, "U.S. Firms Win Some."

CHAPTER SEVEN: JUDGING IRAN, PART II

1. Damien Charlotin, "A Data Analysis of the Iran–U.S. Claims Tribunal's Jurisprudence," *ITA in Review* 1, no. 2 (2019): 6.

2. Charlotin, "Data Analysis of the Iran–U.S. Claims," 6.

3. Mapp, *Iran–United States Claims Tribunal*, 162.

4. Award No. 310-56-3 (July 14, 1987), paras. 145–46, 182.

5. Award No. 310-56-3, paras. 201, 261–64.

6. Award No. 310-56-3, Concurring Opinion of Judge Brower, paras. 4, 10–12.

7. Award No. 310-56-3, Concurring Opinion of Judge Brower, para. 7.

8. Award No. 310-56-3, Concurring Opinion of Judge Brower, paras. 15–17, 19, 23.

9. Award No. 310-56-3, Concurring Opinion of Judge Brower, para. 18.

10. Award No. 425-39-2 (June 29, 1989), para. 126.

11. American Independent Oil Co. v. State of Kuwait, Final Award (March 24, 1982), sec. II, https://jusmundi.com/en/document/decision/en-the-american-independent -oil-company-v-the-government-of-the-state-of-kuwait-final-award-wednesday -24th-march-1982.

12. American Independent Oil Co. v. State of Kuwait, para. 88.

13. American Independent Oil Co. v. State of Kuwait, paras. 89–110.

14. American Independent Oil Co. v. State of Kuwait, para. 178.

15. American Independent Oil Co. v. State of Kuwait, Separate Opinion of Sir G. Fitzmaurice (n.d.), https://jusmundi.com/en/document/opinion/en-the-american -independent-oil-company-v-the-government-of-the-state-of-kuwait-separate -opinion-of-sir-g-fitzmaurice-wednesday-24th-march-1982#opinion_2550.

16. R.J.R. Nabisco Inc. v. Commissioner, 76 TCM 71 (1998), Opinion, sec. 5, https://www.leagle.com/decision/199814776stcm711129.

17. R.J.R. Nabisco Inc. v. Commissioner, secs. 4 & 7.

18. Case Nos. 126 & 129.

19. Remarks, *Proceedings of the Annual Meeting (American Society of International Law)* 105 (2011): 226.

20. Remarks, *Proceedings*, 223.

21. Alfred L. W. Short v. The Islamic Republic of Iran, Case No. 11135, Dissenting Opinion of Judge Brower (July 14, 1987), para. 11.

22. Short v. The Islamic Republic of Iran, para. 34.

23. Short v. The Islamic Republic of Iran, para. 15.

24. Mobil Oil Iran v. The Islamic Republic of Iran, Case No. 74, Partial Award (July 14, 1987), para. 25.

25. Mobil Oil Iran v. The Islamic Republic of Iran, para. 27.

26. Mobil Oil Iran v. The Islamic Republic of Iran, para. 175.

27. Case No. 261.

28. Concurring and Dissenting Opinion of Judge Brower (July 18, 1988), para. 17.

29. Art. V(1)(b).

30. Concurring and Dissenting Opinion of Judge Brower (July 18, 1988), para. 22.

31. Iran Aircraft Industries v. Avco Corp. 980 F.2d 141 (2d Cir. 1992).

32. Iran v. United States, Case No. A27, Award (June 5, 1998).

33. Communiqué No. 16/1 (May 9, 2016).

34. Mapp, *Iran–United States Claims Tribunal*, 55.

35. IUSCT Case No. A33, Decision No. DEC 132-A-33-FT (September 9, 2004).

36. David M. Abshire, *Saving the Reagan Presidency: Trust Is the Coin of the Realm* (College Station: Texas A&M Press, 2005), 69.

37. Charlotin, "Data Analysis," 8–10.

38. Charlotin, "Data Analysis," 8–10.

39. Communiqué No. 16/1 (May 9, 2016).

40. Mapp, *Iran–United States Claims Tribunal*, 35.

41. Charlotin, "Data Analysis," 2, 5.

42. Mapp, *Iran–United States Claims Tribunal*, 176–82, 188.

CHAPTER EIGHT: IRAN-CONTRA: WHAT REAGAN KNEW

1. Mackey, *The Iranians*, 327.

2. Abshire, *Saving the Reagan Presidency*, 67–68.

3. Walter V. Robinson, "Reagan Will Meet Press as Skepticism Mounts," *Boston Globe*, November 19, 1986.

4. Tribunal Rules of Procedure, May 3, 1983, article 13(2).

5. Abshire, *Saving the Reagan Presidency*, 87.

6. "Iran in '88?" *Wall Street Journal*, December 29, 1986.

7. Rowland Evans and Robert Novak, "The Reagan Presidency Is Dead," *Washington Post*, December 31, 1986.

8. Lou Cannon, "Baker Shows Light Touch in New Job: Staff Chief's Debut Contrasts with Style of 'Prime Minister' Regan," *Washington Post*, March 3, 1987.

9. Steven Roberts, "The White House Link to Iran Investigations: David M. Abshire," *New York Times*, January 29, 1987.

10. Abshire, *Saving the Reagan Presidency*, 27, 68.

11. Roberts, "White House Link."

12. Mackey, *The Iranians*, 326–27.

13. Roberts, "White House Link."

14. Lawrence E. Walsh, *Firewall: The Iran-Contra Conspiracy and Cover-up* (New York: W. W. Norton, 1997), 69–70.

15. Abshire, *Saving the Reagan Presidency*, 120–21.

16. Abshire, *Saving the Reagan Presidency*, 123–24.

17. Steven V. Roberts, "Inquiry Finds Reagan and Chief Advisers Responsible for 'Chaos' in Iran Arms Deals," *New York Times*, February 27, 1987, https ://www.nytimes.com/1987/02/27/world/white-house-crisis-tower-report-inquiry -finds-reagan-chief-advisers-responsible.html.

18. Abshire, *Saving the Reagan Presidency*, 136.

19. Steven V. Roberts, "Reagan Concedes 'Mistake' in Arms-for-Hostage Policy; Takes Blame, Vows Changes," *New York Times*, March 5, 1987.

20. David S. Broder, "Public Doubt Lingers on Reagan Iran Affair," *Washington Post*, March 11, 1987.

21. Robert Pear, "How New Testimony Fits into the Iran-Contra Puzzle," *New York Times*, July 19, 1987.

22. Abshire, *Saving the Reagan Presidency*, 179–81.

CHAPTER NINE: OF PARASITES AND LOUSY LOANS

1. UNCTAD, Bilateral Investment Treaties, 1959–1999 (New York: UN, 2000), 1, https://unctad.org/system/files/official-document/poiteiiad2.en.pdf.

2. "The Basics of Bilateral Investment Treaties," Sidley Austin LLP, https://www .sidley.com/en/global/services/global-arbitration-trade-and-advocacy/investment -treaty-arbitration/sub-pages/the-basics-of-bilateral-investment-treaties/.

3. ICSID, "The ICSID Caseload—Statistics."

4. Compañía del Desarrollo de Santa Elena, SA v. Republic of Costa Rica, ICSID case no. ARB/96/1, Final Award (February 17, 2000), paras. 15–19.

5. *Encyclopedia Britannica*, s.v. "Jesse Helms," https://www.britannica.com /biography/Jesse-Helms.

6. Santa Elena, SA v. Republic of Costa Rica, para. 25.

7. "Database of ICSID Member States," International Centre for the Settlement of Investment Disputes, https://icsid.worldbank.org/about/member-states/database -of-member-states.

8. Santa Elena, SA v. Republic of Costa Rica, para. 46.

9. Santa Elena, SA v. Republic of Costa Rica, paras. 54–59.

10. Santa Elena, SA v. Republic of Costa Rica, para. 111.

11. Ian D. Gauld, *The Ichneumonidae of Costa Rica*, vol. 3 (Gainesville, FL: American Entomological Institute, 2000), 434–35.

12. Československá Obchodní Banka v. Slovak Republic, ICSID case no. ARB/97/4, Award (December 29, 2004), para. 38.

13. Conversion carried out using this tool: https://www.nbs.sk/en/statistics/exchange-rates/en-kurzovy-listok/nbs-monthly-cumulative-and-annual-exchange-rates.

14. Československá Obchodní Banka v. Slovak Republic, ICSID case no. ARB/97/4, Decision of the Tribunal on Objections to Jurisdiction (May 24, 1999), para. 37.

15. Československá Obchodní Banka v. Slovak Republic, para. 39.

16. Československá Obchodní Banka v. Slovak Republic, para. 39.

17. Československá Obchodní Banka v. Slovak Republic, para. 4, n2.

18. Československá Obchodní Banka v. Slovak Republic, paras. 46–47.

19. Československá Obchodní Banka v. Slovak Republic, para. 55.

20. Československá Obchodní Banka v. Slovak Republic, para. 351.

21. Československá Obchodní Banka v. Slovak Republic, para. 372.

22. *The American Lawyer: Focus Europe*, Summer 2005.

23. Mondev International Ltd. v. United States of America, ICSID Case No. ARB(AF)/99/2, Award (October 11, 2002), para. 37.

24. Mondev International Ltd. v. United States of America, paras. 37–40, 64.

25. North American Free Trade Agreement, art. 1110.

26. NAFTA, art. 1105.

27. Pope & Talbot Inc. v. Canada, UNCITRAL, Award on the Merits of Phase 2 (April 10, 2001), para. 109.

28. Pope & Talbot Inc. v. Canada, paras. 115–18.

29. Todd Weiler, *The Interpretation of International Investment Law* (Leiden: Martinus Nijhoff, 2013), 167–69, 259–64.

30. Mondev International Ltd. v. United States of America, paras. 100–101.

31. Mondev International Ltd. v. United States of America, para. 114.

32. Mondev International Ltd. v. United States of America, para. 125.

CHAPTER TEN: SUING SADDAM

1. *Encyclopedia Britannica*, s.v. "Kuwait: The Persian Gulf War and Its Aftermath," https://www.britannica.com/place/Kuwait/The-Persian-Gulf-War-and-its-aftermath.

2. UN Security Council Resolution no. 661 (August 6, 1990).

3. UN Security Council Resolution no. 678 (November 29, 1990).

4. Youssef M. Ibrahim, "Gulf War's Cost to Arabs Estimated at $620 Billion," *New York Times*, September 8, 1992, https://www.nytimes.com/1992/09/08 /world/gulf-war-s-cost-to-arabs-estimated-at-620-billion.html.

5. Duncan McLaren and Iran Willmore, "The Environmental Damage of War in Iraq," *The Guardian*, January 18, 2003, https://www.theguardian.com/world /2003/jan/19/iraq5.

6. UN Security Council Resolution no. 687, S/RES/687 (1991), para. 16; UN Security Council Resolution no. 692, S/RES/692 (1991), para. 3.

7. UNCC, *Provisional Rules for Claims Procedure*, S/AC.26/1992/10, art. 31 (note: in technical terms, the UNCC's rules were only ever provisional).

8. UNCC, "Claims Processing," https://uncc.ch/claims-processing.

9. Michael Raboin, Remarks, *Proceedings of the Annual Meeting (American Society of International Law)* 99 (2005): 327.

10. UNCC, *Report and Recommendations Made by the Panel of Commissioners Concerning the Fourth Instalment of 'E1' Claims*, S/AC.26/2000/16 (September 29, 2000), paras. 67–88.

11. UNCC, *Report and Recommendations Made by the Panel of Commissioners Concerning Part Two of the Seventh Instalment of 'E1' Claims*, S/AC.26/2002/13 (June 20, 2002), paras. 22–133.

12. UNCC, *Report and Recommendations* (June 20, 2002), para. 149.

13. UNCC, *Report and Recommendations Made by the Panel of Commissioners Concerning the Fifteenth Instalment of 'E2' Claims*, S/AC.26/2003/29 (December 18, 2003), para. 157 and annex II.

14. UNCC, *Report and Recommendations* (December 18, 2003), paras. 303–308.

15. Victor Mallett, "Kuwait Diary: Shock Lingers Even After the Smoke Clears," *Los Angeles Times*, August 15, 1990, https://www.latimes.com/archives/la-xpm -1990-08-15-mn-680-story.html.

16. "Iraqi Troops Flee Kuwait City," BBC News, February 26, 1991, http://news.bbc .co.uk/onthisday/hi/dates/stories/february/26/newsid_4716000/4716868.stm.

17. UNCC, *Report and Recommendations Made by the Panel of Commissioners Concerning the First Instalment of 'E3' Claims*, S/AC.26/1998/13 (December 17, 1998), para. 27; Google Earth.

18. UNCC, *Report and Recommendations* (December 17, 1998), para. 27; *Encyclopedia Britannica*, s.v. "Hoover Dam," https://www.britannica.com /topic/Hoover-Dam.

19. "In memory of Şarık Tara," Enka, https://www.enka.com/about-us/in-memory -of-sarik-tara/.

20. "Bekhme Dam," Enka, https://www.enka.com/portfolio-item/bekhme-dam/; UNCC, *Report and Recommendations* (December 17, 1998), para. 31; images from Twitter thread by Wladimir, September 12, 2020, https://twitter.com/ vvanwilgenburg/status/1304803124796944385?lang=en.

21. UNCC, *Report and Recommendations* (December 17, 1998), paras. 58–59, 296–97.

22. UNCC, *Report and Recommendations* (December 17, 1998), para. 57.

23. UNCC, *Report and Recommendations* (December 17, 1998), para. 62.

24. UNCC, *Report and Recommendations* (December 17, 1998), para. 77.

25. UNCC, *Report and Recommendations* (December 17, 1998), paras. 163, 148, 183.

26. "Home," UNCC, https://uncc.ch/home.

CHAPTER ELEVEN: JUDGING IRAN, PART III

1. Wolfgang Saxon, "Brig. Gen. George Lincoln Dies; Top Military Planner was 67," *New York Times*, May 26, 1975.

2. David Laylin, "Iranian Environmentalism: Its Origins and Evolution," Atlantic Council, June 20, 2019, https://www.atlanticcouncil.org/blogs/menasource/iranian-environmentalism-its-origins-and-evolution/.

3. Riahi v. Iran, IUSCT Case No. 485, Interlocutory Award (June 10, 1992), paras. 11, 36.

4. Riahi v. Iran, para. 42.

5. Riahi v. Iran, IUSCT Case No. 485, Concurring and Dissenting Opinion of Judge Charles N. Brower (February 27, 2003), para. 153.

6. Riahi v. Iran, para. 1.

7. Riahi v. Iran, Concurring and Dissenting, paras. 70–74.

8. Riahi v. Iran, Concurring and Dissenting, para. 72.

9. Dan Morgan and Walter Pincus, "Friend of Shah was Enriched by 'High Tech' Deals," *Washington Post*, March 11, 1980.

10. Riahi v. Iran, Concurring and Dissenting, para. 5.

11. Riahi v. Iran, Concurring and Dissenting, para. 5.

12. Riahi v. Iran, Concurring and Dissenting, para. 76.

13. Riahi v. Iran, Concurring and Dissenting, para. 5.

14. Riahi v. Iran, Concurring and Dissenting, para. 78.

15. Riahi v. Iran, Concurring and Dissenting, para. 79.

16. Charlotin, "Data Analysis," p. 14.

17. Riahi v. Iran, IUSCT Case No. 485, Dissenting Opinion of Judge Charles N. Brower (November 17, 2004), para. 15.

18. Riahi v. Iran, Dissenting.

19. Riahi v. Iran, Concurring and Dissenting, paras. 2–7, 31, 214.

20. Riahi v. Iran, para. 8.

21. Riahi v. Iran, Dissenting, para. 2.

22. Decision of Appointing Authority on Challenge by Claimant Riahi to Judge Broms (September 30, 2004), 38 Iran–U.S. Claims Tribunal Reports, 398–99.

23. Riahi v. Iran, Dissenting, para. 63.

24. Adam Bernstein, "D.C. Lawyer, Educator Charles Duncan Dies," *Washington Post*, May 7, 2004, https://www.washingtonpost.com/archive/local/2004/05/07/dc-lawyer-educator-charles-duncan-dies/dbbc3b30-49b3-46f6-a344-0a7fc65dbce2/.

25. Iran v. United States, IUSCT Case No. A15, Award (March 10, 2020).

26. Karl Vick, "Why the U.S. Owed Iran That $400 Million," *Time*, August 16, 2016, https://time.com/4441046/400-million-iran-hostage-history/.

27. Iran v. United States, IUSCT Case No. B61, Decision by the Tribunal (May 7, 2007), para. 3.

28. Iran v. United States, para. 6.

29. Iran v. United States, para. 10.

30. Iran v. United States, para. 12.

31. Iran v. United States, para. 12.

32. Decision No. DEC 134-A3/A8/A9/A14/B61-FT, para. 2.

33. David Caron and I had been so appointed in 2014 by Colombia in separate but parallel cases brought against it by Nicaragua, as is discussed later.

34. *Questions of Interpretation and Application of the 1971 Montreal Convention arising from the Aerial Incident at Lockerbie (Libyan Arab Jamahiriya v. United States of America)*, Verbatim Record, March 27, 1992, 37–51.

35. *Questions of Interpretation and Application*, Declaration of Judge Ni (April 14, 1992).

36. Paul R. Hensel et al., "Bones of Contention: Comparing Territorial, Maritime, and River Issues," *Journal of Conflict Resolution* 52, no. 1 (February 2008): 117–43.

37. Article 31.

38. Article 20.

39. Mark Landler, "Trump Abandons Iran Nuclear Deal He Long Scorned," *New York Times*, May 8, 2018, https://www.nytimes.com/2018/05/08/world/middleeast/trump-iran-nuclear-deal.html.

40. Alleged Violations of the 1955 Treaty of Amity, Opinion of Judge *Ad Hoc* Brower (February 3, 2021), paras. 14, 19, 20.

41. Alleged Violations, para. 13.

42. Alleged Violations, paras. 2, 12.

CHAPTER TWELVE: INTERNATIONAL ARBITRATOR, PART I

1. Vacuum Salt Products Ltd. v. Republic of Ghana, Award (February 16, 1994), para. 41, https://jusmundi.com/en/document/decision/en-vacuum-salt-products-ltd-v-republic-of-ghana-award-wednesday-16th-february-1994.

2. Vacuum Salt v. Republic of Ghana, para. 52.

3. Vacuum Salt v. Republic of Ghana, para. 41.

4. United Nations Audiovisual Library of International Law, s.v. "Dr. Kamal Hossain," https://legal.un.org/avl/pdf/ls/Hossain_bio.pdf.

5. Marie Davoise, "Can't Fight the Moonlight? Actually, You Can: ICJ Judges to Stop Acting as Arbitrators in Investor-State Disputes," EJIL Talk, November 5, 2018. https://www.ejiltalk.org/cant-fight-the-moonlight-actually-you-can-icj -judges-to-stop-acting-as-arbitrators-in-investor-state-disputes/.

6. Simeon Djankov, "Hungary under Orbán: Can Central Planning Revive Its Economy?" Peterson Institute for International Economics, July 2015, https ://www.piie.com/publications/pb/pb15-11.pdf.

7. ADC Affiliate Ltd. v. Republic of Hungary, ICSID Case No. ARB/03/16, Award (October 2, 2006), paras. 179–83.

8. ADC v. Hungary, paras. 251–54.

9. ADC v. Hungary, para. 424.

10. ADC v. Hungary, para. 475.

11. ADC v. Hungary, paras. 423–45, 536.

12. ADC v. Hungary, paras. 193–95.

13. ADC v. Hungary, paras. 496–99.

14. ADC. v. Hungary, para. 543.

15. Dow Chemical Co., 2008 form 10-K, p. 60; David Jolly, "Kuwait Backs Out of Venture With Dow Chemical," New York Times, December 28, 2008; Britannica, s.v. "Polyethylene," https://www.britannica.com/science/polyethylene.

16. Dow Chemical Co., 2009 form 10-K, pp. 12, 15, 33.

17. Jolly, "Kuwait Backs Out."

18. "Visualizing Our History," Dow Chemical Company; Dow Chemical Company, 2008 form 10-K, p. 9.

19. Dow Chemical Co., 2012 form 10-K, p. 66; 2013 form 10-K, p. 66.

20. "Shareholders," Equate Petrochemical Company, https://www.equate.com /shareholders/.

21. Congressional Research Service, "The Argentine Financial Crisis: A Chronology of Events," June 5, 2003; "Investment Policy Hub: Argentina," UNCTAD, https://investmentpolicy.unctad.org/international-investment-agreements /countries/8/argentina.

22. "GDP (current US$)—Argentina," World Bank, https://data.worldbank.org /indicator/NY.GDP.MKTP.CD?locations=AR.

23. Historical details in this paragraph and the next two are based on Congressional Research Service "The Argentine Financial Crisis: A Chronology of Events," June 5, 2003.

24. Telefónica S.A. v. Argentine Republic, ICSID Case No. ARB/03/20.

25. Hochtief AG v. Argentine Republic, ICSID Case No. ARB/07/31.

26. Impregilo S.p.A. v. Argentine Republic (I), ICSID Case No. ARB/07/17.

27. Siemens AG v. Argentine Republic, ICSID Case No. ARB/02/8, Award (February 6, 2007), paras. 81, 84, 90–93.

28. Siemens AG v. Argentine Republic, paras. 94–97.

29. Siemens AG v. Argentine Republic, paras. 246–47.

30. Siemens AG v. Argentine Republic, paras. 248, 253.

31. Siemens AG v. Argentine Republic, ICSID Case No. ARB/02/8, Award (February 6, 2007), paras. 254–55.

32. Siemens AG v. Argentine Republic, para. 403.

33. Daimler Financial Services AG v. Argentine Republic, ICSID Case No. ARB/05/1, Award (August 22, 2012), paras. 38–39.

34. Daimler Financial Services AG v. Argentine Republic, paras. 41–42.

35. Daimler Financial Services AG v. Argentine Republic, ICSID Case No. ARB/05/1, Dissenting Opinion of Judge Charles N. Brower (August 15, 2012), para. 26.

36. Daimler Financial Services AG v. Argentine Republic, ICSID Case No. ARB/05/1, Opinion of Professor Domingo Bello Janeiro (August 16, 2012), p. 3.

37. Daimler Financial Services AG v. Argentine Republic, ICSID Case No. ARB/05/1, Award (August 22, 2012), para. 281.

38. Daimler Financial Services AG v. Argentine Republic, ICSID Case No. ARB/05/1, Dissenting Opinion of Judge Charles N. Brower (August 15, 2012), paras. 38, 42.

39. Pierre-Marie Dupuy and Julie Maupin, "Of Wit, Wisdom, and Balance in International Law," in *Practising Virtue: Inside International Arbitration* (Oxford, UK: OUP, 2015), chap. 42.

40. Albert Jan van den Berg, "Dissenting Opinions by Party-Appointed Arbitrators in Investment Arbitration," in Mahnoush Arsanjani et al. (eds.), *Looking to the Future: Essays on International Law in Honor of W. Michael Reisman* (Leiden: Martinus Nijhoff, 2010), 831–32.

41. van den Berg, "Dissenting Opinions," 831.

42. van den Berg, "Dissenting Opinions," 828.

43. Avco Corp. v. Iran Aircraft Industries et al., Case No. 261, Concurring and Dissenting Opinion of Judge Brower (July 18, 1988), paras. 17–22.

44. Perenco Eduador Ltd. v. Republic of Ecuador, PCA Case No. IR-2009/1, Decision on Challenge to Arbitrator (December 8, 2009), para. 27.

45. Perenco Eduador Ltd. v. Republic of Ecuador, paras. 44, 53.

46. Perenco Eduador Ltd. v. Republic of Ecuador, Award (September 27, 2019).

47. David Hill, "Ecuador Pursued China Oil Deal While Pledging to Protect Yasuni, Papers Show," *The Guardian*, February 19, 2014, https://www.theguardian.com /environment/2014/feb/19/ecuador-oil-china-yasuni#.

48. Vale SA v. BSG Resources Ltd., LCIA Case No. 142683, Decision on First Challenge (August 4, 2016), paras. 316–17.

49. "Beny Steinmetz, a Mining Magnate, Found Guilty in Swiss Corruption Trial," *New York Times*, January 22, 2021, https://www.nytimes.com/2021/01/22 /world/europe/beny-steinmetz-guilty-switzerland-guinea.html.

50. Vantage Deepwater Co. v. Petrobras America Inc., Southern District of Texas (unreported), Respondents' Motion to Vacate the Majority Award (August 31, 2018), p. 23, https://jusmundi.com/en/document/other/en-vantage-deepwater -company-vantage-deepwater-drilling-inc-v-petrobras-america-inc-petrobras -venezuela-investments-services-bv-petroleo-brasileiro-s-a-petrobras-brazil -respondents-motion-to-vacate-the-majority-award-friday-31st-august-2018 #other_document_15888.

51. Vantage Deepwater Co. v. Petrobras America Inc., Southern District of Texas (unreported), Order (May 17, 2019), p. 11, https://jusmundi.com/en/document /decision/en-vantage-deepwater-company-vantage-deepwater-drilling-inc-v -petrobras-america-inc-petrobras-venezuela-investments-services-bv-petroleo -brasileiro-s-a-petrobras-brazil-order-of-the-united-states-district-court-for-the -southern-district-of-texas-sunday-17th-march-2019#decision_6503.

52. Vantage Deepwater Co. v. Petrobras, p. 11.

53. Vantage Deepwater Co. v. Petrobras America Inc., Southern District of Texas (unreported), Declaration of Andrew B. Derman (August 31, 2018), para. 8, https://jusmundi.com/en/document/other/en-vantage-deepwater-company -vantage-deepwater-drilling-inc-v-petrobras-america-inc-petrobras-venezuela -investments-services-bv-petroleo-brasileiro-s-a-petrobras-brazil-declaration-of -andrew-b-derman-friday-31st-august-2018#other_document_19041.

54. Transcript reproduced in Vantage Deepwater Co. v. Petrobras America Inc., Southern District of Texas (unreported), Declaration of Lawrence W. Newman (August 31, 2018), para. 71, https://jusmundi.com/en/document/other/en -vantage-deepwater-company-vantage-deepwater-drilling-inc-v-petrobras -america-inc-petrobras-venezuela-investments-services-bv-petroleo-brasileiro -s-a-petrobras-brazil-declaration-of-lawrence-w-newman-friday-31st-august -2018#other_document_19042.

55. Vantage Deepwater Co. v. Petrobras America Inc., Order, p. 11 n4; Vantage Deepwater Co. v. Petrobras America Inc., Declaration of Lawrence W. Newman.

56. Vantage Deepwater Co. v. Petrobras America Inc., ICDR Case No. 01-15-0004- 8503, Final Award (June 29, 2018), https://jusmundi.com/en/document/decision /en-vantage-deepwater-company-vantage-deepwater-drilling-inc-v-petrobras -america-inc-petrobras-venezuela-investments-services-bv-petroleo-brasileiro-s-a -petrobras-brazil-final-award-friday-29th-june-2018#decision_6502.

57. Vantage Deepwater Co. v. Petrobras America Inc., ICDR Case No. 01-15-0004- 8503, Arbitrator James M. Gaitis's Objection to, and Dissent from, the Tribunal Majority's Final Award (undated), https://jusmundi.com/en/document/opinion /en-vantage-deepwater-company-vantage-deepwater-drilling-inc-v-petrobras -america-inc-petrobras-venezuela-investments-services-bv-petroleo-brasileiro-s -a-petrobras-brazil-arbitrator-james-m-gaitis-objection-to-and-dissent-from-the -tribunal-majoritys-final-award-friday-29th-june-2018#opinion_2574.

58. Vantage Deepwater Co. v. Petrobras America Inc., Order, p. 8–11, 12 n5.

59. Vantage Deepwater Co. v. Petrobras America Inc., Southern District of Texas (unreported), Respondents' Motion to Vacate the Majority Award (August 31, 2018), p. 24, https://jusmundi.com/en/document/other/en-vantage-deepwater -company-vantage-deepwater-drilling-inc-v-petrobras-america-inc-petrobras -venezuela-investments-services-bv-petroleo-brasileiro-s-a-petrobras-brazil -respondents-motion-to-vacate-the-majority-award-friday-31st-august-2018 #other_document_15888.

60. Vantage Deepwater Co. v. Petrobras America Inc., U.S. Court of Appeals for the Fifth Circuit (unreported), Decision (July 16, 2020), https://jusmundi.com/en /document/decision/en-vantage-deepwater-company-vantage-deepwater-drilling -inc-v-petrobras-america-inc-petrobras-venezuela-investments-services-bv-petroleo -brasileiro-s-a-petrobras-brazil-decision-of-the-united-states-court-of-appeals-for -the-fifth-circuit-thursday-16th-july-2020#decision_11734.

CHAPTER THIRTEEN: INTERNATIONAL ARBITRATOR, PART II

1. Pia Eberhardt and Cecilia Olivet, *Profiting from Injustice: How Law Firms, Arbitrators, and Financiers Are Fueling an Investment Arbitration Boom* (Brussels/Amsterdam: CEO/TNI, 2012), 11.

2. Eberhardt and Olivet, *Profiting from Injustice*, 7.

3. "Investment Law & Policy," Columbia Center on Sustainable Investment, https://ccsi.columbia.edu/content/investment-law-policy.

4. Eberhardt and Olivet, *Profiting from Injustice*, 38–39.

5. Eberhardt and Olivet, *Profiting from Injustice*, 18–33.

6. "Trading Democracy," February 1, 2002, https://billmoyers.com/content /trading-democracy.

7. Elizabeth Warren, "The Trans-Pacific Partnership Clause Everyone Should Oppose," *Washington Post*, February 25, 2015, https://www.washingtonpost. com/opinions/kill-the-dispute-settlement-language-in-the-trans-pacific-partnership /2015/02/25/ec7705a2-bd1e-11e4-b274-e5209a3bc9a9_story.html.

8. Edward-Isaac Dovere and Doug Palmer, "Warren Was Paid Up to $90,000 as Witness in 2000 Trade Case," *Politico*, April 21, 2015, https://www.politico.com /story/2015/05/warren-was-paid-up-to-90000-as-witness-in-2000-trade-case-118199.

9. "Investment Dispute Settlement Navigator," UNCTAD Investment Policy Hub, https://investmentpolicy.unctad.org/investment-dispute-settlement.

10. ICSID, "The ICSID Caseload—Statistics."

11. ADC Affiliate Ltd. v. Republic of Hungary, ICSID Case No. ARB/03/16, Award (October 2, 2006), paras. 63, 68.

12. Vattenfall AB et al. v. Federal Republic of Germany, ICSID Case No. ARB/12/12.

13. International Centre for Settlement of Investment Disputes, "Hearing: Vattenfall AB and others v Federal Republic of Germany (October 10, 2016) (Part 1)," YouTube video, 1:50:05, October 30, 2019, https://www.youtube.com/watch?v =MsU5JQbJgvY.

14. King v. Sussex Justices, ex parte *McCarthy* [1924] 1 KB 256, 259.

15. Austrian Airlines v. Slovak Republic, UNCITRAL arbitration, Final Award (October 9, 2009), para. 84.

16. Ralph Waldo Emerson, "Self-Reliance" (1841), available at https://emerson central.com/texts/essays-first-series/self-reliance/.

17. Foresti et al. v. Republic of South Africa, ICSID Case No. ARB(AF)/07/1, Letter Regarding Non-Disputing Parties (October 5, 2009).

CHAPTER FOURTEEN: HUMAN RIGHTS

1. "ASIL New York Gala," American Society of International Law, https://www .asil.org/asil-new-york-gala.

2. *Difference Relating to Immunity from Legal Process of a Special Rapporteur of the Commission on Human Rights*, ICJ, Written Statement Submitted on Behalf of the Secretary-General of the United Nations (October 2, 1998), para. 11.

3. *Difference Relating to Immunity*, paras. 16, 21, 23.

4. *Difference Relating to Immunity*, paras. 19–20, 22, 24–25.

5. *Difference Relating to Immunity*, paras. 26–27.

6. Statute of the International Court of Justice, arts. 63 and 66(2).

7. *Difference Relating to Immunity*, 1–2.

8. International Court of Justice, Verbatim Record, December 7, 1998, paras. 6–29.

9. *Difference Relating to Immunity*, Advisory Opinion (April 29, 1999).

10. *Britannica*, s.v. "Bolivia—Post-1952 regimes," https://www.britannica.com /place/Bolivia/Post-1952-regimes.

11. Phil Gunson, "Hugo Bánzer," *The Guardian*, May 5, 2002, https://www.the guardian.com/news/2002/may/06/guardianobituaries.bolivia.

12. Trujillo Oroza v. Bolivia, Inter-American Court of Human Rights, Judgment of February 27, 2002 (Reparations and Costs), para. 46.

13. Trujillo Oroza v. Bolivia, Inter-American Court of Human Rights, Judgment of January 26, 2000 (Merits), para. 2.

14. Trujillo Oroza v. Bolivia, Judgment of February 27, 2002 (Reparations and Costs), para. 46.

15. Trujillo Oroza v. Bolivia, Judgment of January 26, 2000 (Merits), para. 4.

16. *Britannica*, s.v. "Hugo Bánzer Suárez," https://www.britannica.com/biography /Hugo-Banzer-Suarez.

17. Trujillo Oroza v. Bolivia, Judgment of January 26, 2000 (Merits), para. 9; "Bolivia GDP per capita," *Trading Economics*, https://tradingeconomics.com /bolivia/gdp-per-capita.

18. Trujillo Oroza v. Bolivia, Judgment of February 27, 2002 (Reparations and Costs), para. 93.

19. Trujillo Oroza v. Bolivia (Reparations and Costs), para. 46.

20. Trujillo Oroza v. Bolivia (Reparations and Costs), paras. 109, 114–115.

21. Trujillo Oroza v. Bolivia (Reparations and Costs), paras. 94–98, 103, 141.

22. *Legal Consequences of the Construction of a Wall in the Occupied Palestinian Territory*, ICJ, Advisory Opinion (July 9, 2004), para. 72.

23. "Israel's Settlements Have No Legal Validity, Constitute Flagrant Violation of International Law, Security Council Reaffirms," United Nations (December 23, 2016), https://www.un.org/press/en/2016/sc12657.doc.htm.

24. *Legal Consequences of the Construction of a Wall in the Occupied Palestinian Territory*, ICJ, Written Statement Submitted by the Hashemite Kingdom of Jordan, paras. 3.3–3.9, 4.4, 4.10–4.13, 5.178–5.179, 5.264–5.285.

25. *Legal Consequences*, Advisory Opinion, para. 12.

26. *Legal Consequences*, Hashemite Kingdom of Jordan, paras. 5.39–5.107.

27. *Legal Consequences*, Hashemite Kingdom of Jordan, paras. 5.108–5.254.

28. *Legal Consequences*, Hashemite Kingdom of Jordan, paras. 5.255–5.263.

29. *Legal Consequences*, Advisory Opinion, paras. 121–142.

30. *Legal Consequences*, Advisory Opinion, paras. 151–153.

31. Congressional Research Service, "Israel's Possible Annexation of West Bank Areas: Frequently Asked Questions," July 14, 2020.

32. "Equality Report 2017/18," South African Human Rights Commission, p. 17, https://www.sahrc.org.za/index.php/sahrc-publications/equality-reports.

33. Foresti et al. v. Republic of South Africa, ICSID Case No. ARB(AF)/07/1, Petition for Limited Participation as Non-Disputing Parties, para. 4.2.

34. "Roots of Apartheid: South Africa's Mining Industry," CJPME Foundation, May 2014, https://www.cjpmefoundation.org/roots_of_apartheid_south_africa _s_mining_industry.

35. Foresti et al. v. Republic of South Africa, Award (August 4, 2010), para. 56.

36. Foresti et al., Award, para. 54.

37. *Restatement (Third) of the Foreign Relations of the United States*, (American Law Institute, 1987) §712, Comment (g).

CHAPTER FIFTEEN: THE FUTURE

1. "Elihu Root—Facts," The Nobel Prize, https://www.nobelprize.org/prizes/peace /1912/root/facts/.

2. "Elihu Root—Nobel Lecture," The Nobel Prize, https://www.nobelprize.org /prizes/peace/1912/root/lecture/.

3. Maurer, *Empire Trap*, 1, 80–86.

4. Maurer, *Empire Trap*, chaps. 3–9.

5. Maurer, *Empire Trap*, 427.

6. Maurer, *Empire Trap*, 428–29.

7. "List of All Cases," International Court of Justice, https://www.icj-cij.org/en /list-of-all-cases.

8. ICSID, "The ICSID Caseload—Statistics."

9. Charles N. Brower and Jawad Ahmad, "Why the 'Demolition Derby' That Seeks to Destroy Investor-State Arbitration?" *Southern California Law Review* 91 (2018): 1186.

10. Brower and Ahmad, "'Demolition Derby,'" 1154–1156.

11. Charles N. Brower and Jawad Ahmad, "From the Two-Headed Nightingale to the Fifteen-Headed Hydra: The Many Follies of the Proposed International Investment Court," *Fordham International Law Journal* 41, no. 4 (2018).

12. Brower and Ahmad, "'Demolition Derby,'" 1157.

13. Brower and Ahmad, "'Demolition Derby,'" 1154–55.

14. Brower and Ahmad, "'Demolition Derby,'" 1143–44.

15. Brower and Ahmad, "'Demolition Derby,'" 1144–47.

16. White Industries Australia Ltd. v. Republic of India, UNCITRAL, Final Award, November 30, 2011, https://www.italaw.com/cases/documents/1170.

17. Brower and Ahmad, "'Demolition Derby,'" 1149–50.

18. Maurer, *Empire Trap*, 445.

19. Brower and Ahmad, "'Demolition Derby,'" 1147–49.

20. Brower and Ahmad, "'Demolition Derby,'" 1192.

21. Brower and Ahmad, "'Demolition Derby,'" 1192.

22. Brower and Ahmad, "Two-Headed Nightingale," 791ff.

23. Maurer, *Empire Trap*, 447–49.

24. Brower and Ahmad, "'Demolition Derby,'" 1185–86.

25. Brower and Ahmad, "'Demolition Derby,'" 1149.

26. John Morley, *The Life of William Ewart Gladstone*, vol. 2 (New York: Macmillan, 1911), chap. 9, p. 393.

Index

A

Abouzaid, George, 57

Abshire, David M.
  as ambassador to NATO, 135, 137
  role in author's career, 45–46, 50, 55
  Saving the Reagan Presidency, 147
  as special counsellor to Reagan, 137,
    139, 140–144, 146–147

act of state doctrine, 69–71, 94

ADC v. Hungary, 210–211, 228

affirmative action, 242–243

AIG. *See* American International Group

AIOC (Anglo-Iranian Oil Company),
  82–85

CSS *Alabama*, in the U.S. Civil War, 1–5,
  253

Albright, Madeleine, 189

alcohol, ingredient list requirement for,
  52–54

Aldrich, George, 109, 119, 125

Aldrich, Hulbert, 22, 23–24, 63

Algeria
  in freeing U.S. hostages in Iran, 97,
    112
  nationalization of oil industry by,
    78–79

Algiers Accords (1981), xviii, 96–99,
  106, 111–113, 121

*Alleged Violations of the 1955 Treaty
  of Amity, Economic Relations, and
  Consular Rights*, 196, 200–202

Al-Shiraa, 135–136

Amco Asia v. Republic of Indonesia
  (1981), 75–78, 151–152

American Independent Oil Company
  (Aminoil), 125–126

American International Group (AIG)
  claims against Iran, 94–95, 98–99,
    106
  claims against Nigeria, 55–61

*American Law Institute Restatement
  of the Foreign Relations Law of the
  United States*, 26

amicus curiae, 70–71, 91

Aminoil (American Independent Oil
  Company), 125–126

Aminoil v. Kuwait, 125–126

Amity, Frederica "Rica," xiv

*Amoco International Finance v. Iran et
  al.*, 122–125, 127–128, 133, 148, 241

Anglo-Iranian Oil Company (AIOC),
  82–85

Ansari Moin, Parviz
  *Amoco International Finance v. Iran
    et al.*, 124
  *Avco Corp. v. Iran Aircraft Industries
    et al.*, 129–131
  judges' behavior and, 115–116, 118,
    119, 122, 190
  in the Nationality Case, 117

apartheid, 82, 242–243

Arbitration Institute of the Stockholm
   Chamber of Commerce, 51, 116
Argentina
   Daimler Finance AG claims, 215–217
   expropriation of foreign interests, 213
   Siemens v. Argentina, 213–215
ATF (Bureau of Alcohol, Tobacco,
   Firearms and Explosives), 52–53, 54
*Avco Corp. v. Iran Aircraft Industries et
   al.*, 129–131, 219

B
Baker, Howard, 146–147
Baker, Jim, 97, 100–101
Bank Indonesia, 67–69
Bánzer Suárez, Hugo (El Petiso
   "Shorty"), 236–238
Barylypa broweri (paralytic wasp named
   for author), 161–162
Bekhme Dam claims, 177–180
Bellet, Pierre, 117
Bello Janeiro, Domingo, 215–217, 230
Berlin. *See* East Berlin; West Berlin
Berlin Airlift (1948-49), 30, 32
bilateral investment treaties (BITs), 152
   arbitration clauses in, 209, 250–251
   in Argentina, 213, 214, 216
   criticism of, 225–228, 250–253
   between Czech and Slovak Republics,
      162–164
   in Ecuador, 219–220, 251–253
   in India, 251
   "most favored nation" clause, 216
   new U.S. model, 250
   in South Africa, 243
   in West Germany, 152
Birrell, Lowell McAfee, 17–22
Black Economic Empowerment (South
   Africa), 231, 242–243
Blinken, Antony, 203–204
Blough, Roger, 52
Böckstiegel, Karl-Heinz, 122, 139
Bolivia
   ICSID Convention withdrawal by,
      250

nationalization of Brazilian assets,
   252
people "disappeared" by Bánzer's
   regime, 236–239
Bosnian War, 179
Boston, "the Combat Zone" in, 166–167,
   168–169
Boys State summer camp, 24
Brandt, Willy, 27, 31
Brazil
   Bolivian nationalization of assets of,
      252
   expropriation of U.S. telecoms assets,
      66
   Vantage Deepwater v. Petrobras,
      221–222, 223–224
Brezhnev, Leonid, 35–37, 40–44
Brilliant (American merchant vessel), 6–7
Broms, Bengt, 186–188, 193, 197
Brower, Charles H., 99–100
Brower, Charles N. *See also names of
   specific cases and courts*
   acting legal adviser to Nixon, 104
   CSS *Alabama* model, 1, 4, 253
   Alexander lecture (2013) by, 74
   American Bar Association positions,
      51
   American Lawyer magazine praise of
      (2013), 209
   on arbitration of states vs. individuals/
      corporations, 74–75
   at Boys State summer camp, 24
   Certificate of Merit for *The Iran-
      United States Claims Tribunal*,
      278
   challenges to, as arbitrator, 219–224
   "The Dialectics of National Purpose"
      (Brower), 25
   on dissenting opinions in arbitration,
      217–219
   father of, firing Reagan from TV
      show, 100
   The Hague, visit to (1966), 110
   Harvard graduation *cum laude*, 12
   at Harvard Law School, 11–12,
      22–23, 25

Harvard undergraduate studies, 28–29
at Hochschule für Politik, 29
human rights cases, 231, 235–238, 239–241, 242–243
ICSID cases, 75–78, 151–152, 153–169, 189, 206–208, 231
indigent clients of, 15–16
Interagency Task Force on the Law of the Sea, 102
Inter-American Court of Human Rights, 236–238
International Court of Justice, 106, 196, 197–199, 202–203
Iran–United States Claims Tribunal, status in, 139, 148, 188–190, 195
languages spoken by, 27–28
legal adviser under Reagan, offer rescinded, 101–104
as "legal vulture," 225
lifetime achievement awards of, 253
Manley O. Hudson Medal, 253
marriage to Carmen, 138, 148
marriage to Oda, 29
Metropolitan Corporate Counsel interview, 220
misbaha given to, 107
as most-appointed American ICJ judge *ad hoc*, 203
paralytic wasp named for, 161–162
in Pentagon Papers response, 44–45
personal connection with Berlin, 27–30
presidential adviser on the Iran–Contra scandal, 137–139, 140–144, 146–147
on Reagan's transition team, 101
recognition for arbitration, 152, 165, 209, 217, 225, 233
recognition for public service, 203–204
Soest, Germany homestay, 28
Somerset County Republican Committee member, 24
on Soviet–U.S. trade agreements, 40–44

State Department work, 24–26, 31–48, 49–51
United Nations Compensation Commission, 174–180
White & Case, author's positions at, 12–26, 51, 150–151, 205–206
Brower, Chip, xii, 197, 236, 245
Brown–Forman Distillers v. Matthews, 52–54
Brownlie, Ian, 197
Burch, Dean, 103
Bureau of Alcohol, Tobacco, Firearms and Explosives (ATF), 52–53, 54
Burke, Arleigh, 46, 135
Bush, George H. W.
Gulf War and, 172
inauguration of, 149
in Iran–Contra scandal, 143, 147
Jim Baker campaigning for, 100–101
on "voodoo economics," 138
Bush, George W., 145, 240, 246–247
Buzhardt, Fred, 44–45

C
Cambodia, secret bombing of, 47–48
Canada
Mondev v. United States, 166–169
Pope & Talbot v. Canada, 167–168
Québec independence movement, 159
U.S. demand that Britain cede, 3–4
weakening investor protections, 249–250
Caron, David
as author's clerk, 118
background of, 110
in Colombian case, 199
death of, 196
Iran–United States Claims Tribunal commissioner, 172
Carter, Jimmy
Bank Indonesia on, 67–68
continuation of arms sales to shah, 86
freezing Iranian assets, 93–95, 96, 104
Goldwater v. Carter, 89–93, 101–102

Iran–United States Claims Tribunal
formation and, 7
on labeling alcohol ingredients, 54
state visit to Nigeria, 58–60
on Taiwan defense treaty, 89–93
U.S. hostages in Iran and, 87–88,
96–97
Case, Clifford P., xv, 11, 24
Castro, Cipriano, 246
Center for Strategic and International
Studies (CSIS), 45–46, 135, 137
Certain Iranian Assets, frozen, 196,
202–203
Charter of Economic Rights and Duties
of States, 55, 76, 106, 124, 165–166
Chávez, Hugo, 246–247
Chayes, Abe, 104–105
Cheney, Dick, 100
Cheney, Liz, xv
Chiang Kai-Shek, 89
China
lack of participation in international
arbitration, 248
Nixon's recognition of, 89–93,
101–102
Radio Corporation of America suit,
111
Chorzów Factory Case (1927), 55–56,
124–125, 211
Christopher, Warren, 97
Civil War (U.S.), Great Britain's role in,
1–5
Clay, Lucius D., 30, 33
Clooney, Amal (née Alamuddin),
233–234
Clooney, George, 233
coerced testimony, 185, 187
Colombia, maritime dispute with
Nicaragua, 198–199
Commission on International Trade Law
(UNCITRAL), 99, 131–132, 249
compensation. *See* expropriation; Iran–
United States Claims Tribunal; United
Nations Compensation Commission
Contras, 104–106, 136, 142, 166. *See
also* Iran–Contra scandal

copyrights, 41, 42, 43
Cordiner, Ralph, 100
Correa, Rafael, 219–221, 251, 252
Costa Rica
banana exporting, 153
human rights record of, 235
Immunity case participation, 235–236
Santa Elena v. Costa Rica, 153–162
Covid-19, police powers and, 244
Cox, Archibald, 48
Crawford, James, 167–169
Crook, John, 118
CSIS (Center for Strategic and
International Studies), 45–46
CSOB v. Slovakia, 162–165
Cuba, 100, 105
Cumaraswamy, Param, 234–235, 236
Czech Republic, *CSOB v. Slovakia,*
162–165

D

Daimler Finance AG, Argentina and,
215–217
Dames & Moore v. Regan, 98
Dawson, Donald, 67–69
de Graft, Leone, 208
de la Rúa, Fernando, 213–214
"La Députation" (Dubuffet), 95
"The Dialectics of National Purpose"
(Brower), 25
diplomats, policy of immunity for, 23–24
dissenting opinions, in international
arbitration, 217–219
Dole, Bob, 136
Dolgun, Alexander, 39
Donoghue, Joan, 196
double taxation, in international trade,
43
Douglas-Home, Alec, 36
Dow Chemical v. Kuwait, 211–212
Drummond, Nelson Cornelious, 16–17
dual-national cases, 112–113, 117–119,
148
Dudley, Thomas, 2
Duhalde, Eduardo, 214–215

Dun & Bradstreet libel suit, 13
Duncan, Charles T., 183, 188
Dupuy, Pierre-Marie, 194–195, 215–217

E
East Berlin
    author's visits to (1957), 29, 36
    closing of border with West Berlin,
        28–30, 31–33, 36
    Quadripartite Agreement on Berlin,
        35–37
Easum, Donald, 56, 60
Ecuador
    bilateral investment treaties in,
        219–220, 252–253
    Perenco v. Ecuador, 219–221
    withdrawal from ICSID Convention,
        250–251, 252–253
Egbe, Fred, 56–58
Egypt, Pyramids case, 156
Ehrlichman, John, 37
Eisenhower, Dwight D., 31, 84, 123
Ellis, William B., 40
Ellsberg, Daniel, 44–45
The Empire Trap (Maurer), 6, 54–55,
    246
Enka, as contractor for Bekhme Dam,
    177–180, 198
Equate Petrochemical Company, 212
estoppel, doctrine of, 163
European Union (EU)
    European Court of Justice, 252
    Hungary joining, 210
    proposal for a permanent investment
        court, 249
    UN Economic Commission for
        Europe arbitration rules, 42
The Experiment in International Living,
    28
expropriation. See also Iran–United States
    Claims Tribunal; United Nations
    Compensation Commission
    by Algeria, 78–79
    by Argentina, 213
    by Bolivia, 252

by Brazil, 66
Chorzów Factory Case (Poland),
    55–56, 124–125, 211
compensation requirements, 55, 76,
    106, 124, 134, 165
by Costa Rica, 153–154
by Ecuador, 219–221
by Egypt, 156
by Ghana, 206–208
by Hungary, 210–211
by Indonesia, 66–69, 75–78
international law preservation and,
    134
by Iran, under Ayatollah Khomeini,
    87, 94–95, 111, 123, 129, 184
by Iran, under Mosaddegh, 82–83, 84
by Iraq, 171–172, 176
by Israel, 241
by Kuwait, 125–126
lawfulness of, 124–125, 126–127
NAFTA standards in, 167
by Nigeria, 55–61
by South Africa, 243
sovereign immunity and, 94
taxation of compensation, 126
by the U.S., 165–169, 189
U.S. foreign aid policy on, 154
by Venezuela, 246–247

F
Fielding, Fred, 107
Fitzmaurice, Gerald, 126
Food and Drug Administration (FDA),
    53–54
Ford, Gerald, 100–101
Foreign Sovereign Immunities Act (FSIA),
    64–65
Foresti v. South Africa, 231, 242–243
Fortier, Yves, 159–161, 166, 234–235
Frederica Lincoln Riahi v. Islamic
    Republic, 183–188
Frelinghuysen, Peter, 50
Frick, Henry Clay, 233
Friedersdorf, Max, 101–102

FSIA (Foreign Sovereign Immunities Act), 64–65

Fulbright, J. William, 38, 46–48

G

Gaillard, Emmanuel, 163–165

Gaitis, James, 221–223

General Electric Theater, Reagan in, 99–100

"General Hershey Bar," 70

Ghana, Vacuum Salt Products v., 206–208

Gladstone, William Ewart, 253–254

Goldwater, Barry
on maintaining Taiwan defense treaty, 89–90

Goldwater, Barry, *Goldwater v. Carter,* 89–93, 101–102, 103

Gordon, James "Jim," 53–54

Grant, Ulysses S., 4

Greenberg, Maurice "Hank," 55, 57–58, 95

Gromyko, Andrei, 36

Group of 77, 76

Guanacaste, Costa Rica. *See Santa Elena v. Costa Rica*

Guinea, *Vale v. BSG Resources,* 221

Gulf War, 171–172, 174

H

Habib, Philip, 45

Haig, Alexander, 98

Haldeman, Bob, 37

Hallwachs, Winnie, 156

Hamilton, Joe, 153–155, 158

Harriman, W. Averell, 83–84

Hauk, A. Andrew, 70

Helms, Jesse, 153–154, 157–158

Helms Amendment, 154–155

Herlands, William, 18–22

Hess, Rudolf, 34–35

Hezbollah, 135, 202

Hickenlooper, Bourke, 66

Hickenlooper Amendment to the Foreign Aid Act, 66, 67–69, 154

Hidrogradnja, in Bekhme Dam project, 177, 179–180

Higgins, Rosalyn, 197

Highet, Keith, 166

Hoffmann, Leonard H., 212

Holton, A. Linwood, 63, 65

Holtzmann, Howard, 109, 119

Hossain, Kamal, 207

Hughes, Howard, 13

human rights cases
Cumaraswamy defamation immunity, 234–236

Foresti v. South Africa, 242–243

Inter-American Court of Human Rights, 236–238

Israeli wall through the West Bank, 239–241

right to change one's nationality, 112

for tortured and "disappeared" in Bolivia, 236–239

Hungary, ADC v., 210–211, 228

Hurlock, Jim, 150–151

I

IAM (International Association of Machinists & Aerospace Workers) v. OPEC (Organization of Petroleum Exporting Countries), 70

ICJ. *See* International Court of Justice

ICSID. *See* International Centre for the Settlement of Investment Disputes

India, White Industries v., 250–251

Indonesia
Amco Asia v. Republic of Indonesia, 75–78, 151

Bank Indonesia, 67–69

expropriation by, 66–67, 75–78

personal harmony role in, 77

Sea Oil & General suit against, 67–69, 154

U.S. antitrust law suit, 69–71

Inkopad, 75

Interagency Task Force on the Law of the Sea, 102

Inter-American Commission on Human Rights, 237
Inter-American Court of Human Rights, 236–238
international arbitration. *See also* United Nations Compensation Commission
  ADC v. Hungary, 210–211, 228
  annulment of award in, 77
  arbitrators, conflicts of interest in, 79–80, 205–206, 219–224
  arbitrators as "legal vultures," 225–226
  bilateral investment treaties and, 152, 166, 209, 225
  "customary" international law, 169
  Daimler Finance AG and Argentina, 215–217
  dissenting opinions in, 217–219
  Dow Chemical v. Kuwait, 211–212
  by Elihu Root, 246
  getting disputes into, 151–152
  Hickenlooper Amendment and, 68, 154
  importance of courts and tribunals, 7–8, 22–23
  International Chamber of Commerce rules, 68
  International Court of Justice and, 83
  investor/state vs. commercial arbitrations, 74
  Lockheed v. Skanska, 73–74
  Nigeria National Petroleum Corporation with Shell and Exxon, 226–227
  number of cases, 152, 247
  Perenco v. Ecuador, 219–221
  power of private parties in, 249
  "reciprocal" benefits from, 42, 43
  Sea Oil & General suit against Indonesia, 67–69, 154
  Siemens v. Argentina, 213–215
  Sonatrach and Parker Drilling, 78–79, 151
  states vs. individuals/corporations in, 74–75

UN Economic Commission for Europe rules, 42
U.S. claims on U.K. (1871), 3–5
U.S.–Soviet trade talks (1972), 41–42
Vantage Deepwater v. Petrobras, 221–222, 223–224
White Industries v. India, 250–251
International Association of Machinists & Aerospace Workers (IAM) v. Organization of Petroleum Exporting Countries (OPEC), 70
International Centre for the Settlement of Investment Disputes (ICSID), 7. *See also* international arbitration
  Amco Asia v. Republic of Indonesia, 75–78, 151
  boom in cases, 75–78, 247
  challenges to arbitrators in, 219–224
  CSOB v. Slovakia, 162–165
  Mondev v. United States, 165–169, 189
  Pope & Talbot v. Canada, 167–168
  Santa Elena v. Costa Rica, 153–162
  TANESCO v. IPTL, 231
  Vacuum Salt Products v. Ghana, 206–208
  withdrawal of Bolivia, Ecuador, and Venezuela from, 250–251, 252–253
International Court of Justice (ICJ)
  ad hoc judges on, 199
  author on Montreal Sabotage Convention, 39
  author's resignation from, 203
  Certain Iranian Assets case, 196, 202–203
  Cumaraswamy defamation immunity suit, 234–236
  damages to Iranian offshore oil platforms by the U.S., 196
  as descendant of CSS *Alabama* tribunal, 7
  increased caseload of, 247
  Iran Air flight 655 downing by the U.S., 195–196

on Israeli wall through the West Bank, 239–241

on judges also sitting as arbitrators, 207

on Mosaddegh's nationalization of AIOC, 83–84

Nicaragua–Colombia maritime dispute, 198–199

Pan Am flight 103 downed by Libyans, 197–198

at the Peace Palace, 110–111

Time Inc. case, 106

Treaty of Amity violations, 196

Trump's withdrawal from JCPOA, 196, 200–202

U.S. hostages taken by Iran, 88

U.S. sending arms to the Contras, 104–106, 166

International Criminal Courts, 7

International Oil Consortium case, 129, 133

international trade

copyright in, 41, 42, 43

double taxation in, 43

U.S.–Soviet negotiations on, 40–44

U.S. trade imbalance with Japan, 62

International Tribunal on the Law of the Sea, 7

"investomercials," 74

Investor–State Dispute Settlement (ISDS), 248, 249, 251–252

Iran. *See also* Iran, U.S. hostages taken by; Iran–Contra scandal; Iran–United States Claims Tribunal

Certain Iranian Assets case, 196, 202–203

claims from naturalized U.S. citizens, 112–113

cooperation with United States, 85–86

Iran Air flight 655 downing, 195–196

Iranian revolution, 85–88

Iran–Iraq War, 122, 131

land seizures and contract cancellations, 86–87

Mosaddegh ousted, 84–85

nationalization of industry, 82–84, 87

under Shah Mohammad Reza Pahlavi, 82

as "state sponsor of terrorism," 202–203

Treaty of Amity violations, 94, 123–124, 196, 200–202

Trump's withdrawal from JPCOA, 196, 200–202

U.S providing humanitarian relief to, 201

Iran, U.S. hostages taken by. *See also* Iran–Contra scandal

Algiers Accords, xviii, 97–99, 112

arms secretly traded for, 136

Carter and, 87–88, 96–97

U.S. hostages taken from embassy, 87–88

Iran–Contra scandal, 135–147

author's role in advising Reagan, 137–139, 140–141

congressional ban on Contra support, 135

documents in, 142

independent counsel investigation, 140–144, 147

National Security Council in, 141, 145

Nicaraguan suit against U.S., 104–106, 166

Tower Report on, 145–147

U.S. secret arms delivered to Contras, 104

U.S. secret arms sales to Iran, 135–137, 141–142, 155

weapons sale leaked to *Al-Shiraa*, 135–136

Iran–United States Claims Tribunal

A1: ownership of interest on the security account, 112

A18: Nationality Case, 112–113, 117–119

A28: Iran's failure to replenish security account, 186

AIG compensation claims, 106

Algiers Accords and formation of, 97–99, 106, 111–113, 121

Aminoil v. Kuwait, 125–126
Amoco International Finance v. Iran et al., 122–125, 127–128, 133, 148, 241
author's appointment to, 188–190
author's resignation from, 148
Avco Corp. v. Iran Aircraft Industries et al., 129–131, 219
B1: unfulfilled military contracts, 191, 192
B61: delivery of military hardware to Iran, 192–194
as backchannel for diplomatic relations, 132
benefits and frustrations of, 115–117, 131–134
biased and unsatisfactory judges in, 186, 187–188, 192–193
Böckstiegel as president of, 122
Dames & Moore v. Regan, 98
deadline for filing claims, 111
dual-national cases, 112–113, 117–119, 148
employees not allowed to testify, 127
examples of cases at, 14
Frederica Lincoln Riahi v. Islamic Republic, 183–188
International Oil Consortium case, 129, 133
Iranian frustration and belligerence at, 113–117
Iranian judges' attack on Mangard, 81, 117–120
Iran's pending $11 billion claims for unfulfilled military contracts, 111, 188–189
lack of precedent system in, 127
Lagergren as president of, 109, 117, 118–119
lawfulness of expropriation, 124–125, 126–127
lengthy Iranian arguments at, 190–191
miscellaneous Iranian properties and artifacts, 191
Mosk Rule, 117, 148, 193, 195

nationals suing foreign governments in, 111
Sedco v. NIOC, 127–128
Short v. Islamic Republic of Iran, 128
significance of, 7–8
third-country judges in, 8, 114–115, 127–128
UNCC compared to, 172–174, 180–181
UNCITRAL rules adopted by, 131–132
Vale v. BSG Resources, 221
The Iran-United States Claims Tribunal (Brower), 278
Iraq. *See also* Saddam Hussein; United Nations Compensation Commission
expropriation by, 172–181
Gulf War, 172
Iran-Iraq War, 122, 131
UNCC formation, 172–174
ISDS (Investor–State Dispute Settlement), 248, 249, 251–252
Israel, wall through the West Bank, 239–241

J
Jackson–Vanik Amendment to the Trade Act (1974), 43
Jaeger, George, 11–12
Janzen, Daniel, 155–156, 160, 161–162
Japan
Oak Ridge back taxation suit against, 62–66
U.S.–Japanese Friendship Treaty (1953), 65
Javits, Jacob, 47–48
JCPOA (Joint Comprehensive Plan of Action), 196, 200–202
Jennings, Robert Y., 186–187, 207–208
Jessup, Philip C., 245
John Laird, Sons & Company, 2
Johnson, Lyndon B., 30, 66–67
Johnson, Reverdy, 4
Johnson, U. Alexis, 38–39
Johnson–Clarendon Treaty (1868), 3

Joint Comprehensive Plan of Action
(JCPOA), 196, 200–202
Jonkman, P.J.H., 208
Jordan, Hashemite Kingdom of, 239–241

K
Kaplan, Neil, 220
Kartika Plaza (Indonesia), 75–78
Kashani, Ayatollah Abol-Ghasem, 81,
82, 84
Kashani, Mahmoud, 81, 115, 117–119,
121–122
K-Dow, 211–212
Kennedy, John F.
Bay of Pigs, 145
Cuban missile crisis, 104–105
on Hickenlooper Amendment, 66
on steel price rise, 52
in West Berlin, 30
Kennedy, Robert, 52
Khashoggi, Adnan, 73
Khatami, Mohammed, 122
Khemco, 122–124
Khomeini, Sayyid Ruhollah, Ayatollah
Americans expelled by, 128
expropriation by, 87, 94–95, 111,
123, 129, 184
on the shah being admitted to the
U.S., 88
Killham, Edward, 39–40
Kissinger, Henry
admission of the shah into the U.S.,
87–88
in arms deal with the shah, 85
in East Berlin–West Berlin agreement,
35, 37
as Harvard professor, 24–25
replacing Rogers at State Department,
49–50
Kudirka, Simas, 39–40
Kuwait
Aminoil v. Kuwait, 125–126
Dow Chemical v. Kuwait, 211–212
Palestinian refugees from, 171, 174

Saddam Hussein's invasion and
looting of, 171–172, 176
UNCC claims against Iraq for,
174–176, 177–178

L
Lagergren, Gunnar, 109, 117, 118–119,
129
Lau, Christopher, 250
Lauterpacht, Elihu, 159–161, 236
Lee, Rex, 98–99
LeFevre, Carole, 58–59
LeFevre, Louis, 56–61, 94
"level of inflation," in compensation, 126
Libya
Pan Am flight 103 bombing, 197–198
replacement projects from Kuwait in,
179
UN Security Council sanctions
against, 197
Liman, Arthur, 19–20
Lincoln, Frederica "Fritzi" (Riahi,
Frederica Lincoln), 183–188
Lincoln, George A., 184
Litfin, Günter, 30
Lithuanian seaman claiming asylum in
the U.S., 39–40
Lockheed v. Skanska, 73–74
Lowenfeld, Andreas, 79
Lula da Silva, Luiz Inácio, 252

M
Machfud, W. Max, 77
Mahvi, Abolfath, 185–186, 187
Malaysia
in Immunity case, 235–236
in TANESCO v. IPTL, 231
Manchild in the Promised Land (Brown),
15
manganese nodules on the seafloor, 102
Mangard, Nils
assaulted by Kashani and Shafeiei,
116–120, 121–122
Avco Corp. v. Iran Aircraft Industries
et al., 129–130

as third-country arbitrator, 109, 115, 116
Manley O. Hudson Medal, 253
Mardian, Robert, 44–45
maritime sovereignty, 198–199
marshal's tickets, 20–21
Marx, Patsy, 44
Maurer, Noel, 54–55, 246–247
Maw, Carlyle E., 50, 107
McCarthy, Joseph, 12
McFarlane, Robert C., 145
McGraw-Hill libel suit, 13
Me and Other Advertising Geniuses (Charles H. Brower), 99
Meese, Edwin, 136, 142, 143
Metropolitan Corporate Counsel interview, 220
Miranda v. Arizona (1966), 16–17
Mohammad Reza Pahlavi Shah. *See* Shah of Iran, Mohammad Reza Pahlavi
Momtaz, Djamchid, 200
Mondev v. United States, 165–169, 189
Montreal Sabotage Convention (1971), 39–40, 197–198
Morales, Evo, 250
Morris, Larry, 12–13
Mosk, Richard, 110, 117, 194
Mosk Rule, 117, 148, 193, 195
Mosaddegh, Mohammad, 82–85, 113
Motion Picture Association of America (MPAA), 43
Mousavi, Mir-Hossein, 113
Muskie, Edmund, 143

N
Nabavi, Mr. (in Riahi case), 184–185, 187
NAFTA. *See* North American Free Trade Agreement
Nationality Case (Case A18), 112–113, 117
nationalization. *See* expropriation
National Security Council, 145
nemine dissentiente policy, 217
nemo iudex in causa sua, 188

Netanyahu, Benjamin, 241
New York Convention (1958), 42, 130–131, 151
Nicaragua. *See also* Iran–Contra scandal
Contras, 104–106, 136, 142, 166
maritime dispute with Colombia, 198–199
Nicaragua v. United States, 104–106, 111, 166
Nigeria
expropriation of AIG subsidiary, 55–61
extradition agreement, from colonial times, 60
LeFevre and Egbe jailed by, 56–61, 94
National Petroleum Corporation in arbitration with Shell and Exxon, 226–227
"sick-mother routine," 59–60
Nixon, Richard M.
appointment of Rogers, 31, 49–50
arms deals with the shah, 85–86
Cambodia bombing, 47–48
on divided Berlin, 27, 36
election of, 24–25, 31
opening relations with China, 89–90
Pentagon Papers and, 44–45
Quadripartite Agreement on Berlin, 35–37
"Saturday Night Massacre," 48
on Taiwan as part of China, 89
in talks with Brezhnev, 35–36, 40–44
in talks with Tanaka, 62–63
Watergate scandal, 31, 45, 48, 64–65
Ni Zhengyu, 198
non-refoulement principle, 40
Noori, Assadollah, 186, 192–193
North, Oliver, 19, 141, 142, 145–146, 155
North American Free Trade Agreement (NAFTA)
criticism of ISDS provisions in, 226, 250, 251–252
in *Mondev v. United States,* 165–169, 189

in *Pope & Talbot v. Canada,* 167–168

O

Oak Ridge, taxation suit against Japan, 62–66

Obama, Barack, unfulfilled military contracts with Iran, 191

Obasanjo, Olusegun, 55, 57

O'Connell, Jack, 239, 240

Olivet, Cecelia, 251

Operation Ajax, 84–85, 87, 113

Operation Staunch, 136

Organization of Petroleum Exporting Countries (OPEC), 69–71, 126

Oroza de Solón Romero, Antonia Gladys, 236–238

P

Pakistan, BIT with West Germany, 152

Palestinian refugees
in Jordan, 239–241
from Kuwait, 171, 173

Palmerston, Lord (Henry John Temple), 1–2

Panagiotopulos, Gerassimos, 206

Pan Am flight 103 bombing over Lockerbie, 197–198

Park, Rusty, 221–223

Parker Drilling, 78–79, 151

Peace Palace, The Hague, 110, 207

Pentagon Papers, 44–45

Perenco v. Ecuador, 219–221

Permanent Court of Arbitration, 110–111, 220, 247

pesification (Argentina), 215

Petrobras, 221–224

Picado, Sonia, 153, 155

Pierpoint, Robert, 58–59

Poindexter, John, 141, 145, 146

Pope & Talbot v. Canada, 167–168

Price, Dan, 118

Profiting from Injustice (Eberhardt and Olivet), 225, 251

Pyramids case, 156

Q

Quadripartite Agreement on Berlin, 35–37

Québec independence movement, 159

Question of the Delimitation of the Continental Shelf between Nicaragua and Colombia . . . , 198–199

R

Ra'ad al Hussein, Zeid, 240–241

Raboin, Michael, 173

Radio Corporation of America suit against China (1935), 111

Rahimtoola v. The Nizam of Hyderabad, 23

Rappaport, Bruce, 67

Reagan, Nancy, 100

Reagan, Ronald
arming the Contras in Nicaragua, 104–106, 136–137
on Cuba, 100
drinking hot water before a speech, 146
election of, 96–97
fired by author's father, 99–100, 101
Iran–Contra investigation and, 139, 140–144
Iran hostages and, 96, 135–136
naivety of, 144
secret arms sales to Iran, 135–137, 141–142, 155
tax policy of, 138
Tower Report exoneration of, 145–146
zero cooperation with terrorists policy, 136

Regan, Don, 98, 137, 139, 140, 145

Rein, Bert, 25

Restatement of the Foreign Relations Law of the United States, 26

Restatement (Third) of the Foreign Relations Law of the United States, 243

Riahi, Frederica "Fritzi" Lincoln, 183–188

Riahi, Manuchehr, 184–185

Richardson, Elliot, 47–48

Riphagen, Willem, 109, 113

RJR Nabisco, 126

Robinson, Davis, 68, 96–97, 104, 105–106

Rockefeller, David, 87

Rogers, Bill
in bombing of Cambodia, 47–48
Quadripartite Agreement on Berlin, 36
as Secretary of State, 31, 37–38, 49

Rogers & Wells, 159

Rohde-Liebenau, Ulf, 30

Rohm & Haas, 212

Rokison, Kenneth, 212

Roosevelt, Kermit, Jr., 84

Root, Elihu, 245–246

Rovine, Arthur, 91–92, 106, 115

Rowley, Bill, 250

Royal Jordanian Airlines, 239

Russia. *See also* Soviet Union
not participating in international arbitration, 248
takeover of Crimea, 248

The Russians Are Coming, The Russians Are Coming (film), 43

S

Saddam Hussein
invasion of Kuwait, 171–172
Iran–Iraq War, 131
takeover of Baghdad and Kuwait Sheratons, 175–176
use of chemical weapons and human shields, 175, 177

Saleh, Rachmat, 68, 69

Santa Elena v. Costa Rica, 153–162
arbitration of, 158–161
author's visit to Guanacaste, 155–156
"Disneyfying" the Rosetta Stone claim in, 160
efforts at settlement, 157–158
government expropriation of Guanacaste, 153–154
new species named for author, 161–162
panel's visit to Guanacaste, 159–160
possible CIA ownership, 155
UNESCO World Heritage Site designation, 156

Saudi Arabia, in *Lockheed v. Skanska,* 73–74

Saudi Aramco, 174–176

Saving the Reagan Presidency (Abshire), 147

Savoie, Simon, 13–15

Scalia, Antonin "Nino," 71

Schmults, Ed, 107

Schumann, Maurice, 36

Schwebel, Stephen M., 105, 167, 222–223

Scott, Stuart, 49–50

Scowcroft, Brent, 143

Sea Oil & General, suit against Indonesia by, 67–69, 154

Sedco v. NIOC, 127–128

Semmes, Raphael, 2–3, 6–7

"set off" doctrine, in loss claims, 174–175

Shafeiei, Shafei, 115, 117–119, 121–122

Shah of Iran, Mohammad Reza Pahlavi
admitted to the U.S., 87–88
arms sales to, 85–86, 94
claims on unfulfilled contracts with, 132, 188, 191–192
installed by the British, 82
restored to power, 84, 123, 129

Sharon, Ariel, 240

Shearman & Sterling, 163–165, 212

Shelp, Ron, 57

Sheraton Hotels, in Iraq and Kuwait, 175–176

Short v. Islamic Republic of Iran, 128

Shultz, George, 142, 145

Siemens v. Argentina, 213–215

Simon Savoie v. Anheuser Busch, 13–15

Skanska, in suit against Lockheed Martin, 73–74

Skubiszewski, Krzysztof, 190, 194

Slovakia, CSOB v., 162–165
Smith, Anne D., 178–179
Smutny, Abby Cohen, 158–159, 165, 178–179, 189
Soest, author's homestay in (1952-53), 28
Sofaer, Abe, 142
Sonatrach, 78–79
South Africa, Foresti v., 231, 242–243
sovereign immunity
  act of state and, 70
  expropriation and, 94
  in Indonesia and OPEC antitrust defense, 69–71
  in Oak Ridge suit, 63–65
  Rahimtoola v. The Nizam of Hyderabad, 23
  Tate Letter on, 63–65
  U.S.–Japanese Friendship Treaty, 65
Soviet Union
  Dolgun negotiations by author, 39
  East Berlin border and, 31–33, 36
  Lithuanian seaman denied asylum in the U.S., 39–40
  Nixon–Brezhnev summit in Moscow, 40–42
  Quadripartite Agreement on Berlin, 35–37
  U.S.–Soviet Accords on Exchanges in Technical and Cultural Matters, 43–44
  U.S.–Soviet arbitration in Stockholm, 42, 116
  U.S. trade agreements with, 40–44
Spain, negotiations on U.S. bases in, 38–39
Spandau Allied Military Prison (West Berlin), 34–35
stare decisis, 216
Steinstücken (West Berlin), 32–33
Stephen, Ninian, 167
Stevenson, Jack
  author reporting to, 25–26, 37
  as National Gallery of Art board chair, 149
  Pentagon Papers and, 44–45

Sukarno, expropriation by, 66–67
Sullivan, Brendan, 141–143
Sumner, Charles, 3–4
Suy, Eric, 197

T
Taiwan, 89–93, 101–102
Tanaka, Kakuei, 62–63
TANESCO v. IPTL, 231
Tara, Şarik, 177
Tarrant, John, 53
Tate, Jack, 63
Tate Letter on sovereign immunity, 63–65
Time Inc. case, 106
Tomka, Peter, 164–165, 202
Tower, John, 143
Tower Commission, 136, 143–145
treaties, presidential power to end, 89–93
Treaty of Amity, Economic Relations, and Consular Rights, U.S.–Iran (1955), 94, 123–124, 196, 200–202
Treaty of Washington (1871), 4
Triantafilou, Epaminontas, 221
Trujillo Oroza, José Carlos, 236–238
Trump, Donald J.
  denounced U.S.–Iran Treaty of Amity, 94
  vengeance on signers of "never Trump" letter, 200
  war on trade agreements, 251–252
  withdrawal from JCPOA, 196, 200
Turkey
  Bekhme Dam workers from, 177
  in the Gulf War, 177

U
UNCC. *See* United Nations Compensation Commission
UNCITRAL (UN Commission on International Trade Law), 99, 131–132, 249
United Kingdom, role in U.S. Civil War, 2–5

United Nations. *See also* International
Court of Justice; United Nations
Compensation Commission; United
Nations Security Council
Charter of Economic Rights and
Duties of States, 55, 76, 106, 124,
165–166
Commission on International Trade
Law, 99, 131–132, 249
Economic Commission for Europe
arbitration rules, 42
General Assembly, expropriation
resolution of, 55–56
General Assembly, on wall through
the West Bank, 240
UNPROFOR peacekeepers, 179
United Nations Compensation
Commission (UNCC), 172–181
Bekhme Dam claims, 177–180
formation and staffing of, 172–173
good and bad precedents in, 172, 175
increased and lost profits in, 174–175,
180
Iran–United States Claims Tribunal
compared to, 172–174, 180–181
Kuwait claims for Saddam Hussein's
occupation, 7, 171–174, 180
legacy of, 180–181
Palestinian Jordanians with
investments in Kuwait, 239
Saudi Aramco claims, 174–176
Sheraton Hotel claims, 175–176
United Nations Security Council
on Kuwait invasion, 171–172
on Libyan sanctions, 197
on Nicaragua suit, 105
on U.S. hostages in Iran, 88
United States. *See also* Iran–Contra
scandal; Iran–United States Claims
Tribunal
Berlin agreement, 35–37
Berlin Airlift (1948-49), 30, 32
bilateral investment treaties, 152,
249–250

Brazil, expropriation of assets of, 196,
202–203
Cambodia, secret bombing of, 47–48
China, recognition of, by, 89–93,
101–102
Civil War and Great Britain, 1–5
in coup to oust Mosaddegh in Iran,
83–85
expropriation by, 165–169, 189
Hezbollah bombing of Marine
barracks, 202
Indonesia and OPEC antitrust suit by,
69–71
intervention in other countries (1900-
1965), 246
Iran, expropriation of assets of, 85–87
Iran, hostages taken by, 87–88,
96–99, 112, 136
Iran Air flight 655 downing by,
195–196
Iranian assets in, 101, 196, 202–203
Japan, trade imbalance with, 62
JCPOA, Trump's withdrawal from,
196, 200–202
Lithuanian seaman denied political
asylum, 39–40
Mondev v. United States, 165–169,
189
Nicaragua v. United States, 104–106,
166
Oak Ridge suit against Japan, 62–66
Pan Am flight 103 downed by
Libyans, 197–198
Pentagon Papers, 44–45
shah admitted into, 87–88
Soviet arbitration with, in Stockholm,
116
Soviet trade agreements with, 40–44
Spain, bases in, 38–39
Treaty of Amity violations, 94,
123–124, 196, 200–202
Venezuela's confiscation of assets,
246–247
War Powers Act, 46–48
Watergate scandal, 31, 45, 48, 64–65

Universal Copyright Convention, 43

Universal Declaration of Human Rights, on changing nationality, 112

UNPROFOR peacekeepers, 179

U.S.–Iran Treaty of Amity, Economic Relations, and Consular Rights, 94, 123–124, 196, 200–202

U.S.–Japanese Friendship Treaty, 65

U.S.–Republic of China (Taiwan) Mutual Defense Treaty, 89–93

U.S.–Soviet Accords on Exchanges in Technical and Cultural Matters, 43–44

U.S. Steel, 52

U.S. Tax Court, 126

U.S.–U.S.S.R. Double Taxation Convention, 43

V

Vacuum Salt Products v. Ghana, 206–208

Valencia-Ospina, Eduardo, 207

Vale v. BSG Resources, 221

van den Berg, Albert Jan, 218–219

van Houtte, Hans, 194

Vantage Deepwater v. Petrobras, 221–222, 223–224

Venezuela

confiscation of U.S. oil and telecom assets, 246–247

ejection of American asphalt companies, 246

withdrawal from ICSID Convention, 250

verbindung vs. bindung, in East–West Berlin agreement, 35–36

Vienna Convention on the Law of Treaties, 91

Vietnam War, secret bombing of Cambodia in, 47–48

Virally, Michel

in *Amoco International Finance v. Iran et al.,* 122–125, 127, 130, 133

in *International Oil Consortium* case, 129

in Iran–United States Claims Tribunal, 122

Short v. Islamic Republic of Iran, 128

Volio Echeverria, Fabián, 237

W

Wallace, Don, 91

Wallenberg, Raoul, 118

Wallison, Peter, 144

Walsh, Lawrence, 143, 147

War Powers Act, 46–48

Watergate scandal, 31, 45, 48, 64–65

Watts, Arthur, 189, 239, 240–241

Weil, Prosper, 158–161

Weinberger, Caspar, 145, 147

West Berlin. *See also* East Berlin

author's studies in, 28–29

closing of border with East Berlin (1961), 29–30, 31–33

Quadripartite Agreement on Berlin, 35–37

Spandau Allied Military Prison inspection, 34–35

Steinstücken, 32–33

West Germany. *See also* West Berlin

author's homestay in Soest, 28

bilateral investment treaties in, 152

Steinstücken, 32–33

White & Case

author as litigator at, 13–26

author as partner at, 26, 51

author interviewing at, 12–13

as outside general counsel to Indonesia, 69

partners, as international arbitrators, 205–206

recognition of, for international arbitration, 152

White Industries v. India, 250–251

Williams, Rotimi, aka "Timi the Law," 57–59, 61

Williamson, Edwin, 197–198

"Woman III" (de Kooning), 95

About the Author

Judge Charles N. Brower's six-decade career in law and public service has taken him around the world, from the White House to The Hague, with many stops in between.

Admitted to the U.S. Foreign Service when he graduated from Harvard College *cum laude*, Judge Brower was advised to get a law degree, which he did at Harvard in 1961 after a year in Germany as a Fulbright Scholar.

Working at the White & Case law firm on Wall Street in New York City as a prelude to finally becoming a professional diplomat, he was captured by a combination of loving trial work and starting a budding elective political career in his home state of New Jersey. He resigned from the firm four months after being elected a partner, however, to join the Office of the Legal Adviser in the U.S. State Department, where after barely three years he became the acting legal adviser.

Judge Brower then abandoned his elective political ambitions, stayed in the nation's capital, and alternated between law practice and public service. He was readmitted to the White & Case partnership two more times, opening its DC office and eventually moving into international arbitration before later joining Twenty Essex barristers' chambers in London. Judge Brower has served forty years as a judge of the Iran–United

States Claims Tribunal in The Hague, a role briefly interrupted by his time in the White House as sub-cabinet rank deputy special counsellor to the president. He is also the most-appointed American judge *ad hoc* of the International Court of Justice.

Judge Brower has received numerous awards, including the American Society of International Law's highest honor, the Manley O. Hudson Medal, for "outstanding contributions to scholarship and achievement in international law."

Judge Brower's authoritative volume *The Iran–United States Claims Tribunal*, for which he is now preparing a second edition, was awarded the American Society of International Law's Certificate of Merit as "a work of great distinction." He lives in the DC area, where he served recently as distinguished visiting research professor of law at George Washington University's law school. He continues there as adviser to SJD candidates.